Re-Engaging the Middle East

Re-Engaging the Middle East

A New Vision for U.S. Policy

EDITED BY

Dafna H. Rand
Andrew P. Miller

BROOKINGS INSTITUTION PRESS
Washington, D.C.

The Brookings Institution is a private nonprofit organization devoted to research, education, and publication on important issues of domestic and foreign policy. Its principal purpose is to bring the highest quality independent research and analysis to bear on current and emerging policy problems. Interpretations or conclusions in Brookings publications should be understood to be solely those of the authors.

Library of Congress Control Number: 2020938129
ISBN 9780815737407 (pbk : alk. paper)
ISBN 9780815737629 (ebook)

9 8 7 6 5 4 3 2 1

Typeset in Sabon

Composition by Elliott Beard

Contents

PART III
Regional Challenges for the United States

Preface

In the spring of 2010, our State Department supervisors asked us how to shift away from a decade-long overemphasis on the Middle East and North Africa within U.S. foreign policy. A year earlier, President Barack Obama had given a powerful speech in Cairo, outlining a new U.S. approach to key regional priorities—in the process resetting the U.S. relationship with the Muslim world.[1] With this speech, the Obama administration articulated its desire to break from the George W. Bush administration's overinvestment of U.S. power in the region, exemplified by the 2003 Iraq War, which produced disastrous consequences for America and the region.

In 2009 and 2010, we worked for President Obama and Secretary of State Hillary Clinton as they pursued key priorities outlined in the Cairo Speech—the Israeli-Palestinian peace process, enhanced counterterrorism and counter-proliferation efforts—and new projects to promote science, education, and entrepreneurship in the Muslim world. These initiatives were sincere and required a great deal of time and effort. And yet, at the same time, Obama's top officials were considering how to pivot, carefully and deliberately, away from the region. Recognizing the potential offered by the rapidly growing Asian economies, Obama officials were eager to rebalance eastward. For these officials, the Bush administration's overinvestment in the Middle East had damaged U.S. standing globally while wasting American blood and treasure.

Even as our colleagues in the Bureau of East Asian and Pacific Affairs mapped out how to "pivot to Asia," we were among a handful of mid-level State Department Middle East experts working on the other side of the equation. We wrote papers articulating a careful, incremental shift of U.S. energy away from the Middle East in concert with the drawdown of U.S. troops in Iraq and those in nearby Afghanistan.[2] We mapped out how regional powers would manage their own security needs, coordinating collectively and relying less on U.S. security commitments.

The rationale for the pivot seemed sound. Obama was skeptical about America's ability to influence substantially what were fundamentally local political dynamics. He believed strongly in the power and obligation of Middle Eastern states and societies to shape their own futures.[3] Obama feared that in approaching worrisome national security threats in the region, including Iran's steady nuclear buildup, the United States would be led inexorably toward undesirable military confrontation. To Obama, a diplomatic resolution to the threat of Iran's nuclear program, combined with careful diplomatic approaches to other key U.S. priorities, would extricate the U.S. militarily from intractable commitments that could generate a "security dilemma." Indeed, he feared that the U.S. military's significant presence, in and of itself, increased the likelihood of another war in the Middle East, which would be to the detriment of the United States and the region at large.

Whatever the logical appeal of rebalancing toward Asia, in practice, events on the ground revealed the complexities of the Middle East's politics—and America's inextricable link to intra- and interstate dynamics. In some cases, for example, a local dependency on U.S. power and leverage had grown in concert with the expansion of America's security partnerships with the Arab world and Israel. The aftermath of the 2010 Iraqi elections proved a case in point. As a political stalemate persisted for nine months, with Iraqi political parties unable to form a government, Vice President Joe Biden traveled to Baghdad in order to personally mediate a solution among the various political factions. The effort led to a compromise government—and the consequential second term of Prime Minister Nouri al-Maliki—but not before underscoring that U.S. leverage still mattered in the domestic affairs of Middle Eastern states.[4]

That same year, a Turkish-led flotilla of activists tried to break the Israeli security barrier off the coast of the Gaza Strip, prompting international outrage regarding the siege-like conditions facing the 1.5 million Palestinians in the territory.[5] The White House quickly brokered emergency talks with both Egypt and Israel to ease the blockade on Gaza in order to improve the flow of humanitarian and other goods through both borders.[6] And, finally, there was the question of Egypt's leadership. The aging octogenarian who had become one of America's most important allies in the region, President Hosni Mubarak of Egypt, began outlining a plan for his son Gamal to succeed him.[7] This idea provoked outrage among the Egyptian Armed Forces elite, for whom familial rule was anathema—particularly the notion of passing power to someone outside of the military. That spring and fall of 2010, Mubarak held fraudulent parliamentary elections, generating increasing public anger with his apparent move toward greater authoritarianism.[8]

If the prospects for a foreign policy rebalance away from the Middle East seemed challenging in mid-2010, the notion became almost laughable six months later. As we left the State Department for the holidays in late December, demonstrations in Tunisia had suddenly gained momentum: unions, youth leaders, and middle-class professionals joined the protests that had begun after the self-immolation of a produce vendor in the central Tunisian town of Sidi Bouzid.[9] By early January 2011, the localized protests focused on the corruption of local officials in a provincial Tunisian town of 10,000 would inspire Egyptians to demonstrate in Cairo, a city of 20 million people.[10] From there, protests centered on similar themes of chronic corruption and injustice spread across the Arab world.

Quickly, the Middle East's authoritarian order began to erode. In Tunisia, Egypt, Libya, and Yemen, citizens toppled or pushed aside leaders who had ruled for decades. In Syria and Bahrain, ruling regimes mounted counteroffensives to suppress the protesters. The turmoil—and tragedy—sparked by the protests of 2011 became an all-consuming focus for those of us working on the region at the State Department and White House in 2011 and 2012. We abandoned our policy papers explaining how to rebalance away from the region. Instead, it was all-hands-on-deck for every Middle East expert in the U.S. government as we tried to manage the U.S. response to the Arab Spring. Except for Libya, where the White House decided in favor of a limited military intervention to save civilians in Benghazi, the core features of the U.S. approach to the Arab Spring involved caution, deference to local actors, and a preference for quiet diplomacy.[11] As the dynamics between states and societies changed, the United States tried to balance its traditional alliances with regional leaders on the one hand, with support for public aspirations in the region on the other.

Later, critics would accuse the Obama administration of disregarding its friends and interests to blindly support protesters, throwing partners like Mubarak "under the bus."[12] In reality, the Obama administration did not have the capacity to prop up authoritarian regimes indefinitely against surging public opposition. Nor was the United States very successful in stopping the worst abuses, violence, and counterrevolutionary trends that emerged—with catastrophic outcomes—shortly after 2011. In Bahrain, despite aggressive U.S. diplomacy, the repression deepened.[13] In Egypt, the United States was unable to either moderate the overreach and antidemocratic nature of the short-lived Mohamed Morsi presidency or prevent a counterrevolution in 2013.[14] The Obama administration likewise refused to intervene militarily in Syria, as refugees streamed into Europe and the civil war triggered a failed state and a humanitarian catastrophe, one that opened fertile breeding ground for the Islamic State of Iraq and Syria (ISIS).

Meanwhile, diplomatic momentum to finalize the nuclear deal with Iran took on new energy in 2014 and 2015. Negotiations over the Joint Comprehensive Plan of Action (JCPOA) held out the promise that a managed exit from the region still remained possible, and the Obama administration increasingly concentrated on this ambition. At the same time, the initial idealism among many in the Obama administration who rooted for protesters seeking a more democratic future gave way to narrower goals focused on humanitarian aid and limited civilian protection. Ambitions shrank regarding the effects of U.S. policy on largely internal, domestic trajectories—especially as the hopeful, peaceful protest movements increasingly gave way to tragic civil conflicts in Syria, Yemen, and Libya.

A decade after September 11, 2001, and the subsequent overcommitments in the region made by the George W. Bush administration, President Obama remained intent on reducing U.S. investments and military overextension in the Middle East. Yet, in practice, at the policymaking as opposed to the strategic level, by 2010 it became difficult to pick a single area of the Middle East where it would be possible to begin to downgrade the U.S. presence or investment without significant risks and costs. In fact, while U.S. allies accused America under Obama of retreating from the region, by 2016 more arms had been sold, foreign assistance granted, and more diplomatic energy expended (particularly to find a solution to the political conflicts in Syria, Yemen, and Libya) than at any other point in the history of U.S. foreign policy in the Middle East.

In the winter of 2017, the Donald Trump administration took over responsibility for managing U.S. policy in the Middle East. One of us, Andrew Miller, initially stayed on as a career civil servant to work with the new administration, helping them to understand the complexities of the region and why earlier policymakers had tried various approaches. Tending to disregard any logic behind the Obama administration's decisions, the new officials gravitated toward any approach that differed from Obama's as they sought to apply an "America First" frame to U.S. policies in the Middle East.

Trump's general instincts about the Middle East and North Africa were clear from the start, seeing the "troubled region" as a place where "no amount of American blood or treasure can produce lasting peace and security."[15] His decisions over time represented a retreat from America's traditional role in the region. He saw little need for the United States to assert global leadership through its diplomatic, military, or moral position in the Middle East. The promotion of U.S. values would no longer even rhetorically motivate U.S. foreign policy—in the Middle East and elsewhere. Instead, the Middle East offered potential transactions for Americans—first and foremost economic gains for U.S. defense companies, the energy sector, and other select U.S. industries. Trump criticized previous U.S. military and foreign assistance investments in the region as unfair or poorly serving narrowly defined U.S. interests. In Syria, President Trump demanded that Gulf allies pay for reconstruction costs after the defeat of ISIS.[16] In Saudi Arabia, he approached a decades-long alliance as a salesman, eagerly courting an important U.S. arms buyer while ignoring other U.S. interests.[17] This transactional approach colored his limited diplomatic efforts as well. Urging the Palestinian Authority to agree to lopsided negotiation terms, he suspended foreign assistance to the Palestinian people and then presented a "peace plan" that sought in effect to impose terms of surrender on the Palestinians.[18]

Motivated by his underlying desire to beat a hasty retreat from the region, Trump increasingly tried to outsource the management of important regional issues to local actors whose interests were not always the same as ours. For example, at first, Trump officials delegated to the Saudis and the United Arab Emirates (UAE) the question of when, where, and how to end the Yemeni civil conflict. While many of his senior advisers felt differently, Trump was fairly transparent about his approach, which involved disengaging from our traditional leadership role in the Middle East because it was costly and making deals when possible. Most decisions seemed aimed at pleasing various constituencies within Trump's domestic political base, whether withdrawing from the JCPOA (without considering a replacement deal); moving the U.S. embassy to Jerusalem; insisting others pay for Iraqi, Syrian, and other reconstruction efforts; or blindly trusting the threat assessment of local partners over internal judgments offered by his own national security experts.

To be clear, in presenting an alternative vision for U.S. foreign policy in the Middle East and North Africa, we are offering a fundamental critique of President Trump's approach to the region. We abhor his irresponsible methods—policy by tweet, naïve embrace of autocrats, thoughtless saber rattling—but our primary differences go deeper than tactics. While we share Trump's belief that the United States is overcommitted in the Middle East (which was also Obama's position), we diverge from him not only on how to reduce U.S. exposure but also on what type of Middle East would best serve the interests of the American people. Trump's Middle East is an Orientalist caricature, a land of powerful despots keeping their populations in line through brutal repression while buying expensive U.S. goods and selling cheap natural resources. Human rights and political development, even the absence of violent conflict in the region, are not just difficult to achieve, in Trump's view: they are irrelevant to the "America First" agenda.

In contrast, we believe Trump's vision for the Middle East is both unrealistic and undesirable. As we emphasize in this volume, we must be humble about the immediate potential for positive change in the region and, even more so, the capacity of the United States to effect such change. But there is little doubt in our minds that a less violent Middle East with governments that are more accountable to their people is preferable to the chaotic, vicious marketplace that Trump envisions. The strongest partnerships in the region should be with those nations with whom the United States shares values and interests, convergent threat perceptions, and a mutual obligation to advance international norms and global security, including climate, health, and economic security. Such a Middle East would not only be better for the local population, but also require less U.S. intervention and help to forge a region that is more of an exporter of public goods than moral hazards. These conditions would allow the United States to reduce its commitment in the Middle East without fear of events on the ground dragging us back in or inviting challenges to our global stature.

We should not delude ourselves into believing that the United States can foster peace, stability, or the rule of law in the region by itself or quickly. This is especially true as the economic and political effects of the COVID-19 crisis will be far reaching and devastating across the region, and likely include weakened government authority, the rise of non-state actors, waves of public protest, and even greater economic inequality. Acknowledging the limits of U.S. influence in the Middle East is realistic and responsible; pretending that the United States has no influence in the region, and should therefore treat it as a playground, is neither.

Reflecting on our professional experiences navigating these changing winds, we now wonder what comes next. The following chapters are written by those who know U.S. foreign policy in the region best. Some of the U.S. government's most committed experts on the region, the contributors to this volume have worked hard to provide objective analysis, knowledge, and recommendations to their superiors over the past decade. While the views of these experts diverge in important respects, they share a common belief that the Middle East's future is likely to remain highly unpredictable and that a rapid U.S. retreat from the region is too risky and costly. In the following pages, the authors will offer what they view as a responsible strategy for recalibrating the U.S. position in the Middle East, preserving American influence where it most matters while beginning the process of freeing up resources for a new foreign policy century, in which this complex region is no longer the primary international focus of the United States.

Notes

1. Barack Obama, "Remarks by the President at Cairo University," June 4, 2009 (https://obamawhitehouse.archives.gov/the-press-office/remarks-president-cairo-university-6-04-09).
2. Hillary Clinton, "America's Pacific Century," *Foreign Policy*, October 11, 2011.
3. See Obama, "Remarks by the President at Cairo University," and Barack Obama, "Remarks by the President on the Middle East and North Africa," May 19, 2011 (https://obamawhitehouse.archives.gov/the-press-office/2011/05/19/remarks-president-middle-east-and-north-africa).
4. "An Iraqi Government, Finally," editorial, *New York Times*, December 29, 2010.
5. Ian Black, "Israeli Attack on Gaza Flotilla Sparks International Outrage," *Guardian*, May 31, 2010.
6. Mark Landler, "After Flotilla Raid, U.S. Is Torn Between Allies," *Los Angeles Times*, June 1, 2010.
7. Abigail Hauslohner, "In Egypt, Debate Grows over a Successor to Mubarak," *Time*, November 13, 2009.
8. Jack Shenker, "Protests in Egypt against Gamal Mubarak Succession Plans," *Guardian*, September 21, 2010.

9. Christopher Alexander, "Tunisia's Protest Wave: Where It Comes from and What It Means," *Foreign Policy*, January 3, 2011.

10. Ibid.

11. Mark Landler, "As U.N. Backs Military Action in Libya, U.S. Role Is Unclear," *New York Times*, March 18, 2011.

12. Lee Fang, "Santorum Laments Pro-Democracy Movement in Egypt, Says Obama Threw Mubarak 'Under the Bus,'" (https://thinkprogress.org/santorum-laments-pro-democracy-movement-in-egypt-says-obama-threw-mubarak-under-the-bus-743d156205cd/).

13. Ian Black, "Bahrain Protests: 'The Repression Is Getting Worse,'" *Guardian*, August 8, 2011.

14. Patrick Kingsley, "Protesters across Egypt Call for Mohamed Morsi to Go," *Guardian*, June 30, 2013.

15. Jen Kirby, "Read Trump's Statement on Syria Strike: 'They Are Crimes of a Monster,'" Vox, April 13, 2018 (www.vox.com/2018/4/13/17236862/syria-strike-donald-trump-chemical-attack-statement).

16. "Trump: 'Immensely Wealthy' Countries Must Pay for U.S. Protection," Al Jazeera, April 25, 2018 (www.aljazeera.com/news/2018/04/trump-immensely-wealthy-countries-pay-protection-180425080106208.html).

17. Dan De Luce and Robert Windrem, "Under Trump Arms Deal, High-Tech U.S. Bombs to Be Built in Saudi Arabia," NBC News, June 7, 2018 (www.nbcnews.com/politics/congress/under-trump-arms-deal-high-tech-u-s-bombs-be-n1015346).

18. "Donald Trump Cuts More than US$200 Million in Aid to Palestinians," *Guardian*, August 24, 2018.

Acknowledgments

The idea for this volume was born over time, as we worked together for years to shape the U.S. government's approach to the Middle East, including responding to revolutions, coups, civil wars, atrocities, and economic crises. We are both grateful for the opportunity to have served in the State Department and National Security Council during a tumultuous period for the Middle East, between 2009 and 2017. Incapable of knowing the future, and certain that history would harshly judge some of our decisions, we tried to put our best ideas and recommendations forward. We always understood the power of the alternative argument, an experience that deepened our personal and professional humility.

The best part of government service is the people. It was a privilege to work with some of the country's most committed public servants, nonpartisan career diplomats, military personnel, intelligence officers, and others who believe that the United States can and should do good in the world while protecting Americans, our interests, and our allies. Our belief in the hard-working, committed individuals and institutions that sustain U.S. foreign policy motivated this book. When we left the government, we knew that we wanted to give voice to the emerging generation of Middle East experts. Many of the writers we invited to participate here are newer voices, who for many years worked behind the scenes offering careful and thorough recommendations to their superiors. Through this volume we hope to honor the many career government experts, most of whom are toiling away around the world, without public recognition.

When in government, we were lucky enough to work for inspiring senior leaders who invested in our professional growth, particularly Senator Frank R. Lautenberg, Ambassador Susan Rice, Anne-Marie Slaughter, Jake Sullivan, Congressman Tom Malinowski, Phil Gordon, Rob Malley, Ambassador Samantha Power, Gayle Smith, and Yael Lempert. Each of these individuals balances brilliance with a deep humanity. We thank our colleagues with whom we worked closely in the U.S. government on some of the most difficult policy challenges discussed in this book. Dafna thanks members of her various dream teams, without whom she wouldn't have been able to get very much done over fifteen years in and out of the executive and legislative branches of government. Andrew thanks the dozens of people at the National Security Council, State Department, Department of Defense, and U.S. Agency for International Development with whom he worked in the executive branch, whose courage and selfless commitment to public service were an inspiration during moments of optimism and a source of resilience during less favorable times.

Our editor, Bill Finan, has guided us through the publication process with enthusiasm and certainty about the value of this project. Bill is unique in foreign affairs publishing with his innate ability to bridge the gap between scholarship and the world of practice and policy. We are also deeply appreciative of the hard work by his thorough, talented team at the Brookings Institution Press.

To our authors: Thank you for putting up with multiple rounds of suggestions and edits. It was a pleasure to work with each of you. Thank you also to Jeff Prescott, Brian McKeon, Salman Ahmed, Tamara Wittes, and others, who hosted and participated in a workshop for our authors so we could talk collectively about the idea for the volume as a group. We are grateful to our reviewers, who greatly improved this volume with their candid feedback. Thank you, as well, to April Brady, Seth Binder, Louisa Keeler, Sheridan Cole, Claire Stevenson, and Olivia Hinch for your help with research and citations. We are indebted to Karthik Vaidyanathan, Matt Gottfried, Dunia Andary, and Rachid Chaker for helping us to understand opinion polling on American attitudes concerning the Middle East.

Dafna hopes her kids, Maya, Jonah, and Elijah, will someday read this book and understand why their mom is so compelled by the intellectual, strategic, and ethical dilemmas inherent in U.S. foreign policy in the Middle East. In addition to adding joy and meaning to my life, these three provide a daily reason to worry about the future, particularly what the United States's global role will look like when they grow up. This book, like my last one, could not have been written without the support of my husband Doug Rand. He never wavers in his near-mythical aspirations regarding what can be accomplished each day. It is inspiring.

Andrew dedicates this book to his late grandmother, Pauline Rosenmeyer Miller, who introduced him to the world beyond the United States and instilled in him a deep appreciation for the inherent dignity of all peoples. I also want to thank my wife, Lauren, for supporting me, not just during this project but in all of my professional endeavors despite the considerable burden it places on her. My parents, George and Patricia, always nurtured my interest in international affairs, for which I will remain grateful. I also want to express my appreciation for my colleagues at the Project of Middle East Democracy for their forbearance while I worked on this project, especially Executive Director Stephen McInerney.

Re-Engaging the Middle East

ONE

Between Retreat and Overinvestment in the Middle East and North Africa

ANDREW P. MILLER
DAFNA H. RAND

U.S. Interests in the Middle East and North Africa

The George W. Bush administration's approach to the Middle East and North Africa (Middle East) left the United States overextended, provoking a region-wide backlash against U.S. policy. President Barack Obama's effort to execute a cautious, managed "rebalance," slowly and carefully withdrawing investments in the region, proved unworkable. The Trump era has upended both of these approaches. While President Donald Trump's predecessor and a growing number of current political leaders from both parties share his goals of retreating from the region, the callous, often chaotic means through which he has chosen to do so have eroded U.S. leadership and interests and upset global alliances.

The United States has the opportunity, in the wake of the Trump administration, to chart a new strategy for the Middle East, one that begins with a general agreement regarding key U.S. interests in the region. As the authors in this volume will argue, these interests vary by subregion and country. Overall, however, they include preventing terrorism and proliferation from threatening the United States; advancing Israeli-Palestinian peace; de-escalating conflicts, particularly in Syria and Yemen; protecting civilians by promoting a rules-based governance system and universal human rights; and ensuring stable global energy markets.

In order to secure these interests, some recent authors have advocated returning to the Bush-era hegemony that characterized U.S. foreign policy in the region, arguing that only U.S. dominance will ensure success. According to Richard Fontaine and Michael Singh, the United States needs "a Middle East policy that aims to retain U.S. primacy and freedom of action in the region, forges great-power cooperation where possible, and prevents or mitigates damaging competition where necessary."[1] Arguments for preserving U.S. regional dominance often rest on the assumption that U.S. hegemony in the Middle East is necessary to confront China's and Russia's inroads in the region, which is the key to securing U.S. global power. In arguing for muscular power competition with China and Russia in the Middle East, Robert Satloff, for instance, contends that the United States must maintain its role as the singular great power in the region and that a U.S. departure would create a vacuum advantaging our competitors.[2]

Yet, putting aside the theoretical desirability of American primacy in the Middle East, returning to an era of singular U.S. dominance in the region may no longer be possible—especially after the Arab uprisings of 2011, the Syrian civil war, and the retreat of U.S. leadership during the Trump administration. Moreover, such an argument inflates the ambitions of China and Russia in the Middle East. While each may harbor short-term, transactional interests, neither country seeks to replace the United States as a regional security guarantor or dominant external power. In fact, Russia may not have the capacity to play that role even if it so desired. And, given U.S. budget constraints, public opinion trends, and increasing support for isolationism among Republicans and Democrats, the American public is simply not committed to a great game in the Middle East—and certainly not increasing investments in the region in order to advance a global struggle against Russia and China.

Others have doubled down on the logic behind the Obama-era

effort to downsize the U.S. role in the Middle East. Martin Indyk, a former U.S. diplomat who has spent his career arguing for the importance of Arab-Israeli peace, among other key interests in the region, has called for a reduced U.S. investment in the region. In what many see as a significant change of perspective, he now argues that "few vital interests continue to be at stake in the Middle East."[3] Trita Parsi, a consistent critic of U.S. policy in the region under administrations of both parties, now favors policies that deprioritize the Middle East, as "U.S. activities in the region have brought more turmoil than stability" there.[4]

This instinct toward reductionism is understandable, given both the political appeal of this argument and the poor track record of the United States in the Middle East over the past several decades. Yet a call for a new pivot away from the Middle East neglects the fact that long-term U.S. interests endure in the region, and are likely to persist at least for the next decade. Meanwhile, the "known unknowns" include the ever-present, even likely, unpredictability of politics and security crises in the Middle East, compounded by the devastating effects of the COVID-19 pandemic. In addition, the complete drawdown of U.S. power and investments in the region would invite further regional and global competition, generating new types of insecurity. Although we do not necessarily agree with their characterization of U.S. policy in the Middle East as a "purgatory" in their 2019 *Foreign Affairs* article, we agree with Mara Karlin and Tamara Wittes that "Washington can do better than choosing between abandoning its interests there and making a boundless commitment." U.S. policymakers should be debating what the U.S. presence looks like in the Middle East, not whether there should be one.[5]

Why These Interests? A Dose of Humility

Both the recent history of U.S. engagement in the Middle East and the region's present circumstances are humbling. Therefore, we have articulated a set of U.S. interests that are practical, not transformational. While these objectives, if fulfilled, would not remake the Middle East, they could leave both the region's residents and the United States better off than where they started. These are modest goals, surely, but they are still worthwhile.

Counterterrorism and Proliferation

The United States should seek to disrupt those terrorist groups that pose a direct threat to the United States and American citizens, and deny the proliferation of nuclear, chemical, and biological weapons to countries and groups in the region. While it is true that since September 11, 2001, U.S. foreign policy has become unduly focused on counterterrorism at the expense of other interests and values, terrorism continues to top the list of most Americans' foreign policy concerns.[6] U.S. policymakers must consider how to set expectations with the U.S. public, not blowing the threat out of proportion while nonetheless focusing on countering terrorists coming from the Middle East who continue to plot against the U.S. homeland. Moreover, the potential intersection of terrorism and weapons of mass destruction, however remote the prospect, would have cataclysmic implications.

The United States will never succeed in defeating all terrorist groups, banishing the use of terrorism as a political tactic, or eliminating all nuclear, chemical, or biological weapons in the region. But if we are vigilant and focused, we can not only prevent the vast majority of terrorist attacks on American targets, but also degrade the capacity of those groups that could try to conduct such attacks. We also can prevent additional countries from developing nuclear, biological, and chemical weapons capabilities, and stop such weapons from falling into the hands of terrorist groups.

Advance Israeli-Palestinian peace and protect Israel's security. The United States has a long-term commitment to the security of Israel as a Jewish, democratic state, which is rooted in the American public's moral and historical interest in the welfare of the Jewish people.[7] In addition to the moral dimension of U.S. support for a Jewish state in the post-Holocaust era, a stable and democratic actor with a strong military in the heart of the Middle East also benefits hard U.S. security interests, particularly when it comes to threats of mutual concern. U.S. support to Israel is manifested in the commitment to help Israel retain its qualitative military edge in the region—defined in law as its "ability to counter and defeat any credible conventional military threat from any individual state or possible coalition of states or from non-state actors, while sustaining minimal damage and casualties."[8] U.S. military aid to Israel—embodied most recently in the ten-year security assistance package negotiated by the Obama administration—plays an important part in sustaining this dominance.[9]

Ultimately, however, both Israel's long-term security and its democratic character depend on ending the occupation through an agreed resolution to the Israeli-Palestinian conflict. Creating a viable, sovereign Palestinian state is the only way to preserve Israel's Jewish and democratic nature while also respecting the national rights and upholding the dignity of the Palestinian people. Given realities on the ground, the next administration should not expect to be in a position to negotiate an end-of-conflict settlement between Israel and the Palestinians. U.S. leaders nevertheless can perform a critical service by protecting the two-state solution from actions that undermine its practicality—such as settlement expansion and terrorism. This means that a future U.S. president will have to exert pressure on Israeli and Palestinian leaders to rein in these and other self-defeating propensities, including unilateral annexation. The Israeli-Palestinian conflict is not the sole, or even the primary, cause of instability in the Middle East, but the demise of the two-state solution would only add to regional chaos.

De-escalate regional conflicts that have spread insecurity, enabled terrorist groups, impaired economic growth, and created opportunities for malign actors to meddle. The many persistent civil conflicts across the region threaten U.S. interests in the Middle East. Terrorists exploit the security vacuums created by ongoing fighting in Yemen, Syria, and elsewhere to set up shop, train, and plot attacks. Iran capitalizes on the fissures widened by these conflicts to cultivate new proxies, further weakening national governments and extending its influence. These conflicts have ravaged the region's economic life, stunted political development, and ruptured the social fabric of countries, precipitating a self-reinforcing cycle of instability that could take generations to overcome. Every U.S. regional interest, from ensuring Israel's security to sustaining energy supplies to countering terrorism, is more difficult to pursue in the presence of conflict. While the United States will not be able to bring a swift resolution to the Middle East's many burning conflicts through its own diplomacy overnight, at the very least it can help to mitigate the costs and de-escalate the levels of fighting in the short term, while preserving opportunities for conflict termination over the medium term.

Register meaningful and genuine improvements in governance, respect for human rights, and popular inclusion in the political systems of the Middle East. You do not need to be a human rights activist to believe that the quality and nature of governance around the globe affects a variety of U.S. interests, including counterterrorism and economic growth—and therefore should be a priority for the United States. Given the current prevalence in the region of authoritarian rule mixed with conflicts and power vacuums, democracy seems like an aspirational goal. While the United States cannot singlehandedly change this reality, we can still hold out hope for more incremental progress in terms of regional leaders' respect for universal human rights norms, economic reform, and representative, accountable governance. The release of political prisoners, greater transparency and inclusivity of central and local governments, augmented electoral integrity and freedom, and wider space for civil society and media, among other items, should not be a bridge too far.

In pursuing even these comparatively modest governance goals, the United States should remain humble about its influence and sensitive to the danger that our actions, however well intentioned, could be counterproductive. U.S. diplomacy and programming can, nevertheless, be calibrated carefully to empower local actors pushing for change, recognizing that they—and not outside powers—must be the central players in the drama unfolding in the Middle East. Tunisia, where the United States has successfully supported locally driven democratization, could represent a valuable model for future U.S. efforts.

Enable the free flow of oil and natural gas from and through the Middle East and North Africa. For both environmental and political reasons, it is imperative that the United States free itself of dependence on fossil fuels. In at least the short term, however, oil will remain critically important to the U.S. economy and American living standards. Renewed U.S. oil production has made it more difficult for Middle East governments to wield oil as a weapon, but it has not eliminated our vulnerability to developments in the regional Middle Eastern oil market. The major risk Middle Eastern oil presents to the United States is no longer that a country like Saudi Arabia would deliberately reduce oil production to punish us—such action would ultimately hurt the Saudis much more than it would hurt the United States. Instead, the risk is that a reduction in the oil supply caused either by internal unrest in the Middle East or the seizure of regional oil fields by a hostile power could generate a massive spike in world oil prices. The Middle East, as a whole, accounts for 37 percent of global oil production, while Saudi Arabia and the small Arabian Gulf statelets alone produce 23 percent of oil worldwide.[10] It is not hard to see how interruptions in regional oil supplies could wreak havoc on the global oil market, as well as on the international economy. As long as stable oil markets are critical to the health of the U.S. economy, ensuring reliable supplies of oil from the Middle East will remain a core national security priority.

An Opportunity for a New Approach
Based on Limited Principles

Changing circumstances in the Middle East and the United States demand not only identifying the specific interests that we are pursuing in the region, but also using a different approach to achieve these objectives. While the region's relative importance to the United States has declined, for better or worse, the United States does not have the luxury of ignoring the countries and people of the Middle East. On the other hand, a strategy that continues to give the Middle East unquestioned primacy in U.S. foreign policy would be unwise, unaffordable, and unpopular domestically.

If the United States is to achieve the five objectives laid out above, the next administration will have to forge a strategy that can cope with two central dilemmas. First, there is tension between the American public's growing fatigue with the Middle East (exacerbated by the emergence of other global challenges) and the inescapable reality that this region continues to matter.[11] Second, advancing U.S. interests in the Middle East must be done in a way that avoids the perpetual risk of overcommitment.[12] Coping with these dilemmas will require navigating frictions, ambiguities, and some uncertainty.

We believe a strategy that both reduces costs and contains risk, while advancing core U.S. interests in the Middle East, is possible. The best way to overcome the two central dilemmas listed above is to ensure that this strategy adheres to a number of key principles. The following four principles, when taken together, form the foundation of a smart, self-interested, and cost-sensitive approach to U.S. foreign policy in the Middle East. Developing clear U.S. priorities, empowering diplomats and aid workers in the field, and emphasizing conflict-prevention will be even more critical components of this strategy in the COVID-19 era, as unpredictable access, security, and health conditions persist. Through a combination of skillful statecraft, robust diplomacy, and the responsible use of military force, the United States can cut costs without cutting-and-running, and remain a major regional player without the baggage of hegemony.

1. U.S. interests across the Middle East should drive U.S. policy. It seems obvious that U.S. policy in the Middle East should be primarily guided by American interests and values, rather than uncritically shaped based on the interests and agendas of traditional regional partners. Under Donald Trump's presidency, however, U.S. regional policy has been effectively subcontracted to select Middle Eastern partners, especially Saudi Arabia, the United Arab Emirates, and Israel. From the Trump administration's seemingly unconditional support for the strategically disastrous war in Yemen to the short-sighted pressure campaign on the Palestinian Authority, the Trump administration's regional agenda appears to be a product of local actors successfully convincing an impressionable U.S. president to act according to their immediate agendas. At other times, the parochial business interests of President Trump, his family, and his associates seem to drive regional policy choices, making the concept of economic statecraft a proxy for self-interest and self-enrichment. While the United States continues to share certain interests with many Middle Eastern countries, our interests are not identical. Pretending otherwise only harms the American people and risks implicating the United States in costly initiatives that are either immaterial to our interests or directly contrary to them.

Instead, the identification of U.S. interests in the Middle East should be determined largely endogenously. U.S. policy must prioritize those issues that bear on the security, prosperity, freedoms, and values of the American people, such as counterterrorism, counterproliferation, energy security, Israel, and political reform/human rights. Other matters, such as the personal economic interests of a particular foreign leader or the religious agenda of one faction in a friendly country, should not be U.S. priorities. Yes, in order to forge effective partnerships with regional players, we will have to consider their concerns. And the United States should not hesitate to partner with local actors on mutual interests. However, we should never lose sight of our own interests, pretend that traditional allies share them in their entirety, or allow regional actors in the Middle East to use us in the pursuit of objectives of dubious strategic logic or morality.

2. The division between values and interests is a false dichotomy. Assuming these two elements of U.S. foreign policy are inherently at odds has been an easy, though often inaccurate, prism. This oversimplified binary is often used by decisionmakers to justify de-prioritizing human rights in U.S. foreign policy in the Middle East. Yet, while de-escalating regional tensions, focusing on conflict prevention, and prioritizing human rights and governance reforms are morally sound approaches reflecting the universal values animating U.S. foreign policy, they are often also the most direct way to achieve U.S. interests. Too often, past administrations have largely ignored brewing conflicts until they have escalated to the highest levels of violence, a point at which nonmilitary options are sometimes no longer available. This pattern of last-minute interventions tends to be more costly to American taxpayers, particularly to the extent that it leads to an overreliance on the military. All else being equal, diplomatic forms of engagement are far cheaper than the military alternatives. And while the American public is war weary, public opinion polls show continued support for nonmilitary U.S. leadership in the Middle East.[13]

With the exception of Trump's quixotic attempt to negotiate the "ultimate deal" between Israel and the Palestinians, the Trump administration has sidelined efforts to resolve regional conflicts, including in Libya, Syria, and Yemen.[14] In the absence of U.S. engagement, we have seen the intensity of these conflicts increase, existing political processes diverge from U.S. preferences, or both.

By placing a renewed emphasis on conflict prevention and management in the Middle East, a new administration can reassert American influence, better contain destabilizing regional dynamics, and economize on resources. The first step in revitalizing U.S. conflict management capacity will be to reverse the damage the Trump administration has done to the State Department, USAID, and the U.S. diplomatic corps. Beyond strengthening our civilian international affairs institutions, the next administration will have to be sensitive to those fleeting opportunities when conflict resolution is possible, while not shying away from the less glamorous but equally important work of conflict mitigation.

Similarly, the next administration can make an important and relatively cheap investment in a more peaceful future for the Middle East by making governance and human rights concerns a core part of all of our bilateral relationships. Specifically, U.S. diplomats should stop censoring themselves on these points in private meetings. As noted above, governance failures and human rights abuses can exacerbate, and may even be the primary source of, regional security challenges, including terrorism, ethnic conflict, and state failure. In the interest of avoiding friction with traditional partners, however, policymakers have often pulled punches when it comes to internal political issues. Seeking to avoid unpleasant conversations with friendly governments, U.S. officials often signal tacit acceptance of unstable domestic practices, even if these domestic practices will irritate U.S. relationships in the Middle East in the short term and are likely to produce medium-term negative security externalities for our partners and ourselves. When we raise these uncomfortable domestic concerns with Middle Eastern partners, we should begin by explicitly disavowing regime change, to allay unnecessary tension with our partners and to emphasize that our focus on human rights in no way detracts from our commitment to their external security. In short, pursuing both U.S. values and interests are mutually reinforcing and inextricably intertwined approaches to the Middle East.

3. The United States should adopt a new approach to security partnerships with regional actors. The Trump administration deserves widespread criticism of its transactional approach to foreign policy, a global approach that has rankled U.S. allies and severely weakened the post–World War II global order. On the other hand, in the Middle East, where most states tend to be transactional in their foreign relations, taking such an approach may be warranted at times. Ironically, Trump has treated several regional countries who do not share American values—Saudi Arabia and the United Arab Emirates in particular—as strategic partners deserving of a blank check, forgoing transactionalism with them while descending into tit-for-tat squabbles with our European allies. The results have been unfortunately predictable, as Middle Eastern states have pocketed blanket U.S. support while continuing to pursue agendas contrary to U.S. interests.

A different approach to security and political cooperation with most countries in the Middle East is long overdue. Instead of blindly supporting those leaders or states designated as friends, we should begin specifying clear conditions and delineating what we expect for our support, including transparency on how recipient states will use our support and assistance. And, critically, we will need to impose consequences when our partners violate these expectations, something the United States has been loath to do in the Middle East. In an effort to preserve the "relationship" with putatively friendly but problematic countries, the U.S. government has often lost sight of whether any given relationship is working to the benefit of the United States. In the past, preserving the relationship became the end, not the means to achieve U.S. goals. The guiding principle for our relationships in the Middle East should be mutual benefit, in the short and long terms. The United States should not hesitate to make changes to partnerships where this is not the case. Having difficult conversations with countries we think of as partners is never easy. If we are more explicit about our aims and what we will support, however, the United States may be able to avoid the type of unnecessary misunderstandings that erode trust over time.

4. The United States should more critically evaluate its military posture in the region and, where possible, elevate civilian power instead.
U.S. military strength enhances our diplomatic power, but it is not a substitute for it. Conflicts will not resolve themselves, and certainly not peacefully, just because we are strong. American diplomats need to become once again our first resort in dealing with conflict.

Since at least September 11, 2001, and perhaps even earlier, U.S. foreign policy in the Middle East has over-relied on military tools. Today, effective deterrence against potential external aggressors, whether Russia or Iran, does not necessarily require a large permanent footprint in the region, as long as U.S. redlines are clearly and publicly articulated, and prepositioning agreements as well as emergency basing rights remain in force. Technological changes on the horizon, such as a growing array of floating platforms, will further reduce the importance of maintaining a large military footprint in the Middle East. There will still be circumstances in which the United States needs to employ military force in the Middle East (or at least threaten to do so), particularly in the Gulf. However, we should eschew a binary choice between withdrawing all troops and the status quo, understanding the array of arrangements in between that could give us greater flexibility to advance U.S. interests at a more acceptable cost to the American public.

In the meantime, the U.S. government should also review its security assistance practices in the Middle East in the hope that we can help regional countries develop more effective and responsible militaries that can later take over some security responsibilities from the United States. Despite receiving billions of dollars in arms and countless training programs from the United States, the military performance of most Middle Eastern countries has not improved markedly. We need a new approach if this is to change, one that emphasizes institutional reform, not just operational training. Bilateral compacts should embed security assistance programs and these compacts should establish a clear strategic vision for U.S. support. More rigorous and systematic reviews of past security assistance programs would enable these changes. While it will not be easy to reform these programs, the status quo is simply not working; it is time to start experimenting with new models of cooperation. Finally, traditional security assistance, typically focused on military-to-military training and equipment programs, must be complemented by other crucial assistance programs: development, intelligence sharing, and law enforcement. A new approach to foreign assistance would build in rigorous expectations that the United States is advancing its own goals and objectives through its foreign aid programs, whatever the nature of the assistance.

The Inheritance: Constraints to U.S. Foreign Policy in the Middle East in a Post-Trump Era

The above principles may seem clear-cut, but navigating them will encounter many constraints. The Coronavirus pandemic is likely to generate yet more challenges for the United States in the region. As of mid-2020, some immediate-term effects of the COVID-19 crisis in the Middle East were beginning to emerge, including the dramatic downturn in the region's economy, particularly as oil prices sank and major sectors such as tourism crashed.

The first constraint is that U.S. foreign policymakers in a post-Trump world will not be able to start from a clean slate; they will have to contend with the legacy President Trump leaves in the Middle East, correcting for his many missteps to the extent possible. This volume proceeds from the assumption that President Trump will continue to ply a chaotic, unpredictable path in the Middle East, swinging erratically between his two somewhat inconsistent goals of disengaging from the region and taking on Iran. There may be a military confrontation, and further precipitous decisions to deploy and redeploy troops.

Overall, we assume that the inconsistent stops and starts in this approach will generally serve to undermine U.S. credibility in the region. We expect Trump to remain capricious in his decisions on military deployments, recklessly withdrawing troops from places they are needed (such as in northeastern Syria), while surging more forces to countries where they are either not needed or potentially carry significant unintended consequences (such as in Saudi Arabia). In the diplomatic realm, Trump will continue to cultivate closer ties with Saudi Arabia—in spite of the brutal murder of Jamal Khashoggi—and the United Arab Emirates, whose activist authoritarianism and fulsome flattery appeal to the U.S. president. The rest of the Arab world will either receive Trump's rhetorical endorsement but not much else (currently the case with Egypt), or Trump will ignore them entirely (the status of Tunisia and Morocco). President Trump will maintain his unstinting political embrace of Israel's right-wing government, and enable Israel's most hawkish policies within the West Bank and across the region. The president's almost obsessive hostility toward Iran will persist. Human rights issues will continue to be marginalized, and the United States will take a back seat to other actors in conflict management and resolution in Syria, Yemen, and Libya. Instead, the focus of U.S. diplomacy will increasingly revolve around the promotion of arms sales and other commercial activities.

Trump may not yet have caused irreversible damage to U.S. interests, though he is getting perilously close. Partners forsaken by the Trump administration, including Jordan, Tunisia, the Syrian Kurds, and the Palestinians, will probably give the next administration some benefit of the doubt. Future policy officials will have to countermand Trump's most egregious decisions, including suspending funding to the Palestinians, embracing Khalifa Haftar as the solution to Libya's problems, and granting a blank check to the Saudis and Emiratis. Other decisions, such as recognizing Jerusalem as the capital of Israel and moving the U.S. embassy there, will be politically hard to reverse. Instead, U.S. officials will have to balance out these past decisions with new measures to neutralize much of the harm inflicted on U.S. interests. As of this writing, the JCPOA (Joint Comprehensive Plan of Action) may still be salvageable, but ongoing developments may ultimately render it obsolete. And if the Trump administration recognizes Israel's annexation of parts of the West Bank, it could fundamentally change what options are available to his predecessors in dealing with the Israeli-Palestinian conflict. The next administration should not rely on inheriting a clean slate from its predecessor.

The second constraint for any new U.S. strategy involves the continuing turmoil in the Middle East. The Arab world's decades-old nation-state system is under assault both from within—from the forces of tribalism, sectarianism, and dramatic socioeconomic change—and from without—from destabilizing actors like Iran and Russia. Economic stagnation, an immense youth bulge, venal governance, and the persistent appeal of extremist groups are simultaneously the cause and result of the growing instability that has come to characterize the region. The Middle East appears to be in the middle of a prolonged process in which the relationship between societies and political authority is being contested and renegotiated. This contestation could take a generation to resolve fully. And the ensuing instability will play out against a backdrop of intensified regional rivalries not only between Iran and Saudi Arabia, but also between two blocs—Qatar/Turkey and the UAE/Egypt/Saudi Arabia.

In the immediate term (two to three years), however, there is likely to be substantial divergence at the subregional level. In Syria and Iraq, the durability of gains by the U.S.-led counter-ISIS coalition will be tested by a combination of geopolitical intrigue, persistent sectarian-ethnic tensions, and dysfunctional politics. Starting in the spring and summer of 2019, the Syrian regime, aided by Russian airpower, begin to reconquer Idlib Province. Meanwhile, the October 2019 offensive by Turkey in the north, encouraged by Trump's bizarre decision to draw down U.S. forces with little notice, will empower the Syrian regime, Iran, Russia, and ISIS. Israel will continue its air strikes against Hezbollah in Syria as Iran slowly fortifies its presence in the war-torn country. In Iraq, the challenges of addressing the Sunni Arab community's long-standing grievances, an increasingly restive Shia community dissatisfied with corrupt and feckless governance, and Kurdish national aspirations will remain nettlesome. Recent violence between the United States and Iran and its Iraqi proxies that began in late December 2019 has further undermined Iraq's stability and could lead to a wider confrontation.

Unresolved failed states in Yemen and Libya will continue to fester, as the divergent agendas of regional and international actors exacerbate centrifugal forces in countries whose internal national coherence has always been tenuous. Libya will face difficulty establishing a single set of national institutions that reach to all corners of the country, particularly as Libyan militias and factions have become increasingly bogged down in intraregional and interregional competition over time, while in Yemen southern secession is a distinct possibility. A variety of other states that have so far averted state failure but still suffer from deep structural problems will manage on the brink of instability. Countries in this category include the kingdoms of Jordan, Morocco, and Bahrain; authoritarian republics in Egypt and Tunisia, which continues its inspiring transition to democracy amid a faltering economy. In Lebanon, an economic emergency has brought long-standing discontent to a head, and it is unclear whether any conceivable government can manage popular expectations and the pressures of the international financial system. All of these states will most likely survive this period, but we cannot discount the possibility that a shock, whether external or internal, will bring regime change or even chaos to at least one of these states.

In Israel, Prime Minister Benjamin Netanyahu's desperate attempts to stay in power and to avoid conviction on corruption charges have overtaken Israeli politics. Beneath these personality conflicts, however, it is not clear that there are major policy differences between Netanyahu and his former primary challenger-cum-coalition partner, Benny Gantz of the Blue and White Party. With the Trump administration's ongoing support for right-of-center political positions, parties on the center-right are primed to further their consolidation of power in Israel. Meanwhile, the combination of the continued growth of Israeli settlements in the West Bank, possible Israeli annexation, and potential Palestinian succession makes the prospects for progress toward ending the occupation and realizing a two-state solution to the Israeli-Palestinian conflict seem remote at best.

In the Gulf, we will continue to see enhanced regional activism by Saudi Arabia and the UAE, countries that until recently were traditionally passive players. President Trump's unwillingness to come to the defense of Saudi Arabia after Iran struck a major oil installation has induced some momentary caution in Riyadh and Abu Dhabi, but these countries' risk-acceptant leaders are unlikely to retreat from the scene. Qatar, on the other hand, has temporarily scaled back its regional ambitions in response to Saudi-Emirati pressure and greater scrutiny of its activities. In spite of the blockade on Qatar, Emir Tamim's government, which presides over a population of just 300,000 citizens and has sufficient proven natural gas reserves to last several more decades, may prove to be the Gulf's most stable country.[15] Other countries in this subregion, already struggling with low oil prices, are on the wrong side of their production plateaus, straining their ability to sustain decades-old social welfare contracts with their publics. These pressures are, and will remain, particularly acute for Saudi Arabia, which has a rapidly growing population and an economy that has been severely damaged by COVID-19. The Saudi public's political, social, and economic expectations are not being met.[16]

The third constraint, as discussed above, is the fact that the American public has little appetite for more military adventures in the Middle East after nearly two decades of war. Many Americans have concluded that the post-9/11 "forever wars" achieved comparatively little at great cost. Public opinion, therefore, will militate against new military entanglements in the region.[17] In contrast to past years, the burden of proof will increasingly rest with those advocating military action in the Middle East, not those counseling restraint. The use of force will remain part of the next administration's toolkit, but a new president should not expect to enjoy the same free rein as his or her predecessors.

Fourth, the so-called return of great power competition will also constrain U.S. policy in the Middle East. As the Pentagon's National Defense Strategy makes clear, China and Russia are likely to displace the Middle East as the central focus of U.S. foreign policy. And, as priorities change, so, too, will the distribution of resources. The more manpower, money, and attention that is devoted to near-peer competition, the less that will be available for the Middle East. Absent major increases in not just defense but also the foreign affairs budgets—a remote possibility, given the current domestic political reality—U.S. officials working on the Middle East will have to make do with less.

Fifth, the checkered standing of the United States among the people of the Middle East limits what the United States can achieve there. Regional mistrust of the U.S. government, if not the American people, is not new, but it remains a handicap for policymakers. Whether it is U.S. support for Israel and repressive dictatorships, or anti-colonial sensitivities, there is deep opposition to U.S. policy in the Middle East. Authoritarian leaders play on popular suspicions of U.S. motivations to discredit even the most well-intentioned aid programs. The presence of U.S. forces in the Middle East often provokes a strong nationalist backlash, endangering our troops while destabilizing host countries. Increasingly, this mistrust has spread to regional leaders, who accuse the United States of abandoning long-standing friends and warming up to their Iranian enemy. Friction is inherent in U.S. relationships with Middle Eastern countries and, while this will not stop cooperation, it will continue to complicate it.

Based on the preceding analysis, it is clear that the next administration will face an extremely challenging policy environment in the Middle East. The region is likely to remain mired in turmoil, leaving few opportunities for major policy victories. A new administration will not be in a position to solve the region's many problems in its first four years, and probably not in eight years. Simply put, the United States should view the Middle East as a region to be managed over time, not one awaiting deliverance.

This Volume

In this volume, we have gathered the most passionate, most thoughtful emerging voices. These authors worked for policymakers across the Clinton, Bush, Obama, and Trump administrations. They have reflected for years on policy trade-offs and challenges in the Middle East. In this compendium, they lay out a path for future U.S. engagement with regional countries, reflecting distinctions within the subregions. The authors as a cohort represent the new generation of Middle East policymakers. While each has worked on the region from within the U.S. government over the past fifteen years, their analysis does not dwell on past mistakes. Rather, each author considers anew how to resolve key regional and subregional challenges, understanding that the future will not look like the past.

The following chapters, when taken together, are not meant to be exhaustive. Left out of this volume are key issues and key countries that are likely to merit key consideration and attention in the future. In particular, we did not have the space to address intra-Gulf tensions; the changing politics within Algeria; and the local political dynamics, and spillover from regional conflicts, affecting Jordan and Lebanon. Moreover, we have dedicated little space to the significant economic and trade trends in the region as well as the Trump administration's focus on commercial diplomacy. Its approach to the Middle East has overempowered U.S. industries' voices in key decisions, whether it comes to prioritizing the concerns of the U.S. defense industry in human rights policies toward the Gulf or elevating the importance of investments in the United States by key Middle Eastern states or rich individuals. In this volume, rather than commercial diplomacy or economic decisionmaking, we home in on the political and security elements of U.S. strategy. We have organized this volume around three themes based on three big picture challenges that future policymakers will have to tackle: de-escalating key regional crises; reimagining key U.S. security partnerships; and addressing crosscutting regional issues.

The authors in part I ask how U.S. foreign policy can manage, mitigate, and eventually resolve the many civil conflicts that persist across the Middle East. Wa'el Alzayat argues that the next U.S. administration will find few opportunities to change the bad outcomes facing U.S. foreign policymakers in Syria. Nonetheless, we cannot afford to give up. We must try to move the needle, where possible, on U.S. interests such as counterterrorism, protecting civilians, providing humanitarian aid, and eventually generating a diplomatic environment more favorable to U.S. goals in Syria and beyond. Christopher Le Mon makes a case for prioritizing ending the Yemen war—in part because of its deadly human costs and in part because de-escalating the conflict will allow the United States to achieve its other interests in Yemen. Even if the next administration fully extricates the United States from the war, sustained and creative U.S. diplomacy—particularly U.S. pressure exerted on the Kingdom of Saudi Arabia—will be necessary for any meaningful de-escalation on the ground. Megan Doherty argues that the United States must work with the European Union to stabilize Libya. However, in order to counter ISIS's growth in Libya over the medium term, and in order to achieve a modicum of stability, the United States and its allies must help the Libyan parties address deficits in governance and the weakness of local institutions.

The authors in part II reconsider U.S. security partnerships in the Middle East, analyzing how the United States can prioritize its own interests and values rather than submit to the objectives and preferences of the partner country. Dan Shapiro reimagines a U.S. alliance with Israel that revisits Israeli-Palestinian peace as a way to protect Israeli security. Jon Finer argues that key U.S. interests in the Middle East converge in Iraq, where, in spite of the risks of being caught in U.S.-Iranian tensions, the still-fragile transitioning democracy needs U.S. political, military, and economic support. Amy Hawthorne and Andrew Miller show how the U.S.-Egypt partnership—once a security lynchpin of U.S. strategy in the region—might not matter as much for U.S. interests. At the same time, Egypt's authoritarian governance, combined with its economic and demographic crises, means that President Abdel Fattah al Sisi's rule will continue to be destabilizing. Finally, Daniel Benaim argues that the United States must recalibrate its partnership with Saudi Arabia. Partners should agree to disagree candidly where interests diverge, even as they find areas for cooperation on limited goals.

The authors in part III consider crosscutting U.S. foreign policy issues relevant to the entire region. Alexander Bick argues against overinvesting in the Middle East in order to fight a new Cold War with Russia, limiting U.S. competition with Russia in the region to those few cases where core American interests are implicated. Sahar Nowrouzzadeh and Jane Rhee contend that it is possible to manage the Iranian nuclear threat while also countering its dangerous regional behavior. They argue that a future Iran policy should retain an emphasis on dialogue, even if the channels of communication are limited. Mara Karlin and Melissa Dalton advocate for a smaller, smarter U.S. defense posture that confronts the threats the United States faces in the Middle East with more limited and strategic defense tools. Stephen Tankel argues for a more coherent, rigorous, and ultimately smaller U.S. security sector portfolio in the region. Currently, the United States is achieving too few returns on its extensive and growing investments in security assistance in the Middle East. Dafna H. Rand argues that policymakers should scrutinize the return on investment derived from the current civilian assistance portfolio, which is a derivative of many earlier policies; better strategy can ensure that U.S. aid achieves U.S. objectives, particularly in the realm of rule of law and institutional reform.

While the ends prescribed by the authors in this volume—a reduced, more strategic, more disciplined and principled Middle East
policy—might not differ much from at least the intent of the past two
administrations, new tactics and programs will be needed to achieve
these policy ends where earlier generations of policymakers fell short.
The conclusion considers key innovations to the bureaucracy and
policy process that can advance more limited American goals in the
Middle East over the coming decade.

Notes

1. Richard Fontaine and Michael Singh, "Is America No Longer the
Middle East's Greatest Power?" *The National Interest*, February 15, 2017.

2. Robert Satloff, "Don't Pull Back," in "Commitment Issues," *Foreign
Affairs*, May/June 2019.

3. Martin Indyk, "The Middle East Isn't Worth It Anymore," *Wall Street
Journal*, January 17, 2020.

4. Trita Parsi, "The Middle East Is More Stable When the United States
Stays Away," *Foreign Policy*, January 6, 2020.

5. Mara Karlin and Tamara Cofman Wittes, "America's Middle East Purgatory," *Foreign Affairs*, December 11, 2018.

6. In April 2000, 24 percent of Americans worried they or someone they
knew could be a victim of terror. Following September 11, 2001, 58 percent
of Americans believed they could be a victim of terror. In 2017, 42 percent of
Americans believed that they could become a victim of terror. See Gallup
polling "Terrorism" (https://news.gallup.com/poll/4909/terrorism-united-states
.aspx).

7. United States Senate. 115th Congress. 1st Session S. RES. 5.

8. United States Senate. 116th Congress. 1st Session. S. RES. 234.

9. Peter Baker and Julie Hirschfeld Davis, "U.S. Finalizes Deal to Give
Israel US$38 Billion in Military Aid," *New York Times*, September 13, 2016.

10. "International Energy Statistics," EIA Beta (www.eia.gov/beta/inter
national/data/browser/#/?c=41000000020000600000000000000g00020000
0000000000001&vs=INTL.44-1-AFRC-QBTU.A&vo=0&v=H&start=1980
&end=2016&showdm=y).

11. A 2019 poll by Surveys of U.S. Veterans found 62 percent of adults
thought the war in Iraq was not worth fighting and 58 percent thought the war
in Afghanistan was not worth fighting. Ruth Igielnik and Kim Parker,
"Majorities of U.S. Veterans, Public Say the Wars in Iraq and Afghanistan
Were Not Worth Fighting," PEW Research Center, July 10, 2019 (www.pew
research.org/fact-tank/2019/07/10/majorities-of-u-s-veterans-public-say-the-
wars-in-iraq-and-afghanistan-were-not-worth-fighting/).

12. Karlin and Cofman Wittes, "America's Middle East Purgatory." This
article provoked a much needed debate about the U.S. role in the Middle East
establishment foreign policy circles.

13. As of 2015, 50 percent of Americans considered the Middle East as very important to national security interests, while only 29 percent desired an increase in the U.S. military presence in the region. Dina Smeltz and Craig Kafur, "American Anxiety over Middle East Buffets Public Support for U.S. Presence in the Region," Chicago Council on Global Affairs, November 9, 2015 (www.thechicagocouncil.org/publication/american-anxiety-over-middle-east-buffets-public-support-us-presence-region).

14. Bill Law, "Trump's 'Ultimate Deal' Faces Ultimate Failure," Al Jazeera, March 4, 2019 (www.aljazeera.com/indepth/opinion/trump-ultimate-deal-faces-ultimate-failure-190303130838617.html).

15. "The World Factbook" Central Intelligence Agency, September 9, 2019 (www.cia.gov/library/publications/the-world-factbook/geos/qa.html).

16. Michael Amon and Nicolas Parasie, "Saudi Arabia's Economic Overhaul Is Backfiring," *Wall Street Journal*, March 23, 2019.

17. Igielnik and Parker, "Majorities of U.S. Veterans, Public Say the Wars in Iraq and Afghanistan Were Not Worth Fighting."

PART I

Defusing Regional Conflicts and
Rebuilding Diplomatic Influence

TWO

The Syrian Crucible and Future U.S. Options

WA'EL ALZAYAT

The Syrian conflict, one of this century's great tragedies, started as peaceful protests against single-family rule. Nine years later, it has morphed into a Gordian knot of competing interests between various Syrian, regional, and international actors. It has pitted pro-democracy activists against a mafia-like police state and religious extremists, rural folk against urban elite, and a religious majority against coopted minorities. It has exacerbated tensions between regional rivals, strained traditional alliances, empowered non-state actors, and enabled a former superpower to challenge a world order it has chafed under for three decades. To date, over 500,000 people have been killed, although the United Nations stopped tallying Syria's dead in 2015.[1] More than 100,000 are missing, with the majority thought to either be languishing in or to have died in Syrian regime prisons.[2] And over half of the country's prewar population of 24 million has been displaced, with over 6 million seeking refuge outside of Syria.[3]

Several developments in Syria present a threat to regional stability and potentially U.S. national interests. The war has precipitated massive forced displacement, which in turn has placed great strain on neighboring Turkey, Lebanon, and Jordan, as well as Europe. The refugee crisis has been weaponized by far-right and populist leaders in Europe and the United States in their bid to attain power. Chaos in Syria, largely due to Bashar al-Assad's violent response, which included the cynical release of extremists from his jails, has provided fertile ground for al Qaeda and ISIS to thrive. Today, the presence of tens of thousands of extremists complicates efforts to protect close to 3 million people in Idlib Province, and the ideology of ISIS is alive in the Syria-Iraq border region. Nonproliferation norms have been repeatedly broken with the regime's continued use of chemical weapons, including sarin and chlorine gases. The conflict has severely weakened ties between the United States and its NATO ally Turkey. Russia and Iran have exploited these divisions by seeking separate arrangements on Syria with Turkey via the Astana Process.

The Syrian conflict has not ended, notwithstanding Assad's claims that he is on the cusp of victory. In 2019, Syrian regime and Russian offensives to retake Idlib have forced 400,000 Syrians from their home, killed 4,000, and destroyed dozens of schools and hospitals.[4] Even in areas reconquered by the regime (such as the southern province of Daraa), active fighting persists.[5] The fighting inside of Syria continues to spill beyond its borders; Israel has launched several air attacks against pro-Iranian militias, including at least two in September 2019,[6] and Turkey invaded Syria in October 2019 to push the People's Protection Units (YPG)—the Syrian affiliate of the Kurdistan Workers' Party (PKK)—away from the border.[7] Meanwhile, the Syrian regime has allied itself with and given space to U.S. competitors and adversaries who seek to undermine U.S. interests, including states such as Iran and Russia and militant groups such as Hezbollah. And, while ISIS has been militarily defeated for now, the sustainability of this defeat remains in question, particularly given the ability of its cells to regroup and evidence that ISIS is actively recruiting across northeastern Syria.[8]

Complicating matters was President Trump's decision following the Turkish invasion to withdraw all U.S. forces from Syria, except for the small contingent operating out of the al Tanf base along the Jordanian border. The precipitous withdrawal and fear of advancing Turkish-backed forces caused the YPG to allow regime and Russian forces to move into their areas before the Turkish side could. Although the decision was partially reversed a month later with U.S. troops repositioned to eastern Syria, the events altered the landscape and the balance of power on the ground.[9] With the American military presence reduced, counter-ISIS partners co-mingled with the regime and Russia, and with relations with Turkey in tatters, U.S. options in Syria have become even more limited.

Notwithstanding these limits, U.S. policymakers will still need to address a number of issues that affect American interests, including ensuring the enduring defeat of ISIS, countering Iranian hard and soft power in Syria, protecting U.S. allies on Syria's borders, maintaining diplomatic and economic pressure on the regime, and protecting civilians. The last objective may be the most consequential over the long run, as the inability of the United States to end the atrocities against the Syrian people has weakened its moral standing and contributed to political instability from Lebanon to Western Europe. Indeed, the failure of the international community to protect Syrian civilians has damaged the perceived efficacy of the Western liberal order, increasing the appeal of alternatives offered by rivals, most notably Russia.

To pull off this juggling act will require the resumption of coordination on Syria with Turkey, even if other bilateral issues remain unresolved. With 3 million people in Idlib under de facto Turkish protection, the United States and Europe will suffer if the regime achieves a complete victory there. Given the politicization of the issue, such a scenario would likely produce a massive humanitarian crisis that can destabilize Europe.

This chapter begins by reflecting on why U.S. policy options narrowed over the course of the Obama and Trump administrations. It then offers lessons learned from the almost decade-old conflict. The chapter concludes with recommendations to policymakers intent on making the best of the limited policy options available to the United States. Rebuilding greater U.S. leverage is the only way the United

States will be able to secure a longer-term solution that protects the Syrian people and advances core U.S. interests in the realm of counterterrorism and maintaining regional stability.

The U.S. Response to the Syrian Civil Conflict, 2011–19

The United States has had limited, fraught relationships with the Syrian Arab Republic since Hafez al Assad took power in 1971 and transformed the country into a totalitarian system. Every component of the Syrian state, including its military, intelligence services, foreign policy, state-owned enterprises, educational system, religious establishment, media and entertainment sectors, and even urban development, were either coerced or coopted to ensure that "the family" would rule in perpetuity. A key tactic was linking the family's survival to that of the Alawite sect, to which Hafez al Assad belonged. Using this sect as a buffer against the country's majority Sunnis, Hafez filled the officer corps and key government posts with Alawi apparatchiks reporting primarily to members of his family or close associates. Through a combination of patronage and violence, Hafez positioned his regime as a predictable, if unsavory, player in the international community. Even though Syria would spew rhetoric against its neighbor Israel, it would not threaten military action against it, thus maintaining regional order.

While the transition to Hafez's son Bashar in 2001 offered a possibility for Damascus to warm its relations with the West, Syria continued to harbor al Qaeda cells in the wake of the 2003 Iraq war. Moreover, Syria was implicated along with Hezbollah in the killing of former Lebanese prime minister Rafik al Hariri.[10] Some Syrians had hoped for change when Bashar, a British-trained ophthalmologist, succeeded his father—and indeed the Damascus Spring of 2000–01 did include limited economic reforms.[11] Instead, over the course of Bashar's first ten years in office, the authoritarian state tightened its grip over all aspects of political and civic life.

In 2011, a group of teenagers scribbled "It's your turn, Doctor" on a wall in the southern city of Daraa, and with it challenged the forty-year rule of the Assads. The regime's harsh treatment of the boys and subsequent repression of peaceful protests led to an increasingly violent state-led response.[12] By the end of 2011, at least five thousand people had been killed and thousands arrested.[13] The regime's brutality, including the mobilization of irregular militias called *shabiha* (ghosts), led to significant defections among Sunni members of the military. Another phenomenon that caught the regime off guard was the organic proliferation of civil society groups that organized protests, documented regime atrocities, and ran makeshift hospitals for those injured at protests. These Local Coordination Councils (LCCs) formed the backbone of the revolution in 2011–13.[14] Outside of Syria, long-exiled figures such as Burhan Ghalioun and recently released Damascus Spring oppositionists like Riad al Seif came together with intellectuals, activists, and members of the Syrian Muslim Brotherhood to form the nucleus of the political opposition outside of Syria.[15]

The United States, its Western allies, and most of the Arab world were stunned by the Syrian regime's brutality—in some cases, the military would shell entire neighborhoods.[16] From early 2011, some of these countries began supporting the growing political and military forces cohering into a "Syrian opposition." (The term often meant different things to different constituencies.) Through 2012, policymakers from London to Washington to Geneva expected Bashar al Assad's imminent fall, assuming he would follow in the footsteps of Mubarak, Ben Ali, Saleh, and others.[17] Assad, after all, was from a minority sect ruling over a Sunni majority, and his repressive response to the peaceful protests had outraged the Sunni world, from Turkey to the Arabian Gulf. There was near-unanimous international support for Western sanctions on Damascus to squeeze the regime and build up both the political and military elements of the Free Syrian Army (FSA). All of these factors led President Obama, in August 2011, to declare that "Assad must go."[18] The Obama administration followed that pronouncement a year later with a decision to provide material support to the FSA while increasing pressure on the regime.

No Appetite for Military Intervention

From 2012 to 2013, regime violence drove Syrian refugees into neighboring Jordan, Turkey, and Lebanon, sparking a migration crisis that eventually reached Europe. As the Syrian regime horrified the world, and the geopolitical costs of the war continued to grow, President Obama faced growing public pressure, as well as pressure from members of his own administration, to respond militarily. However, having just ended the U.S. military mission in Iraq, Obama was reticent to entangle the United States in another Middle Eastern war, partly out of doubt that U.S. intervention would ultimately succeed in stabilizing Syria. He also worried about the absence of a clear political transition plan for a post-Assad state that would preserve Syria's institutions.[19]

Obama's strategy thus rested on building enough military, economic, and diplomatic pressure on Assad to force him to agree to either step aside or implement serious reform rather than committing U.S. forces to topple the Syrian dictator immediately. Diplomatically, in March 2012, the United States backed former UN Secretary-General Kofi Annan's six-point plan, and then convened an "action group" at the Geneva I Conference on Syria in June of that same year. Its communiqué called for a "transitional government body with full executive powers" that could include members of the Syrian government and the opposition.[20] Differences, however, quickly emerged between Russia and the United States regarding the role of Assad in a future government of Syria. Ultimately, there would be Geneva I, II, III, and IV, with the Russians neither conceding that Assad would have to step aside nor pressuring him to seriously contemplate political reform. Instead, Russia provided diplomatic cover for the regime, including vetoing numerous Syria-related resolutions at the UNSC, as it sought to first slow down rebel advances and then go on the offensive to regain lost territories. The failed Geneva II talks, for example, took place against the backdrop of the regime and Hezbollah finalizing their assault on the city of Homs after an eighteen-month siege.[21]

With Russian diplomatic protection, Assad calculated that the United States was unlikely to attack him, given President Obama's established aversion to unilateral actions. Any uncertainty regarding this possibility disappeared after the president reversed course and decided against striking Syria following the 2013 Ghouta chemical weapons attack that killed an estimated 1,400 people as they slept.[22] To many, Obama's failure to follow through on his "redline" in the fall of 2013 conveyed to Russia and Iran the United States's unwillingness to use military force to deter or punish attacks against civilians. The decision also signaled to allies, who were supportive of the opposition, that there were limits to what the United States was prepared to do, which prevented other countries from contemplating unilateral action against Assad. As military pressure from opposition fighters intensified, Assad escalated attacks against civilians in opposition-held areas, perhaps convinced that there would be no international community response to increasing violations of international norms. By January 2012, the regime was regularly using tanks and artillery against heavily populated areas, and by 2013, it even deployed Scud ballistic missiles against Aleppo.[23]

Despite its military superiority, the regime continued to lose territory to the opposition, and by mid-2015 was heavily relying on as many as five thousand Hezbollah fighters and thousands of Iraqi, Pakistani, and Afghan Shia militias sent by Iran's Islamic Revolutionary Guards Corps (IRGC).[24] Russia's military intervention in late September 2015 and its subsequent buildup of personnel and military hardware, including sophisticated anti-aircraft systems, secured the regime's survival. By 2015, Obama officials now publicly ruled out military action against Assad, fearing that U.S. intervention could lead to a war with Russia. Instead, President Obama authorized Secretary of State John Kerry to engage the Russians in negotiations intended to de-escalate the fighting even if a permanent political solution remained elusive.

Contrary to predictions of a quagmire for the Russians by senior U.S. officials, Russia's intervention achieved its main objective of preventing regime collapse, bolstering Moscow's regional and international reputations. Obama officials established a high-level, multilateral forum known as the International Syria Support Group (ISSG), which included—among other key players—Russia, Iran, Saudi Arabia, and Turkey.[25] In parallel, the United States held intensive bilateral diplomatic talks with Russia that led to the 2016 Cessation of Hostilities Agreement (CoH).[26] While these diplomatic efforts achieved a short-lived ceasefire in 2016, the U.S.-Russia agreement eventually unraveled, primarily due to violations by the regime and Russia and the absence of an enforcement mechanism to hold them to account. In one particular incident, a UN and Syrian Arab Red

Crescent aid convoy near Aleppo was destroyed by the Syrian air force in what the UN described as a "meticulously planned and ruthlessly carried out" air strike.[27] Without deterrence against or punishment for such violations, the regime, with help from Russia and Iran and support from Hezbollah, accelerated its campaign to reclaim lost territory. With the fall of Aleppo, Syria's largest urban center and an important symbol of opposition strength, in December 2016, the Syrian regime was reinvigorated, inspired to reconquer territory that the opposition had held for years. Meanwhile, Obama exited office acknowledging that his efforts in Syria had failed to achieve the end of the Assad regime or stop a catastrophic war with extensive human and geopolitical consequences.[28]

Shift to an ISIS-First Policy

From the early days of the revolution, Assad released former al Qaeda in Iraq (AQI) fighters and other extremists from jail while focusing his repression against nonviolent protesters, civil society activists, and nonextremist militias. This strategy proved effective, as it simultaneously weakened the moderate opposition while empowering extremists. As elements of al Qaeda infiltrated the Syrian armed opposition, hardline extremist groups became the more capable fighting forces on the ground, with the more moderate oppositionists struggling militarily.[29] This trend gave further pause to those in the U.S. administration weighing whether to use military power against Assad, worrying that only al Qaeda-linked opposition groups would inherit Syria after Assad was gone.[30]

Meanwhile, ISIS was on the rise in Iraq, and, after capturing Mosul, ISIS swept through northeastern Syria, declaring a Caliphate across both Iraq and Syria.[31] Suddenly, U.S. policy toward Syria shifted to prioritizing the fight against the insurgent group. In September 2014, the United States mobilized over seventy nations to form the Global Coalition against Daesh (the derogatory Arabic name for ISIS).[32] Initially seeking to focus on ISIS in Iraq only, the Obama administration came to recognize that it could not effectively combat the group without addressing its operations in Syria, where it was flourishing.

A focus on eliminating this threat led the Obama administration to look for local partners on the ground in lieu of deploying substantial numbers of U.S. combat troops in Syria. Having decided against military confrontation with the Syrian regime or its allies, the Obama administration looked for groups that were disinterested in fighting Assad. Although moderate opposition groups were keenly interested in partnering against ISIS, U.S. insistence on avoiding conflict with Assad precluded many from joining the Department of Defense Train and Equip (T&E) program that was set up to train local fighters. From their perspective, opposition fighters found it impossible to pledge not to defend themselves or their communities against Assad's forces.[33] The failed effort to partner with the opposition coincided with another one to work with the YPG, which eventually became the main on-the-ground effort against ISIS. The relationship with the YPG was first established when the United States provided air cover and some weapons to YPG fighters pinned down by ISIS in the northern Syrian town of Kobane.[34] Though it was originally conceived as a one-off collaboration, senior U.S. officials saw the potential of a longer-term partnership with the YPG, given their military experience and ideological cohesion. The partnership posed significant political challenges, not least because of the PKK's aspirations for an independent Kurdish state, its status under American law as a foreign terrorist organization, its intolerance of rival Kurdish political parties, and its problematic history of armed conflict with Turkey. To assuage Turkish concerns, the United States tried unsuccessfully to recast the effort as a more inclusive Kurdish-Arab venture under the name of the Syrian Democratic Forces (SDF), even as it remained dominated by YPG fighters and their political arm, the Democratic Union Party (PYD).[35]

Ultimately, by late 2017, the multinational coalition was successful in destroying ISIS in Syria. Yet, the decision to work with the YPG and the predictable fallout with Turkey has become one of the most vexing issues confronting the Trump administration. An erratic decision by President Trump in early October 2019 to withdraw the limited number of U.S. troops who had remained in northeastern Syria from 2017–19 gave the green light to the Turkish military to begin an attack in northeastern Syria against America's SDF partners.[36] At the time of this writing, the government of Syria had re-entered the northeast for the first time in seven years, albeit in small numbers, and the U.S. strategic position to accomplish its goals in Syria had deteriorated.

Trump's Near Retreat from Syria

As a presidential candidate, Donald Trump argued that the United States should not get drawn into another Middle Eastern conflict. From the beginning of his administration, Trump was clear that countering ISIS would be the key goal for the United States in Syria. He has made clear that pressuring the Assad regime is no longer a top U.S. priority. At one point, he called Assad a "natural ally" against ISIS.[37] In July 2017, Trump abruptly ended a covert CIA program, reportedly at the urging of then CIA director Mike Pompeo, to arm and train the moderate opposition without seeking anything in return from the Russians or the regime.[38] Up to that point, the program had enabled FSA brigades to hold on to territory in northern and southern Syria, including a key border crossing with Jordan.[39] Cut off from U.S. support, many FSA fighters were absorbed by regime-sanctioned militias, extremist groups, or the Turkish-backed Syrian National Army (SNL).[40]

There have nevertheless been a few exceptions to Trump's ISIS-only policy. In April 2017 and again in April 2018, the United States carried out air strikes against the regime for using chemical weapons on Syrian civilians in Khan Sheikhoun and Douma, respectively.[41] But these attacks failed to deter Assad from escalating his gruesome campaign against Syria's civilians, which continued unabated in the offensive in Daraa Province in 2018 and again in Idlib in 2019. U.S. airstrikes also targeted regime forces and their allies when they threatened U.S. military positions. The most notable episode occurred on February 7, 2018, when U.S. airstrikes decimated Syrian forces and allied militias, as well as a large contingent of Russian mercenaries near the eastern city of Deir al-Zour.[42]

On the diplomatic front, Trump's approach to Syria during his first two years in office vacillated between indifference and incoherence. U.S. diplomats were noticeably absent from the Astana Process meetings in 2017 and 2018—ceding the diplomatic ground to Russia and Iran. Meanwhile, there were splits within the administration between those who wanted to maintain a focus on fighting ISIS and those who also wanted to counter Iran. President Trump routinely made contradictory statements, sometimes emphasizing the importance of expelling the Iranians from Syria and at other times declaring that it did not matter if Iran stayed in Syria.

By 2018, it seemed that Trump not only had no interest in a conflict with the Assad regime, but, in fact, wanted to get out of Syria altogether. The president had seemed eager to declare mission accomplished against ISIS as early as 2017.

Then, in late 2018, Trump tweeted that the United States would immediately withdraw its military presence in northeastern Syria, shocking U.S. allies in the coalition against ISIS, aggrieving SDF partners on the ground, and surprising officials in his own administration.[43] Many had felt, correctly, that a sudden withdrawal would leave the SDF vulnerable to the regime and its allies, or Turkey, which in turn would jeopardize whatever gains had been made against ISIS. The United States had been able to preserve this piece of real estate at a relatively low cost, which could be leveraged in the future in any serious political negotiations. The Department of Defense disagreed vehemently with the president's tweets, which led to a nine-month effort by the Pentagon to keep limited troops. Ultimately, the president decided in October 2019 to withdraw U.S. troops from SDF areas in the northeast, giving a green light to the Turkish military. They launched an offensive against SDF strongholds, creating another round of displacement and insecurity in the region, which has ultimately led to the Syrian government's efforts to reinstate itself in northeastern Syria after seven years.

In terms of the growing Iranian presence inside Syria, increased U.S. assertiveness in combatting the Iranian militias in Iraq had some degree of spillover effect into Syria by the end of 2019 and early 2020. Following the targeted assassination of IRGC Commander Qassem Soleimani in Iraq in January 2020, the United States launched a strike on Iranian-backed militias, including Iraqi groups such as Kata'ib Hezbollah.[44] The U.S. government also continued to provide (as it did under President Obama) tacit support to Israel to attack discrete sites affiliated with Hezbollah and Iran. Beyond kinetic operations, the Trump administration's "maximum pressure"

policy against Iran, including increased sanctions, has severely cur-
tailed Iran's economy, which could force Iran to reduce its military
and economic assistance to Assad in the long run. While Trump's
policies since taking office have largely signaled an American exit
from Syria and a disinterest in protecting the Syrian people, the decision to leave some U.S. troops combined with a more robust response
to Iran's influence in Syria leaves the door open to whether the United
States can preserve a degree of influence on the ground.

What Comes Next in Syria

While the regime and its backers have gone to great lengths to convey
that they have won the war, in reality the conflict is likely to continue for some time. Unaddressed grievances, coupled with unfet-
tered access to weapons, all but guarantee that sporadic violence
will continue well into the future. The Syrian state lies in ruins with
a reconstruction bill of at least US$250 billion—four times Syria's
GDP.[45] The Syrian regime will struggle to maintain control over the
entirety of the country, even if it completes its current effort to retake
the final area of opposition control in Idlib. Indeed, the Syrian regime
has already been dealing with resurgent rebellions or unrest in areas
it had recently come to control, such as swaths of southern Syria
it subdued through "reconciliation" agreements.[46] Syrian Arab and
Kurdish factions will coexist uneasily, particularly in tense northeastern Syria, where land has changed hands—in some cases, several
times—between ethnic groups.

Regional dynamics will likely continue to exacerbate intra-Syrian
tensions. Syria's neighbors will closely monitor and manage threats to
their interests. Israel, for instance, will continue to use force to combat
the increasing military assets of Iran and Hezbollah in Syria. Though
Israel might be able to diminish the tactical and operational capacities of Hezbollah and the IRGC across Syria, limited air strikes are
unlikely to change the strategic calculus in Tehran regarding the cen-
trality of the survival of Assad's regime to Iranian regional ambitions.

Meanwhile, across the region, the instability caused by the Syrian
unrest is likely to continue. ISIS and al Qaeda, although significantly
degraded, will continue to radicalize, recruit, and plot on Syrian soil,

requiring continued U.S. and regional counterterrorism and counterinsurgency efforts. Indeed, ISIS is likely to adapt and survive by decentralizing its organizational structures, embedding itself into Syrian communities by updating its recruiting strategy abroad, and inspiring attacks that require less logistical planning. Turkey will continue to monitor the YPG's status in the northeast as a far greater threat to its national security than ISIS, which means that U.S. policymakers will need to contend with future skirmishes between Turkey and Kurdish groups and/or the regime across its border. In Lebanon and even Turkey, there is growing political pressure to repatriate Syrian refugees, despite the fact that the conditions in Syria are not conducive to their return.

Given these unpredictable challenges, the United States cannot afford to completely retreat from Syria as President Trump seems to want to do. Future Syria policy must realistically accept that the Assad regime has survived the war for now. Yet that does not mean that the worst excesses and barbarism of the Syrian regime should be ignored or that it is impossible for the United States to try to protect Syrian civilians, minimize the risk from ISIS, and work with regional allies to limit the extent of Iranian influence and capabilities over time. By sequencing its objectives and investing in public and private diplomacy, the next administration can build up its leverage over time, allowing the United States more, though by no means decisive, influence over Syria's trajectory.

A Foreign Policy Approach for the Next Administration

The most important principle that should guide a future administration's approach to Syria after nine years is that it must fully resource and faithfully execute whatever policy approach it adopts. The Obama administration announced that "Assad must go" in 2011, but never committed to using all the tools of U.S. statecraft to achieve this goal. The policy has become even more confusing under Trump, with his contradictory statements and those of his senior officials. He has ended support to the moderate opposition yet bombed the regime and its allies, suspended assistance funding to the northeast, and announced that U.S. troops would leave Syria in 2018 and again in 2019, only to reverse those decisions.

While it would be convenient to compartmentalize into distinct categories the policy challenges Syria poses, in reality they are inter-related and mutually reinforcing. Future U.S. administrations should pursue policies that holistically consider civilian protection, the terrorist threat, and a political solution to the civil war, while remaining realistic about what they can achieve in Syria. Taking into consideration the likely trajectory of the conflict as well as lessons learned from previous policies, the next U.S. administration should seek to achieve the following:

Ease human suffering and protect civilians. Given Syria's unenviable status as the largest and most complex humanitarian disaster of our time, it is simply untenable for the United States to maintain its moral authority in the world while relinquishing leadership on humanitarian issues. While the United States may not be able to stop or prevent all the violence in Syria, it can provide de facto safe havens for civilians in areas already under SDF and Turkish control, and undertake a number of efforts to bolster its support to millions of Syrian refugees.

The United States should work with Turkey to prevent a complete takeover of Idlib Province by the regime with Russian help. Should Idlib fall, close to 3 million people may seek to enter Turkey, with catastrophic consequences for President Erdogan at home and in turn Europe. The United States should send clear signals to the Russians that the regime's offensive in Idlib threatens a NATO ally and that there will be consequences for the regime's continued crimes against civilians there. U.S. officials should make it clear publicly that they consider the forced displacement of 3 million people into Turkey a security threat to the alliance.

Future administrations can and should do more to help the millions of Syrians in need. They should start by reversing the Trump administration's travel ban on citizens from Syria and, in parallel, restore the cap on refugee resettlement in the United States from the planned 18,000 for 2020 to at least its historical average of approximately 85,000. In addition, the United States should not only continue to fund UN humanitarian appeals, but maintain and increase funding for civil society, free journalists, local councils, and mechanisms to prosecute war crimes and enforce accountability. Finally, the United States should be an international leader in preventing the forced return of refugees to Syria, either to the Turkish occupied "safe zones" or elsewhere.

Prevent the resurgence of terrorism. A future administration should seek to prevent the resurgence of terrorist organizations in Syria. Although significantly degraded, ISIS and al Qaeda are likely to continue to radicalize, recruit, and plot on Syrian soil. At the time of its territorial defeat in 2019, the U.S. military estimated that ISIS retained tens of thousands of fighters. In January 2019, U.S. Central Command assessed that "absent sustained pressure, ISIS could likely resurge in Syria"—and this was before the reported escape of ISIS prisoners in October 2019 during the Turkish offensive.[47]

Given the reduction in U.S. troops, the United States will need to rely on regional partnerships, intel sharing, and remote collection platforms to keep an eye on emerging counterterrorism threats. The Assads are well known for coopting terrorist groups, just as they did following the Iraq invasion, and using them to ensure the survival of their regime. The United States or allied countries may need to conduct overt or covert counterterrorism operations inside Syria even after its troops have departed.

U.S. support for Turkey in Idlib has to include a joint effort to contain and ultimately destroy al Qaeda's presence in the province, which will be complicated and messy but ultimately necessary. Idlib still has thousands of moderate and conservative (but not terrorist) opposition fighters and activists, who have confronted al Qaeda on numerous occasions. Protecting the province from regime attacks while conducting joint counter–al Qaeda operations with the help of moderate fighters is the most viable way to prevent massive displacement and atrocities, deny further regime gains, and potentially stabilize a NATO ally. The United States should also consider supporting Turkish engagement with Syrian groups in the northwest to create an edifice of local governance, as long as these groups renounce terrorism.

Reinvest in long-term local partnerships. The United States has deep and now long-standing relationships with Syrian civil society, citizen journalists, community leaders, human rights advocates, and political activists. By and large, these communities share democratic values and desire changes that would make Syria more closely aligned with the U.S. vision for the region. Where possible, the United States should reverse the decision to cut stabilization funds, and support with financial assistance, mentoring, and technical training communities in Idlib and parts of the northeast that are not under regime control. It should also continue to actively engage these communities to inform U.S. and international policy deliberations. The United States cannot hope to develop sound or successful strategies without input from Syrians. This is especially true as COVID-19 threatens to compound the humanitarian crisis in Idlib and other parts of Syria's northwest, as well as in the country's northeast.

Maintain pressure on the Syrian regime and Iran. The United States would have a greater number of avenues to pursue its objectives if there were a government in Syria with which it could partner. Yet, barring dramatic changes to the current regime, the United States should avoid cooperating with or legitimizing Damascus. To do so would undermine the moral authority of the United States and embolden dictatorships around the world. Aside from ethical considerations, it is worth recalling that even in the best of times, the Assad regime was ineffective, corrupt, and no friend of the United States. Similarly, the United States should maintain economic and at times military pressure against Iran and Iranian-backed militias in Syria to signal to Tehran that supporting Assad's violent repression does come at a price.

The United States should continue funding humanitarian appeals for Syria, but divert assistance that goes through Damascus and channel it to the northeast and Idlib to bolster efforts against al Qaeda. Focusing on the health needs of Syrians will be particularly crucial given the threat of COVID-19. Lastly, the United States should strongly counter Assad's regime and Russian efforts to rehabilitate Assad by rejecting efforts to restore diplomatic ties or secure reconstruction funds absent serious and verifiable changes to the nature of the regime, including the ending of military operations against civilians in Idlib and the release of political prisoners. The Syrian lira had plummeted precipitously by the end of 2019, likely because of a lack of access to hard currency following the Lebanese banking crisis and increased sanctions against Iran. With the passage of the Caesar Syria Civilian Protection Act, future U.S. administrations have the leverage to maintain pressure against the regime and any country that supports its repression of its people.[48]

A strategy of isolation, while necessary, is unlikely to have a moderating effect on the Assad regime in the short term. Indeed, future administrations should be clear-eyed about the overall grim prospects for reform of Syria's authoritarian system, regardless of the policy options it chooses to pursue. That said, the United States should not give up on its search for potential political solutions. While the prospects for a breakthrough are low, the potential payoff is high.

Keep diplomatic channels open. Washington should continue to invest in multilateral mechanisms that allow the international community to share analysis, coordinate assistance, and align strategies. If a diplomatic opening, however unlikely, does occur in the future, the United States will want to work with the international community to maximize the chances of success. Yet, while there is value in working with like-minded partners, if there is a political deal to be had, it will not materialize without credibly pressuring Assad and his supporters.

Opening channels of communication with Syrians supportive of the Assad regime should be a relatively easy policy change. The United States loses nothing by doing so, but stands to gain potentially game-changing insights into the constituency most critical to the Assad regime's continued survival. Throughout this engagement, however, the United States should maintain clarity about the need for genuine political reform and accountability in order to avoid giving false hope that Assad can be rehabilitated.

———

Diplomatic channels to Russia on Syria were established by the Obama administration and continue under Trump. These channels have been critical to deconflicting military operations, as noted by Alexander Bick in chapter 9, but have thus far resulted in little on the political track. There are ample reasons to be skeptical of the possibility that the United States and Russia will ever find enough common ground to reach agreement on almost anything related to Syria. However, Russia's pivotal role in securing Assad's survival, its close and continued operational alliance with the regime apparatus, and its veto power in the Security Council make ignoring or working around Moscow virtually impossible.

It is similarly difficult to imagine what a deal acceptable to both Iran and the United States would involve, especially after the killing of Soleimani. Arguably, Iran has a greater interest in maintaining the current status quo in Syria, given that its reach into the region, and therefore its ability to project its power and influence, is partially dependent on the government in Damascus. Although Iran is unlikely to consider proposals that threaten the Assad regime and, by extension, its position in Syria, it may be compelled to back de-escalation measures and a more serious political process if the United States links the easing of sanctions and resumption of the Joint Comprehensive Plan of Action (JCPOA) to movement on the Syrian track. In fact, there is a direct connection between the degree of U.S. investment in northeastern Syria, the degree of leadership the United States exerts to protect civilians and support refugees, and its ability to more credibly convince Iran, and for that matter Russia, that a political agreement is the only viable and sustainable way to end the conflict.

Notes

1. Megan Specia, "How Syria's Death Toll Is Lost in the Fog of War," *New York Times,* April 13, 2018 (www.nytimes.com/2018/04/13/world/middle east/syria-death-toll.html).

2. UN News, "UN Security Council 'Utterly Failed' Syrian Detainees; A Victim Voices Her Plea to 'End Impunity and Stop This Horror,'" August 7, 2019 (https://news.un.org/en/story/2019/08/10438910).

3. Phillip Connor, "Most Displaced Syrians Are in the Middle East, and about a Million Are in Europe," Pew Research Center, January 29, 2018 (www.pewresearch.org/fact-tank/2018/01/29/where-displaced-syrians-have-reset tled/).

4. Amnesty International, "Syria: Unlawful Attacks by Government Forces Hit Civilians and Medical Facilities in Idlib," March 28, 2019 (www.amnesty.org/en/latest/news/2019/03/syria-unlawful-attacks-by-government-forces-hit-civilians-and-medical-facilities-in-idlib/).

5. Suha Maayeh and Nicholas A. Heras, "The Fall of Daraa" *Foreign*

Affairs, July 23, 2018 (www.foreignaffairs.com/articles/syria/2018-07-23/fall -daraa).

6. Agencies and TOI Staff, "Iraq-Syria Border Crossing Reopens Amid Series of Reported Israeli Strikes," September 30, 2019 (www.timesofisrael. com/iraq-syria-border-crossing-reopens-amid-series-of-reported-israeli-strikes/).

7. Ben Hubbard, Charlie Savage, Eric Schmitt, and Patrick Kingsley, "Abandoned by U.S. in Syria, Kurds Find New Ally in American Foe," *New York Times,* October 13, 2019 (www.nytimes.com/2019/10/13/world/middle east/syria-turkey-invasion-isis.html).

8. Joby Warrick and Souad Mekhennet, "ISIS Eyes Breakout Opportunity as Turkish Forces Batter Kurds," *Washington Post,* October 17, 2019 (www .washingtonpost.com/world/national-security/isis-eyes-breakout-oppor tunity-as-turkish-forces-batter-us-allied-kurds/2019/10/17/b68c6358-f048-11e9-89eb-ec56cd414732_story.html).

9. Laurel Wamsley, "Some U.S. Troops May Remain in Northeast Syria to Protect Oil Fields," NPR, October 21, 2019 (www.npr.org/2019/10/21/ 771901687/some-u-s-troops-may-remain-in-northeast-syria-to-protect-oil-fields).

10. United Nations, *Report of the International Independent Investigation Commission Established Pursuant To Security Council Resolution 1595 (2005),* October 19, 2005 (www.un.org/unispal/document/auto-insert-180707/).

11. Carnegie Middle East Center, "The Damascus Spring," April 1, 2012 (https://carnegie-mec.org/diwan/48516?lang=en).

12. Kelly Mcevers, "Revisiting the Spark that Kindled the Syrian Uprising," NPR, March 12, 2012 (www.npr.org/2012/03/16/148719850/revisiting-the-spark-that-kindled-the-syrian-uprising).

13. CNN Wire Staff, "U.N. estimates 5,000 Killed in Syrian Uprising," CNN, December 13, 2011 (www.cnn.com/2011/12/12/world/meast/syria-unrest /index.html); Anthony Shadid, "In Syria, Reports of Arrests Proliferate," *New York Times,* May 2, 2011 (www.nytimes.com/2011/05/03/world/middle east/03syria.html).

14. Carnegie Middle East Center, "Local Coordination Committees in Syria," December 20, 2012 (https://carnegie-mec.org/diwan/50426?lang=en).

15. Carnegie Middle East Center, "The Syrian National Council," September 25, 2013 (https://carnegie-mec.org/diwan/48334?lang=en).

16. Hugh Naylor, "Islamic State Has Killed Many Syrians, But Assad's Forces Have Killed More," *Washington Post,* September 5, 2015 (www.wash ingtonpost.com/world/islamic-state-has-killed-many-syrians-but-assads-forces-have-killed-even-more/2015/09/05/b8150d0c-4d85-11e5-80c2-106 ea7fb80d4_story.html).

17. Helene Cooper, "Washington Begins to Plan for Collapse of Syrian Government," *New York Times,* July 18, 2012 (www.nytimes.com/2012/07/ 19/world/middleeast/washington-begins-to-plan-for-collapse-of-syrian-government.html).

18. President Barack Obama, "The Future of Syria Must Be Determined by

Its People, But President Bashar Al-Assad Is Standing in Their Way." Obama White House Archives, August 18, 2011 (https://obamawhitehouse.archives. gov/blog/2011/08/18/president-obama-future-syria-must-be-determined-its-people-president-bashar-al-assad).

19. Ben Rhodes, *The World as It Is* (New York: Penguin Random House, 2018).

20. United Nations, "Final Communiqué of the Action Group for Syria," June 30, 2012 (https://peacemaker.un.org/sites/peacemaker.un.org/ files/SY_120630_Final%20Communique%20of%20the%20Action%20 Group%20for%20Syria.pdf).

21. Nicholas Blanford, "Retreat from Homs Assad Conquers Cradle of Revolution," *The Times*, May 8, 2014 (www.thetimes.co.uk/article/retreat-from -homs-assad-conquers-cradle-of-revolution-zzmhp9qc5tm).

22. The White House, "Remarks by the President in Address to the Nation on Syria," September 10, 2013 (https://sy.usembassy.gov/syria-anniversary-of-the-ghouta-chemical-weapons-attack/).

23. Khaled Yacoub Oweis, "Syria 'Scud-Type' Missile Said to Kill 20 in Aleppo," Reuters, February 19, 2013 (www.reuters.com/article/us-syria-cri sis/syria-scud-type-missile-said-to-kill-20-in-aleppo-idUSBRE91I0GK 20130220).

24. NPR, "With Syria's Army Losing Ground, a Boost from Hezbollah," May 24, 2015 (www.npr.org/sections/parallels/2015/05/24/408794283/with-syrias-army-losing-ground-a-boost-from-hezbollah); Pamela Constable, "Recruited by Iran to Fight for Syrian Regime, Young Afghans Bring Home Cash and Scars," *Washington Post,* July 29, 2018 (www.washingtonpost.com /world/asia_pacific/recruited-by-iran-to-fight-for-syrian-regime-young-afghans-bring-home-cash-and-scars/2018/07/29/ecf9e34c-64e0-11e8-81ca-bb14593acaa6_story.html).

25. United Nations, "Statement of the International Syria Support Group Vienna," November, 14, 2015 (www.un.org/undpa/en/Speeches-statements /14112015/syria).

26. "Syria War: Cessation of Hostilities Comes into Effect," BBC, September 12, 2016 (www.bbc.com/news/world-middle-east-37335829).

27. Stephanie Nebehay, "Syria Air Force Bombed Convoy, U.N. Says in Aleppo Probe," Reuters, March 1, 2017 (www.reuters.com/article/us-mideast -crisis-syria-aleppo-warcrimes-idUSKBN1684G0).

28. Ben Rhodes, *The World as It Is* (New York: Penguin Random House, 2018); Robert M. Gates, *Duty: Memoirs of a Secretary at War* (New York: Penguin Random House, 2014); Bill Burns, *The Back Channel: A Memoir of American Diplomacy and a Case for Its Renewal* (New York: Penguin Random House, 2019).

29. Roy Gutman, "Assad Henchmen: Here's How We Built ISIS," *The Daily Beast,* April, 13, 2017 (www.thedailybeast.com/assad-henchman-heres -how-we-built-isis).

30. Thom Shanker, C. J. Chivers, and Michael R. Gordon, "Obama Weighs

'Limited' Strikes Against Syrian Forces," *New York Times,* August 27, 2013 (www.nytimes.com/2013/08/28/world/middleeast/obama-syria-strike.html).

31. Oliver Holmes and Thomson Reuters, "This Disowned Al Qaeda Branch Is Killing More Al Qaeda Fighters in Syria than Anyone Else," *Agence France-Presse,* May 12, 2014 (www.pri.org/stories/2014-05-12/disowned-al-qaeda-branch-killing-more-al-qaeda-fighters-syria-anyone-else).

32. U.S. Department of State, "The Global Coalition to Defeat ISIS," September 10, 2014 (www.state.gov/about-us-the-global-coalition-to-defeat-isis/).

33. Ibrahim Hamidi, "Syrian Opposition Fighters Withdraw from U.S. 'Train and Equip' Program," *The Syrian Observer,* June 22, 2015 (https:// syrianobserver.com/EN/news/29743/syrian_opposition_fighters_withdraw_ from_us_train_equip_program.html).

34. Liz Sly and Brian Murphy, "Intensified U.S. Airstrikes Keep Kobane from Falling to Islamic State Militants, *Washington Post,* October 8, 2014 (www.washingtonpost.com/world/airstrikes-target-islamic-state-positions-near-embattled-kobane/2014/10/07/122c9a76-1bba-4c8c-a3df-16e5a054 5bb0_story.html).

35. Ruby Mellen, "A Brief History of the Syrian Democratic Forces, the Kurdish-Led Alliance that Helped the U.S. Defeat the Islamic State," *Washington Post,* October 7, 2019 (www.washingtonpost.com/world/2019 /10/07/brief-history-syrian-democratic-forces-kurdish-led-alliance-that-helped-us-defeat-islamic-state/).

36. Mehmet Guzel and Bassem Mroue, "Turkey Widens Invasion as Syrian Army Returns to Northeast," AP News, October 14, 2019 (https://apnews. com/a7033640aad04506b2e8aa139d9edabe).

37. Helene Cooper and Eric Schmitt, "Syrian President Calls Donald Trump a 'Natural Ally' in Fight Against Terrorism," *New York Times,* November 16, 2016 (www.nytimes.com/2016/11/17/world/middleeast/assad-don ald-trump-syria-natural-ally.html).

38. Greg Jaffe and Adam Entous, "Trump Ends Covert CIA Program to Arm Anti-Assad Rebels in Syria, a Move Sought by Moscow," *Washington Post,* July 19, 2017 (www.washingtonpost.com/world/national-security/trump-ends-covert -cia-program-to-arm-anti-assad-rebels-in-syria-a-move-sought-by-moscow /2017/07/19/b6821a62-6beb-11e7-96ab-5f38140b38cc_story.html).

39. Fabrice Balanche, "The End of the CIA Program in Syria," *Foreign Affairs,* August 2, 2017 (www.foreignaffairs.com/articles/syria/2017-08-02/ end-cia-program-syria).

40. Elizabeth Tsurkov, "Who Are Turkey's Proxy Fighters in Syria?" *New York Review of Books,* November 27, 2019 (www.nybooks.com/daily/2019 /11/27/who-are-turkeys-proxy-fighters-in-syria/).

41. Daniel Arkin, F. Brinley Bruton, and Phil McCausland, "Trump Announces Strikes on Syria Following Suspected Chemical Weapons Attack by Assad Forces," NBC News, April 13, 2018 (www.nbcnews.com/news/world /trump-announces-strikes-syria-following-suspected-chemical-weapons -attack-assad-n865966).

42. Thomas Gibbons-Neff, "How a 4-Hour Battle between Russian Mercenaries and U.S. Commandos Unfolded in Syria," *New York Times*, May 24, 2018 (www.nytimes.com/2018/05/24/world/middleeast/american-com mandos-russian-mercenaries-syria.html).

43. Julian Borger and Martin Chulov, "Trump Shocks Allies and Advisers with Plan to Pull U.S. Troops Out of Syria," *The Guardian*, December 19, 2018 (www.theguardian.com/us-news/2018/dec/19/us-troops-syria-withdraw al-trump).

44. Michael R. Gordon, Nancy A. Youssef, and Isabel Coles, "U.S. Strikes Shiite Militia Targets in Iraq and Syria," *Wall Street Journal*, December 29, 2019 (www.wsj.com/articles/u-s-strikes-shiamilitia-targets-in-iraq-and-syria -11577642168).

45. Krishnadev Calamur, "No One Wants to Help Bashar al-Assad Rebuild Syria," *The Atlantic,* March 12, 2019 (www.theatlantic.com/inter national/archive/2019/03/where-will-money-rebuild-syria-come/584935/).

46. Neil Hauer, "What South Syria Insurgency Could Mean for Russia," *Asia Times*, August 21, 2019 (www.congress.gov/bill/115th-congress/house-bill/1677).

47. Operation Inherent Resolve, Lead Inspector General Report to the United States Congress, October 1, 2018–December 31, 2018 (www.stateoig .gov/system/files/fy2019_lig_oco_oir_q4_sep2018.pdf).

48. Library of Congress, "H.R. 1677: Caesar Syria Civilian Protection Act of 2018," March 22, 2017 (www.congress.gov/bill/115th-congress/house-bill /1677).

THREE

Moving from Partisan to Peacemaker in Yemen

CHRISTOPHER J. LE MON

Beyond its horrific human toll, the five-year war in Yemen has directly undermined U.S. national security interests, imposing significant moral costs on U.S. leadership in the region and beyond as a result of American support for the military intervention led by Saudi Arabia and the United Arab Emirates (UAE). Already the Middle East's poorest country, today Yemen faces the world's worst humanitarian crisis. The crisis is a direct result of the conflict between the Ansar Allah armed group (known colloquially as the Houthis) and a Saudi-UAE–led coalition (including multiple Yemeni proxy armed groups) seeking to restore Yemen's recognized government.

This chapter argues that, given the devastation of the civil war in Yemen, the depths of the humanitarian crisis, and Yemen's increasing risk of entanglement in Saudi-Iranian and U.S.-Iranian tensions, a future administration must fundamentally change the U.S. policy approach. The next president should prioritize ending the Saudi-UAE conflict with the Houthis, because U.S. national interests in Yemen all require the resolution of the country's rampant instability, violence, and governance gaps.

Though healing the devastation in Yemen will take decades, the United States can and should begin to extricate itself from its ill-fated policy choice to support the Saudi-UAE offensive in Yemen, which has proven to be one of the greatest U.S. strategic and moral missteps of the past decade. There is no guarantee that this policy prescription will secure a final negotiated ceasefire in Yemen, or a durable peace on which Yemenis can begin to rebuild a future state. But each month that the Saudi-UAE conflict with the Houthis persists, and that the United States provides military support for Saudi Arabia and the UAE, the negative consequences compound: more Yemeni civilians die from direct attacks, preventable starvation, and disease; more opportunities emerge for Yemen to serve as a flashpoint for a broader regional conflagration or as a safe harbor for terrorist groups; U.S. credibility is further tarnished for its association with the violations by the Saudi-UAE coalition; and a unified and peaceful future for Yemen becomes a more distant prospect.

U.S. Interests in Yemen

Multiple U.S. interests—relating to regional security, counterterrorism, nonproliferation, human security, and international trade—all converge in Yemen. Yemen is located alongside a key maritime route in the Red Sea and through the Gulf of Aden. It is home to the most lethal branch of al Qaeda (al Qaeda in the Arabian Peninsula, or AQAP) and to an offshoot of ISIS. And Yemen, particularly a Yemen embroiled in civil war, is a potential flashpoint for both regional conflict between Saudi Arabia and Iran and direct conflict between the United States and Iran. U.S. policymakers, however, have focused too little and too late on Yemen, despite the presence of these and other critical U.S. national security interests in the country.

During President Ali Abdullah Saleh's twenty-plus-year rule over Yemen, U.S. policymakers dedicated relatively little attention to the country, betting on a strongman to deliver stability and, where needed, cooperation on U.S. interests, especially counterterrorism in the post-9/11 period.[1] This misguided emphasis sacrificed the promotion of U.S. values (particularly respect for the rule of law and human rights). Saleh's cronyism and divisive, authoritarian rule undermined the possibility of compromise and a shared commitment to Yemen's stability among the country's diverse political factions and regions. One particular political grievance generated the Houthi movement, which emerged in the 1990s from the Zaydi sect in Yemen's northern Saada governorate marginalized by the central state in Sanaa.[2] Saleh's unilateral and incompetent governance, particularly in the country's south, also allowed al Qaeda in the Arabian Peninsula (AQAP) the ideological room to attract local recruits and the operational space needed to plan major attacks against the U.S. homeland. In 2009, AQAP attempted to down a U.S. passenger aircraft, and in 2010 it attempted to blow up multiple planes using bombs hidden inside printer cartridges.[3]

Today, after five years of war, Yemenis face staggering levels of human suffering. Four-fifths of the country's population (over 24 million people) require some form of humanitarian assistance or protection. Eleven million civilians are malnourished and struggle daily to find sufficient food, while the largest cholera outbreak in recorded history has infected more than 2.2 million people since 2017, over one-quarter of whom have been children under the age of five.[4] The humanitarian toll stems directly from the war, as civilians are displaced by fighting and cut off from aid by restrictions imposed by the warring parties. All sides have attacked hospitals and water and sanitation systems, leaving Yemen woefully unequipped for the COVID-19 outbreak. A failure to end the Saudi-UAE conflict with the Houthis thus threatens the lives of millions of Yemeni civilians. The UN recently assessed that by the end of 2019, fighting had killed over 100,000 Yemenis, while another 130,000 died from starvation and preventable disease as a direct result of the conflict.[5]

Yemen's humanitarian suffering is, in part, the unfortunate outgrowth of a decades-long failed U.S. approach that has subordinated the country's long-term development to short-term exigencies. There is not only a moral imperative to end Yemen's humanitarian crisis, but also a strategic one—given the role the humanitarian crisis has played in deepening Yemen's instability.

Conflicting Priorities: Obama's Yemen Challenges

For nearly a decade, the United States has lacked a coherent Yemen policy. Instead, two successive administrations have sought to achieve a variety of policy goals, such as ensuring the free flow of commerce around Yemen's maritime perimeter, pursuing counterterrorism objectives, or countering Iranian-backed or supported proxies perceived to be a threat to U.S. interests, but without deconflicting or ranking these efforts. The pursuit of these U.S. interests in Yemen was, moreover, never a high priority within overall U.S. foreign policy, as higher-order crises diverted policymakers' attention elsewhere in the region. Until at least 2014, the Obama administration, like the George W. Bush administration before it, viewed Yemen foremost as a battlefield for counterterrorism.[6] The emergence of AQAP in 2009, and its attempted bombings in the United States in 2009 and 2010, made Yemen a principal front for U.S. counterterrorism operations during Obama's first term.[7] And though the counterterrorism priority might have had the short-term effect of tactically weakening AQAP, U.S. drone strikes ultimately caused significant civilian casualties in Yemen, which generated large-scale public anger and undermined Saleh's public standing due to his association with U.S. counterterrorism policy.[8]

In 2012, after a year of Arab Spring–related civilian protests and significant internecine violence, Saleh's rule ended. The Obama administration supported a Gulf Cooperation Council initiative that elevated Vice President Abdrabbuh Mansur Hadi as a compromise leader thought capable of temporarily (given his original election to a two-year term) answering Yemenis' calls for a new order. The Obama administration also provided significant political support and development assistance during the subsequent National Dialogue Conference (NDC), hopeful that Yemen might be a rare Arab Spring success story.[9] Nevertheless, the political transition ended prematurely when the Houthis rejected what they claimed was an unfair NDC proposal for decentralization of authority and resources, and then subsequently seized the capital Sanaa by force in 2014.[10] Faced with the dissolution of years of painstaking negotiations among Yemenis, the United States found itself backing Hadi against the Houthis' armed uprising, given his status as the elected president and the U.S. perception that Hadi was a supportive, even pliant, partner for counterterrorism purposes.[11, 12]

U.S. opposition to the Houthi coup initially was limited to the imposition of sanctions and the rejection of the Houthis' claim to represent Yemen's government; the Obama administration did not consider using force to restore Hadi to power. In March 2015, however, when Saudi Arabia and the UAE informed the White House that they would intervene militarily in Yemen to support Hadi against the Houthis—and asked for U.S. support in what they promised would be a quick victory—the Obama administration agreed to provide refueling, intelligence, and arms.[13] At the time, U.S. policymakers justified their decision on several grounds. First and foremost, the United States wanted to signal its opposition to the violent deposition of an internationally recognized government. According to U.S. officials at the time, Obama intended U.S. military support to be limited and defensive in nature, aimed at helping Saudi Arabia protect itself against cross-border attacks by the Houthis.[14] The Obama administration thus also wanted to reassure Saudi Arabia and other Gulf states that they could depend on the United States to support their self-defense, at a time when the United States was finalizing the Joint Comprehensive Plan of Action (JCPOA) agreement with Iran. Additionally, U.S. policymakers had been pushing the Gulf states for years to take up greater collective security arrangements, and the Saudi-UAE coalition formed to intervene in Yemen appeared to represent a possible version of exactly that.

Soon, however, the Saudi promise of a quick defeat of the Houthis proved illusory. The Obama administration found itself simultaneously pursuing three policies in Yemen, which at times worked at cross-purposes with one another: conducting counterterrorism strikes (largely in the south and the east of the country); providing military support to the Saudi-UAE coalition in its intervention against the Houthis; and undertaking diplomatic efforts to negotiate an end to the Saudi-UAE conflict with the Houthis. Obama defended the increase in U.S. air strikes against AQAP in 2015 and 2016 as necessary to reverse AQAP's expansion during the ongoing conflict between the Saudi-UAE coalition and the Houthis. As the government of Yemen withdrew to Aden (and ultimately fled the country to Jeddah, Saudi Arabia), AQAP took advantage of the security vacuum to seize territory.[15] As the Saudi-UAE coalition offensive intensified from the air, civilian casualties mounted. And as large numbers of Yemenis were killed or maimed by air strikes on funerals, weddings, or other civilian sites, President Hadi's popularity decreased. Similarly, what had been intended by Obama as "defensive" assistance for the Saudi-led coalition expanded to include the sale of air-to-ground munitions that Saudi and Emirati aircraft used to bomb Yemen, not only causing significant civilian casualties and destruction of key civilian infrastructure, but also damaging U.S. credibility as the death toll rose.[16] The Obama administration sought to reduce civilian casualties through extensive coaching and training programs, but Saudi Arabia and its partners appeared unwilling and incapable of reducing civilian harm.[17]

Even as the United States armed and fueled the Saudi-UAE bombing campaign, and continued to conduct direct counterterrorism strikes, senior U.S. officials sought to support (and later lead) unsuccessful international efforts to negotiate an end to the conflict. In this, the Obama administration failed to recognize the impossibility of serving as an impartial international arbiter while also arming and backing one party to the war. After several years of inconclusive UN-led negotiations and failed ceasefires, the United States seized the reins following the August 2016 collapse of peace talks in Kuwait. Then Secretary of State John Kerry sought to advance a more even-handed proposal, which the Obama administration believed stood a chance of bringing along the Houthis.[18] But the dramatic rejection of Kerry's plan by President Hadi, and a subsequent U.K. rejection of a new UN Security Council resolution to reset the terms of negotiations, made clear that U.S. diplomatic capital was dwindling, given the impending end of Obama's term in office. The perceived necessity of Saudi and UAE cooperation for the U.S. counterterrorism mission—as well as already-frayed relations with both governments over the Iran nuclear deal—also limited how far the Obama administration was willing—or able—to pressure its allies and partners to back a new plan for peace in Yemen.[19]

Despite these limitations, the Obama administration eventually did draw a partial redline over U.S. arms sales, following egregious October 2016 Saudi air strikes on a funeral hall in Sanaa, which killed and injured hundreds of civilians. After a two-month review, Obama suspended a nearly US$400 million transfer of precision-guided munitions to Saudi Arabia—but continued to refuel Saudi and UAE aircraft used to attack the Houthis, and essentially maintained intelligence-sharing in support of both the anti-AQAP and anti-Houthi campaigns.[20] This decision represented the Obama administration's most significant rebuke of the Saudi-UAE campaign in Yemen since it commenced. Yet even the White House decision to block this single munitions sale, unsurprisingly, did not alter the Saudi or Emirati conduct of the war, in part because refueling and other U.S. military support continued, blunting the operational and political impact of the munitions ban. More importantly, however, the Saudis already knew that the next U.S. president was unlikely to follow Obama's course. Indeed, the Trump administration quickly reversed even this cautious and circumscribed attempt to apply U.S. pressure on the Saudi-UAE coalition.

Taking Off the Gloves: Trump's Approach to Yemen

Trump's election swept away any lingering Saudi or Emirati worry that U.S. Middle East policy might seek more regional balance. The United States would no longer moderate or reduce its support for the Saudi-UAE intervention in Yemen because of the widespread Saudi and UAE violations of international norms that were already evident by the time of Trump's inauguration.[21] The Trump administration appears to see Yemen as little more than a playground for pursuing other objectives: Yemen presented an avenue for unequivocally elevating U.S. ties with Saudi Arabia and the UAE (including resuming all U.S. arms sales); a place to strike AQAP; and an arena for escalating tensions with Iran. U.S. counter-AQAP strikes increased markedly in 2017, causing greater Yemeni civilian casualties, including a U.S. Special Forces raid carried out just a week after Trump took office that killed sixteen women and children.[22]

Meanwhile, the Trump administration threw U.S. support un-equivocally behind the Saudi-UAE coalition. As discussed by Andrew Miller and Dafna Rand in chapter 1, under Trump, U.S. support for Gulf partners (particularly Saudi Arabia) has become an important end unto itself. Given Trump's fixation on reversing decisions made by the Obama administration, it should have surprised no one when his administration quickly ended the suspension on certain arms sales to Saudi Arabia within weeks of taking office.[23] While Obama had emphasized the limited nature of U.S. military aid for the Saudi-UAE coalition, Trump expanded U.S. intelligence-sharing, targeting, and other military support for Saudi and UAE forces.[24] When Saudi crown prince Mohammed bin Salman visited the White House in a high-profile trip in March 2018, Trump held a bizarre press confer-ence announcing additional arms sales to Saudi Arabia with wildly exaggerated price tags.[25] For its part, the UAE also took advantage of the Trump administration's hawkishness, openly seeking U.S. back-ing for its escalation against the Yemeni key port city of Hudaydah. Had key voices in Congress not objected in both 2017 and 2018, the Trump administration likely would have blessed (and perhaps even supported militarily) a UAE-led offensive against Hudaydah that the UN warned could have killed 250,000 civilians.[26]

U.S. support for a negotiated peace in Yemen also withered, or at least fell in terms of policy priorities. The Trump administration unequivocally aligned itself with Saudi Arabia and the UAE against the Houthis, mischaracterizing the Houthis as mere Iranian proxies. By taking sides in this way, the United States not only alleviated polit-ical pressure to end the Saudi-UAE intervention, but also reinforced the Saudi-UAE view that they must defend themselves against Iran by handing the Houthis a complete military defeat in Yemen. This perspective ignored or dismissed concerns that the perpetuation of the Saudi-UAE conflict with the Houthis was strengthening Iranian-Houthi ties, diminishing the international standing of Saudi Arabia and the UAE, and bolstering Tehran's interests. Trump also failed to criticize the regular and egregious Saudi and UAE violations of the laws of war.[27] In so doing, the Trump administration both signaled to the Saudi-UAE coalition that no consequences would be forthcoming no matter their conduct, and helped create an environment of impunity in Yemen that made clear to the Houthis and other non-state armed groups that their violations, too, would go unpunished.[28] This one-sided approach by the Trump administration also undermined whatever limited and primarily rhetorical support U.S. diplomats lent to ongoing UN-led peace efforts.

But even as the Trump administration threw the U.S. lot in completely with the Saudi-UAE coalition, the increasing death toll from the conflict and humanitarian crisis in Yemen sparked attention and opposition in Congress. With concerns over civilian casualties from Saudi and UAE air strikes driving congressional unease, a June 2017 Senate attempt to block US$500 million in precision-guided munitions sales to Saudi Arabia only narrowly failed, as did a March 2018 vote to curtail U.S. refueling and logistical support for the Saudi-UAE coalition.[29] Rumors in early summer 2018 of a potentially catastrophic UAE-led assault on Hudaydah led to a warning from a large bipartisan group of senators demanding that the UAE suspend the planned attack, given these "unacceptable consequences for any responsible member of the community of nations."[30] Congress subsequently acted by conditioning continued U.S. refueling of Saudi and Emirati aircraft on both countries' tangible progress in improving access for humanitarian aid and reducing civilian casualties.[31] As pressure mounted in late 2018 for a second Senate vote to end all U.S. military support to the Saudi-UAE coalition, the Trump administration announced a voluntary end to U.S. refueling. Yet this concession was not enough to forestall a historic vote by the Senate in December 2018 to end U.S. military involvement in the Saudi-UAE conflict with the Houthis.[32] Faced with the reality that a durable majority in the Senate had turned against the war, and that the incoming Democratic majority in the House of Representatives would follow suit, the Trump administration urged Saudi Arabia to support UN efforts to secure a Hudaydah ceasefire at talks in Stockholm in December 2018.[33] Still, efforts to disentangle the United States from the war in Yemen continued under the 116th Congress, with the new Democratic majority in the House holding multiple hearings in the early months of the session.[34] And, for the first time ever, both chambers of Congress voted under the War Powers Act to curtail authorization of U.S. logistical support for the Saudi-UAE coalition, but the measure was vetoed by President Trump, as were three subsequent resolutions passed by Congress in mid-2019 that would have suspended specific sales of U.S. munitions to Saudi Arabia and the UAE.[35]

In no small part due to the growing congressional opposition to the war, the UAE announced in July 2019 that it would cease its participation in the anti-Houthi coalition and withdraw the majority of its forces based in Yemen.[36] Initial hope that this move might pressure Saudi Arabia and the Hadi government to adopt a less intransigent approach to peace talks quickly gave way to rekindled concerns for the future viability of a unified Yemen, as UAE-backed separatists in southern Yemen attacked forces loyal to the Hadi government and seized key positions in the temporary seat of government in Aden in August 2018.[37] The subsequent fighting included not only ground battles between these two former allies, but even air strikes by Saudi Arabia and the UAE on the other's preferred Yemeni partner. Although both Riyadh and Abu Dhabi vocally reiterated their partnership and shared goals, the diverging positions between these long-standing allies was increasingly visible—and potentially growing as the battles in southern Yemen continued into autumn 2019.[38] Although Saudi Arabia succeeded in convincing the Hadi government and the Southern Transitional Council to sign an agreement to reset relations, as of mid-2020 this ceasefire grows more fragile by the day. It is unclear whether Saudi Arabia and the UAE will be aligned if and when the Riyadh Agreement collapses.[39] After tarnishing U.S. credibility on human rights and damaging Saudi Arabia's reputation at a time of national transition, the war in Yemen claimed the Saudi-UAE coalition as its latest political casualty.

In the final months of 2019, new hope emerged that the warring parties had finally accepted the impossibility of a military solution to the conflict in Yemen. Soon after the September 2019 attacks on Saudi oil infrastructure—for which the Houthis took credit, despite their clear origins in Tehran—the Houthi leadership announced a unilateral pause to cross-border attacks on Saudi territory. Riyadh responded with a pledge to halt air strikes in certain key Yemeni governorates.[40] Although air strikes and other attacks did not end entirely, the significant curtailment markedly reduced civilian casualties from fighting, and reports of Saudi-Houthi talks aimed at a cessation of hostilities gave rise to predictions that the war would end in a matter of months.[41] Yet despite these promising signs, as of mid-2020, Yemen is facing renewed and significant fighting between the Houthis and government-aligned forces, the tentative peace in Aden threatens to unravel at any moment, and COVID-19 threatens significant infections and deaths across the country.[42] And, beyond its rhetorical support for negotiations to end the conflict—and, notably, reports of ongoing, mid-level direct U.S.-Houthi backchannel talks—the Trump administration has been unable, or unwilling, to convert the United States from a partisan to a peacemaker.

A New Approach for a New Administration

Obama's and Trump's approaches to Yemen, and to the war between the Saudi-UAE coalition and the Houthis, evolved in very different ways. Yet each administration failed to realize that it was the war itself—particularly its scarring effects on the Yemeni state, institutions, economic capacity, and civilian life—that was impeding the pursuit of almost every U.S. national interest implicated in Yemen. Beyond its catastrophic impact on Yemeni civilians, the Saudi-UAE war against the Houthis has managed to empower Iran and bolster Iran's relations with and support to the Houthis; set back, or at least counteract, U.S. counterterrorism efforts against AQAP and ISIS; diminish the influence and standing of traditional U.S. security partners in Riyadh and Abu Dhabi, while also introducing serious tensions in the relationship between them; increase the threat to the territorial security of Saudi Arabia and the UAE posed by the Houthis; expand the potential flashpoints for broader regional conflict; threaten the free passage of naval and commercial vessels through key shipping channels; and damage U.S. standing, credibility, and values.

A new administration, however, should not look at these consequences and conclude that the United States should simply turn away from Yemen entirely. If some or all of the continuing U.S. interests in Yemen are to be achieved, it will require the United States to prioritize diplomatic efforts to end the conflict, and to not lose focus or deprioritize Yemen. Although the odds of success are not high, especially given increased fragmentation among the parties supporting or aligned with the Hadi government,[43] the United States can neither write off Yemen, nor can it continue the current approach and expect more positive outcomes. While U.S. military support for the Saudi-UAE coalition can and should end on day one of the next adminis-tration, the conflict in Yemen is not likely to de-escalate without a reorientation and substantial increase in U.S. diplomatic investments toward that end.

The next president should adopt a new position not only on the war, but also on how the United States pursues its interests in Yemen more generally. This approach would focus on addressing the root causes of threats to U.S. interests rather than simply dealing with the out-ward symptoms. On counterterrorism, for example, both the Obama and Trump administrations have relied on limited kinetic operations in Yemen, effectively "mowing the grass" without fatally damaging AQAP's ability to reconstitute itself inside Yemen.[44] Although U.S. air strikes and a UAE-led offensive have reversed much of AQAP's momentum and territorial control within Yemen, the ongoing Saudi-UAE conflict with the Houthis nurtures the conditions—absence of state authority, crushing poverty, insecurity, and violence—that have allowed AQAP to thrive in the past.[45] Without a credible national government and reestablished public institutions and security forces, the threat from AQAP will remain. Additionally, although ongo-ing fighting with AQAP has weakened ISIS, its fighters nonetheless have continued to try to establish themselves in southern and east-ern Yemen, risking expanding the group's threat to civilians within Yemen as well as the terrorist danger emanating from the country.[46]

Troublingly, Saudi Arabia and the UAE have exacerbated the drivers of radicalization. Instead of rebuilding state institutions in the areas of Yemen that have been under the nominal control of the Hadi government, the UAE especially has armed, funded, backed, and empowered a multitude of non-state armed groups that have in-creased instability and prevented the reconstitution of the Yemeni state. These militias also have committed extensive violations against Yemeni civilians with impunity, reduced rather than enhanced civil-ian security, and emerged as additional potential spoilers to peace, as they profit from the war economy.[47] In some instances, U.S.-sold arms have even been transferred by the UAE to militias affiliated with AQAP.[48] The August 2019 outbreak of fighting in Aden between the Hadi government and secessionist southern militias, coming soon after the UAE announcement that it was withdrawing the majority of its troops in Yemen, highlights the longer-term risk of instability that will result from years of UAE support for non-state armed groups in Yemen's south.

The civil war and breakdown of state authority also has unleashed the question of southern autonomy or independence, increasing the likelihood of another bloody conflict between Yemen's north and south, or between forces loyal to the Hadi government and those seeking an independent southern Yemen. In other words, even if today's conflict between the Saudis and the Houthis de-escalates, conflict will still loom in Yemen for decades—with counterproductive effects on U.S. national interests.

The length and scope of the Yemeni civil conflict also have presented an opportunity for Iranian opportunism and interference—one that it has seized enthusiastically. Originally, the much-vaunted Saudi-UAE concerns about Iran's ties with the Houthis were not fully founded. Yet over time, the Gulf states' worries about Iranian exploitation of the Houthis' fight have become a "self-fulfilling prophecy."[49] When the war began in 2015, Iran was offering only minimal arms and other military and economic support. The scale of that support has markedly increased over five years.[50] Although the precise scope of Iranian support is not public, experts believe this support now involves Iranian training and military capacity building.[51] By one expert's account, the Houthis not only import weapons or weapons parts from Iran, but also, as of the spring 2019, can produce two offensive armed UAVs per week, thanks to Iran's training. The Houthis have used these weapons to regularly attack Saudi territory, including airports, oil infrastructure, and other civilian sites.[52]

Finally, the continuation of the Saudi-UAE war with the Houthis also threatens American economic interests, particularly the free flow of goods through safe international shipping lanes.[53] The absence of governmental oversight and control of the shipping lanes on the coasts of Yemen puts a significant percentage of global sea trade at risk of attack as it transits the Red Sea. This means that, by one count, approximately 8 percent of all global trade, including nearly

5 percent of the world's crude oil, transits highly insecure waters.[54] It is easy for an armed group such as the Houthis to threaten every ship that passes choke points like the Bab al Mandab—twenty miles wide at its narrowest point. In the absence of a negotiated peace, the Houthis can threaten to disrupt the U.S. and global economy.[55]

The remainder of this chapter outlines a recommended Yemen approach for a new administration.

Immediately end U.S. military support for the Saudi-UAE intervention. First and foremost, U.S. policy must prioritize an immediate end to all U.S. military involvement in the Saudi-UAE war against the Houthis. This approach should be made for strategic reasons, for ethical reasons, for reasons of congressional intent, and because U.S. diplomatic leadership in the region requires it. Regional (and even global) perceptions of the United States as a party to the conflict—bolstered by high-profile media coverage of Saudi-UAE air strikes using U.S. munitions, which have resulted in significant civilian casualties—severely diminishes U.S. credibility in the Middle East and globally. U.S. participation in a war whose parties have regularly violated basic global norms of warfare, such as the international humanitarian law, will threaten U.S. military personnel in future armed conflicts.

A U.S. exit from the Yemen conflict by the next administration should begin with a complete suspension of arms sales, transfers, and licenses to both Saudi Arabia and the UAE (exempting only ground-based missile defense systems based within either country's territory), and a termination of all U.S. logistical, intelligence, and other support for the Saudi-UAE intervention in Yemen. As of this writing, repeated votes by both chambers of Congress to curtail U.S. arms sales and other military support to Saudi Arabia and the UAE have been met with vetoes by President Trump.[56] The next administration need not wait for opposition in Congress to grow further, and instead should announce immediately an across-the-board suspension of U.S. arms sales to Saudi Arabia and the UAE, going beyond the Obama administration's limited suspension of Saudi munitions sales in December 2016.

As of 2019, the UAE has announced its withdrawal from the anti-

Houthi coalition. Yet any U.S. arms suspension should include the UAE, which continues to engage in combat in Yemen.[57] With the UAE having quietly, then overtly, provided military support to southern secessionist militias even when those groups turned their arms against the same Hadi government that the UAE claims to support, the next administration must take a hard line with Abu Dhabi, akin to its approach to Saudi Arabia. Despite the UAE's often-heralded military prowess, it remains highly dependent on U.S. arms sales and on its close defense relationship with the United States, both of which provide significant U.S. leverage to change UAE behavior. U.S. diplomats should use this influence, pushing the UAE to lead its neighbors in ending the conflict with the Houthis and in backing a unified, functional postwar Yemeni government. Moreover, the international community should seek accountability for the UAE's involvement in significant violations against civilians in Yemen, and its willingness to divert U.S.-sold arms to Yemeni proxies.

The suspension of U.S. arms transfers should be conditions-based. The resumption of arms should depend on the parties: (1) ending their participation in the conflict in Yemen, including the cessation of Saudi air strikes and other attacks on Yemen; (2) participating in credible independent investigations of and accountability for civilian mass casualty incidents resulting from Saudi and UAE air strikes; and (3) adhering to new U.S. controls to ensure (and monitor) Saudi and UAE compliance with U.S. export controls for past and future arms sales.[58] Such an approach would maximize the pressure on U.S. partners to support peace efforts. Similarly, completely ending all U.S. military support for the Saudi-UAE coalition—including all refueling, targeting, and intelligence support—would signal to Riyadh and Abu Dhabi that the United States is serious about ending the war. A comprehensive prohibition on U.S. military support for the Saudi-UAE–led coalition would avoid the ambiguity from which the Obama administration suffered when it blocked one major arms sale while continuing refueling and other support. This arms policy would also be consonant with the multiple congressional attempts to suspend U.S. arms sales during the Trump administration, all of which the president vetoed.

This termination of bilateral U.S. military support for the Saudi-

UAE coalition is also a prerequisite for enhanced U.S. diplomacy to bring about a negotiated settlement to the civil conflict. For the United States to claim credibly that it is pursuing peace in Yemen, it cannot at the same time be fueling the war through arms sales and military support to one side of the conflict. Even though Saudi air strikes dropped significantly during the final months of 2019—as Saudi-Houthi negotiations continued—2019 still saw numerous air strikes with significant civilian casualties. These strikes demonstrate that years of U.S. military training and top-shelf American munitions and other military hardware have failed to improve Saudi Arabia's ability and willingness to protect civilians and abide by international humanitarian law standards.[59] So long as American weapons continue to be used by the Saudi and Emirati militaries to kill Yemeni civilians, U.S. calls for ceasefires and negotiations will carry little weight with either side. And so long as Riyadh and Abu Dhabi do not perceive any tangible consequences to their relationships with Washington resulting from their continued misconduct of the war in Yemen, U.S. diplomatic pressure to stop the fighting will be perceived by these governments as empty words.

Enhance U.S. diplomatic efforts to end the Saudi-UAE and Houthis war. Although U.S. interests in Yemen depend on ending the Saudi-UAE war with the Houthis, the United States obviously does not hold all the cards. But, despite the complexity of the conflict and the multiplicity of actors, the United States does have significant leverage to push for an immediate ceasefire and toward a peaceful resolution of the war. To do so, the next administration must find new ways to convince the parties to the conflict that they have more to gain by ending the war than they do in continuing it. This means refining both the carrots and sticks of U.S. policy toward all parties to the conflict. It will require a marked shift in U.S. diplomatic posture— away from the Trump administration's unequivocal support for the Saudi-UAE coalition and toward a more balanced role that allows for both U.S. pressure and incentives to be deployed on both sides of the conflict.

A new U.S. diplomatic approach must begin by addressing the

structural impediments to peace. This includes establishing a new framework for peace negotiations, replacing the flawed and outdated UN Security Council Resolution 2216, which treats Houthi disarmament as a prerequisite rather than a milestone, and creates disincentives for the Hadi government to negotiate an end to the war.[60] Beyond revisiting the framework for diplomacy, the next administration must rebalance its approach to the conflict. Leveraging both the arms sale suspension and growing congressional and American public outrage toward the war, a diplomatically deft administration could push Saudi Arabia to change course in Yemen before additional action by Congress further cements the divide between Washington and Riyadh. This divide risks jeopardizing a bilateral relationship perceived by most in Riyadh as integral to Saudi Arabia's security and the kingdom's survival.[61]

This diplomatic pivot will not be easy. For Saudi Arabia, its intervention in Yemen is connected so personally with Crown Prince Mohammed bin Salman that he may be prepared to retaliate in response to U.S. pressure. Diplomatic sources indicated in late 2019 that the crown prince had finally accepted that the war against the Houthis is unwinnable, and that the Saudi intervention needed to end. Yet it remains unclear if Saudi Arabia will stay committed to negotiations, especially in the event of new escalation such as a new round of Houthi cross-border attacks on Saudi territory.[62] Regardless, the next administration must find a way to drive home to Saudi leaders that the time has come for Riyadh to choose between its military partnership with the United States and the continuation of a hopeless war in Yemen. U.S. diplomats and officials must make the case that Saudi Arabia's security owes far more to the former than the latter. For instance, offering Saudi Arabia increased U.S. support for purely defensive military systems that are unhelpful to the Yemen war (such as ground-based missile interceptors) might help to demonstrate that ending its intervention in Yemen would improve Saudi security. Additionally, the diplomatic approach suggested below, which (ironically) could allow Saudi Arabia to claim a central role in ending the war, might placate bin Salman's reported desire for a "victory" in Yemen.

The UAE, for its part, appears to have decided that the political and reputational costs of its intervention in Yemen outweigh any security gains that continued military action could achieve. Moreover, without the ceaseless international criticism for its misconduct in the Yemen war, the UAE can better pursue its national interests. Yet, as discussed above, given the UAE's ongoing involvement in Yemen, the next administration should emphasize to Abu Dhabi that the resumption of U.S. security assistance will be conditioned on demonstrable UAE actions to rein in its secessionist proxies in southern Yemen. In this vein, a new president should indicate that the UAE's "rhetorical support" for peace talks are insufficient to shield it from the same bilateral consequences as its erstwhile ally Saudi Arabia.[63] Instead, Emirati leadership will need to make its rhetoric reality. As with the Saudis, the next administration should offer to continue U.S. assistance to defend UAE territory against increasingly dangerous Houthi missile and armed UAV strikes, but only so long as both governments engage in Yemen peace negotiations in good faith.[64]

Bolstering Saudi and UAE defenses against the threat of Houthi attacks should drive Riyadh and Abu Dhabi to greater pragmatism in negotiations over the Yemen conflict. At the same time, by at least partially neutralizing the Houthis' capacity to harass Riyadh and Abu Dhabi, a U.S. investment in border and missile defense could also increase Houthi willingness to negotiate by depriving them of the ability to threaten Saudi and Emirati territory.

It is important to note that pivoting the United States to a more even-handed posture—by stepping back from reflexive support for the Saudi-UAE coalition—could give the next administration additional tools to pressure the Houthis, over whom the United States historically has had almost no leverage.[65] To date, the Houthis have shrugged off U.S. criticism and pressure over their rampant violations against civilians, interference with humanitarian aid, and escalation of the conflict, deeming it biased, due to U.S. support for (and lack of criticism by the Trump administration of) the myriad violations committed by the Saudi-UAE coalition.[66] The next administration could attempt to incentivize the Houthis, rather than merely criticize them for their transgressions, by making clear that an end to violations against civilians and interference with humanitarian aid, and good-faith engagement in negotiations, would increase U.S. support for Houthi participation in a postwar Yemeni government. All outside parties would have to recognize, of course, that Yemenis themselves must make decisions about governmental composition and structure.[67]

Humanitarian Aid and Accountability

In the end, a more balanced U.S. approach to the conflict should begin to help improve the humanitarian situation. To do so, U.S. officials will have to condemn civilian casualties, publicly and privately, regardless of who is the responsible party. A more balanced U.S. approach to the conflict also will help address the severe funding shortfalls in the humanitarian response. In 2019, the cost of providing for the more than 24 million Yemenis whose survival depended on humanitarian assistance exceeded US$4 billion, making it the most expensive humanitarian response in the world.[68] Although two key parties to the conflict—Saudi Arabia and the UAE—promised to provide US$1.5 billion, both countries took months to make good on most of those pledges, despite extensive diplomatic pressure from UN officials and U.S. and other diplomats.

U.S. officials indicated throughout 2019 that they continued to urge their Saudi and Emirati counterparts to provide the necessary funds, but refrained from public criticism of either country based on fear that it could have been counterproductive.[69] The next administration must be willing to call out publicly any obstacle to the funding and delivery of lifesaving humanitarian aid, no matter whether it is by a partner or an adversary. Saudi Arabia and the UAE will bristle at public criticism, but the efficacy of a naming and shaming strategy should be measured by their material response to the humanitarian crisis, not their rhetorical one. Moreover, U.S. criticism of increasing Houthi obstruction of and interference with humanitarian aid delivery will have little impact unless Washington is willing to criticize aid interruptions by Saudi Arabia, the UAE, and the Hadi government as well. With the 2020 humanitarian response estimated to require an additional US$3.2 billion beyond the incomplete funding for prior years, Yemenis cannot afford a repeat of the unfulfilled promises of 2019.

The next administration also should enhance accountability for gross violations of human rights in Yemen to start restoring the credibility of the U.S. commitment to international law. Longtime U.S. leadership on human rights and international humanitarian law has been damaged by the Trump administration's continued unwillingness to criticize violations by Saudi Arabia or the UAE, a silence that also diminishes the effect of U.S. criticism of Houthi violations.[70] As a start, the next administration must provide Congress with an honest public report on Saudi and UAE violations, fulfilling a FY2019 congressional reporting requirement ignored thus far by the Trump administration. In addition, the White House owes Congress the FY2020 reporting requirement on Saudi and UAE compliance with international humanitarian law and steps to reduce civilian casualties.[71] Finally, the United States should use the annual State Department report on human rights abuses worldwide to present a comprehensive and impartial accounting of violations by all sides to the conflict.

Beyond these steps, the next administration also should support the creation of a robust UN accountability mechanism for Yemen, reversing both the Obama and Trump administration's opposition to such a body.[72] By engaging with Yemeni civil society to understand Yemeni priorities for accountability and redress, the next administration can both pursue stronger accountability measures from a global perspective, while at the same time strengthening Yemeni nongovernmental organizations and other actors who will play an essential role in the country's future.

Conclusion: Resisting Defenders of the Status Quo

As of early 2020, there is no sign that the Trump administration will reverse its one-sided backing of the Saudi-UAE coalition. It will therefore fall to the next president to reset U.S. policy.

To be sure, a reset of the U.S. approach to the war in Yemen will face opposition. Saudi Arabia and the UAE (and their phalanxes of paid and unpaid champions in Washington) will condemn the change as a reward for Houthi intransigence, encouraging future Houthi aggression. The defense industry will warn that interrupting U.S. arms sales will create openings for Chinese or Russian companies to step in, or hurt U.S. manufacturing jobs. In addition, the Pentagon might again claim that because arm sales create U.S. leverage over our partners, we ought not to cede this influence merely to avoid a perceived moral stain over civilian casualties.

Nonetheless, all of these arguments give undue weight to tactical risks—or contradict ample research and data—while ignoring the ultimately more important strategic liabilities implicit in continuation of the status quo. The figures cited by the Trump administration, asserting that Saudi arms sales support hundreds of thousands of American jobs, are without statistical grounding and wildly exceed academic estimates.[73] Given Saudi-UAE dependence on U.S. arms, any shift to Chinese or Russian weapons could take years, if not decades.[74] Claims by the Trump administration and its supporters that U.S. arms sales, training, and other military support has reduced civilian casualties lacks any supporting data or evidence. Repeated investigations by the UN, and international and Yemeni human rights and humanitarian aid organizations, have all identified significant numbers of cases where high-end U.S. precision munitions have been used not to avoid civilian casualties, but instead to precisely strike civilians and civilian sites.[75] Moreover, couching U.S. arms sales exclusively in commercial or economic terms disregards that such sales are a foreign policy tool deployed in order to enhance U.S. national security and other national interests. In Yemen's case, because it is clear that U.S. interests are being set back rather than advanced by the Saudi-UAE conduct of the war, the case for continued U.S. arms sales rings hollow.

In the end, some degree of friction and tension in bilateral relations with Saudi Arabia and the UAE is inevitable, should the next administration suspend U.S. military support and arms sales and adopt a more balanced approach to the conflict in Yemen. Nevertheless, the next administration must make clear to its partners, to Congress, and to the American public that a rebalancing of U.S. Yemen policy derives from a more clearheaded assessment of America's national interests than does the current inherited policy that stymies rather than advances those interests. Setting this policy change in the context of a broader reassessment of twenty-first century U.S. interests and goals in the Middle East and U.S. relations with Saudi Arabia and the UAE, a new administration can allay concerns that the pursuit of a different U.S. policy toward Yemen would come at the expense of other regional or global policy goals.

The status quo approach undermines U.S. medium- and long-term national interests and further tarnishes America's reputation—not to mention increasing the risk of widespread famine among innocent civilians and perpetuating instability that provides sanctuary to terrorists. These costs—measured in human lives, and diminished U.S. influence and security—are simply too high a price to pay for the sake of maintaining bilateral relationships with governments whose interests and values long ago diverged from those of the United States, and who by all accounts need the United States far more than the United States needs them. To date, two American presidents have failed to end the catastrophic war in Yemen. The next administration must avoid those errors, in the interests of U.S. national security and the Yemeni people.

Notes

1. See, for example, Robert Worth, "Yemen Under Siege," *New York Review of Books*, February 21, 2019; Adam Baron, Maged Al-Madhaji, and Waleed Alhariri, "The Destabilizing Legacy of U.S. Military Aid and Counterterrorism Efforts in Yemen," Sana'a Center for Strategic Studies, August 5, 2017.

2. Marieke Brandt, *Tribes and Politics in Yemen: A History of the Houthi Conflict* (Oxford University Press, 2017); Sama'a Al-Hamdani, "Understanding the Houthi Faction in Yemen," *Lawfare*, April 7, 2019; Ahmed Nagi, "Yemen's Houthis Used Multiple Identities to Advance," March 19, 2019 (https://carnegie-mec.org/2019/03/19/yemen-s-houthis-used-multiple-identities-to-advance-pub-78623); Michael Knights, "The Houthi War Machine: From Guerilla War to State Capture," *CTC Sentinel*, v. 11 (September 2018).

3. For a thorough account of the Christmas 2009 "underwear bomber" attempted attack on a U.S. passenger jet, see Scott Shane, "Inside Al Qaeda's Plot to Blow Up an American Airliner," *New York Times*, February 22, 2017. The October 2010 attempted bombing of two aircraft using bombs planted in printer cartridges is detailed in Mark Mazetti, Robert Worth, and Eric Lipton, "Bomb Plot Shows Key Role Played by Intelligence," *New York Times*, October 31, 2010. The October 2000 bombing of the USS *Cole* in

Aden Harbor was an even earlier example of al Qaeda using Yemen as a base for attacking the United States.

4. UN Office for the Coordination of Humanitarian Affairs, "2019 Yemen Humanitarian Needs Overview," December 2018 (https://reliefweb.int/sites/reliefweb.int/files/resources/2019_Yemen_HNO_FINAL.pdf).

5. UN Development Programme, "Assessing the Impact of War on Development in Yemen," May 2019 (https://reliefweb.int/sites/reliefweb.int/files/resources/ImpactOfWarOnDevelopmentInYemen.pdf).

6. President Obama himself referenced the U.S. counterterrorism approach as a model for other fronts as late as September 2014. "Statement by the President on ISIL," September 10, 2014 (https://obamawhitehouse.archives.gov/the-press-office/2014/09/10/statement-president-isil-1). For a critical assessment of this "Yemen model" of counterterrorism (comprising air strikes and targeted raids against terrorist leaders), see Leonard Cutler, *President Obama's Counterterrorism Strategy in the War on Terror* (New York: Palgrave Macmillan U.S., 2017), especially chapter 3.

7. Despite Saleh's reputation at the time as a strong U.S. counterterrorism partner, it has been widely reported that the U.S. government was aware that Saleh was diverting American support intended to be used to combat AQAP to instead attack the Houthis. Ellen Knickmeyer, "Yemen's Double Game," *Foreign Policy*, December 7, 2010.

8. Amrit Singh, *Death by Drone: Civilian Harm Caused by U.S. Targeted Killings in Yemen*, Open Society Justice Initiative, 2015 (www.justiceinitiative.org/uploads/1284eb37-f380-4400-9242-936a15e4de6c/death-drones-report-eng-20150413.pdf); Farea Al-Muslimi, written testimony before the Senate Judiciary Subcommittee on the Constitution, Civil Rights, and Human Rights, April 23, 2013 (www.judiciary.senate.gov/imo/media/doc/04-23-13 Al-MuslimiTestimony.pdf).

9. U.S. assistance to Yemen totaled more than US$890 million from FY12 to FY14, and Obama authorized targeted sanctions against individuals or groups under EO 13611. Jeremy Sharp, "Yemen: Background and U.S. Relations," Congressional Research Service, February 11, 2015.

10. April Longley Alley, "Yemen's Houthi Takeover," Middle East Institute, December 22, 2014 (www.mei.edu/publications/yemens-houthi-takeover).

11. Spencer Ackerman, "U.S. Gives 'Strong Support' to Yemen Government Despite Shia Rebel Uprising," *Guardian*, September 26, 2014.

12. International Crisis Group, *Ending the Yemen Quagmire: Lessons for Washington from Four Years of War*, April 15, 2019 (www.crisisgroup.org/united-states/003-ending-yemen-quagmire-lessons-washington-four-years-war). U.S. air strikes in Yemen actually peaked in 2012, targeting AQAP operatives who had taken advantage of governmental instability amid the transition but killing and injuring significant numbers of Yemeni civilians as well.

13. Melissa Dalton and Hijab Shah, *U.S. Support for Saudi Military Operations in Yemen*, Center for Strategic and International Studies, March 23, 2018.

14. International Crisis Group, "Ending the Yemen Quagmire," 7.

15. The counter-AQAP campaign has been a significant driver of closer U.S. military ties with the United Arab Emirates, which has been willing to deploy forces on the ground where the United States was reluctant; the Trump administration and its supporters consistently cite the desire to maintain this close cooperation in arguing against ending U.S. military support for Saudi-UAE attacks on the Houthis.

16. International Crisis Group, "Ending the Yemen Quagmire," 11. (Obama's "guidance to provide defensive support to the coalition was not understood to preclude the administration from moving forward on offensive arms sales that it might have made even in the absence of a campaign on Yemen.")

17. The most extensive account is by Larry Lewis, who led U.S. coaching efforts. Larry Lewis, "Promoting Civilian Protection during Security Assistance: Learning from Yemen," May 2019 (www.cna.org/CNA_files/PDF/IRM-2019-U-019749-Final.pdf). The Saudi failure to improve is also detailed in International Crisis Group, "Ending the Yemen Quagmire," 8–14.

18. International Crisis Group, "Ending the Yemen Quagmire," 14–15; "Kerry Announces New Yemen Peace Initiative," *Middle East Eye*, August 25, 2016.

19. International Crisis Group, "Ending the Yemen Quagmire," 6.

20. Missy Ryan, "With Small Changes, U.S. Maintains Military Aid to Saudi Arabia despite Rebukes over Yemen Carnage," *Washington Post*, December 13, 2016; International Crisis Group, "Ending the Yemen Quagmire," 12.

21. According to the most comprehensive database of battle-related casualties, Saudi-UAE air strikes are responsible for around 67 percent of civilian casualties in Yemen since 2015. Armed Conflict Location and Event Data Project (ACLED), "Yemen War Death Toll Exceeds 90,000 According to New ACLED Data for 2015," June 18, 2019 (www.acleddata.com/2019/06/18/press-release-yemen-war-death-toll-exceeds-90000-according-to-new-acled-data-for-2015/).

22. Iona Craig, "Death in al Ghayil," *Intercept*, March 9, 2017. The Hadi government said it wanted U.S. counterterrorism operations "reassessed" following publication of the civilian casualties caused by the raid. Julian Borger and Ben Johnson, "Yemen Wants U.S. to Reassess Counterterrorism Strategy after Botched Raid," *Guardian*, February 8, 2017.

23. Missy Ryan and Anne Gearan, "Trump Administration Looks to Resume Saudi Arms Sale Criticized as Endangering Civilians in Yemen," *Washington Post*, March 8, 2017.

24. International Crisis Group, "Ending the Yemen Quagmire," 20.

25. William Hartung, "U.S. Military Support for Saudi Arabia and the War in Yemen," Center for International Policy, Arms and Security Project, November 2018 (https://docs.wixstatic.com/ugd/3ba8a1_5e9019d625e84087af647e6cb91ea3e2.pdf).

26. Dion Nissenbaum, "UN Pushes to Avert 'Catastrophic' UAE Attack on Yemen Port," *Wall Street Journal*, June 10, 2018.

27. The single exception to this—Trump's direct criticism of the Saudi-UAE total blockade of Yemen that was begun in November 2017—demonstrates

the unused potential of U.S. diplomatic leverage, since the Saudis began to lift the blockade within days of the White House statement criticizing it. Michael D. Shear and Ben Hubbard, "Trump Urges Saudi Arabia to End Blockade of Goods into Yemen," *New York Times*, December 6, 2017; Missy Ryan and Josh Dawsey, "Why Trump Lashed Out at Saudi Arabia about Its Role in Yemen's War," *Washington Post*, December 29, 2017.

28. Radhya Almutawakel, written testimony before the House Foreign Affairs Middle East Subcommittee, March 6, 2019 (https://docs.house.gov/meetings/FA/FA13/20190306/109038/HHRG-116-FA13-Wstate-AlmutawakelR-20190306.pdf) ("The warring parties depend on the total absence of accountability and expect their allies to allow the status quo to continue. Their disregard for international law and for the millions of civilians suffering in Yemen will only grow with each new abuse they are allowed to commit with impunity. Saudi Arabia, the UAE, the Houthis, and other armed groups feel they have a green light to do whatever they want, however horrible it may be, because they do not believe anyone will stand up in the face of their abuses."). On the Saudi failure to credibly investigate its own violations, see Human Rights Watch, *Hiding Behind the Coalition: Failure to Credibly Investigate and Provide Redress for Unlawful Attacks in Yemen*, August 24, 2018 (https://hrw.org/report/2018/08/24/hiding-behind-coalition/failure-credibly-investigate-and-provide-redress-unlawful).

29. Helene Cooper, "Senate Narrowly Backs Trump Weapons Sale to Saudi Arabia," *New York Times*, June 13, 2017; Nicholas Fandos, "Senators Reject Limits on U.S. Support for Saudi-Led Fight in Yemen," *New York Times*, March 20, 2018.

30. Letter from Senators Corker, Menendez, and others to Secretaries Pompeo and Mattis, June 12, 2018 (www.foreign.senate.gov/download/menendez-bipartisan-letter-on-hudaydah); see also Margaret Coker and Declan Walsh, "Humanitarian Crisis Worsens in Yemen After Attack on Port," *New York Times*, June 13, 2018.

31. The provision was included in the FY19 National Defense Authorization Act. See Pub. L. 115-232, sec. 1290. On Congress's backlash to what it viewed as a baseless certification by the Trump administration, see Dion Nissenbaum, "U.S. Lawmakers Challenge Trump's Support for Saudi War in Yemen," *Wall Street Journal*, October 10, 2018.

32. John Hudson and Missy Ryan, "Trump Administration to End Refueling of Saudi-Coalition Aircraft in Yemen Conflict," *Washington Post*, November 10, 2018; Karoun Demirjian, "Senate Votes to Condemn Saudi Crown Prince for Khashoggi Killing, End Support for Yemen War," *Washington Post*, December 13, 2018.

33. Robert Malley and Stephen Pomper, "Yemen Cannot Afford to Wait," *The Atlantic*, April 5, 2019.

34. The first 2019 hearing of the House Foreign Affairs Committee focused on U.S. policy toward the Arabian Peninsula (https://foreignaffairs.house.gov/2019/2/u-s-policy-in-the-arabian-peninsula), while the first 2019 hearing of the Middle East and North Africa Subcommittee focused on the war and

humanitarian crisis in Yemen (https://foreignaffairs.house.gov/2019/3/the-humanitarian-crisis-in-yemen-addressing-current-political-and-human itarian-challenges).

35. Karoun Demirjian and Missy Ryan, "Senate Fails to Override Trump's Veto of Resolution Demanding End to U.S. Involvement in Yemen War," *Washington Post*, May 2, 2019; Catie Edmondson, "Senate Fails to Override Trump's Veto on Saudi Arms Sales," *New York Times*, July 29, 2019.

36. Becky Anderson, "UAE Partially Withdrawing from Yemen, Official Says," CNN, July 8, 2019.

37. Sudarsan Raghavan, Kareem Fahim, and Ali Al-Mujahed, "Yemen: Seizure of Aden by Separatists Exposes Rift within Saudi Arabia and UAE Coalition," *Washington Post*, August 11, 2019; Declan Walsh and Saeed Al-Batati, "Ally Attacks Ally in Yemen's War within a War," *New York Times*, August 29, 2019.

38. Bethan McKernan, "Yemen: Aden's Changing Alliances Erupt into Four-Year Conflict's Newest Front," *Guardian*, October 1, 2019.

39. Raiman al-Hamdani and Helen Lackner, "War and Pieces: Political Divides in Southern Yemen," European Council on Foreign Relations, January 22, 2020 (www.ecfr.eu/publications/summary/war_and_pieces_politi cal_divides_in_southern_yemen); International Crisis Group, "Breaking a Renewed Conflict Cycle in Yemen," January 24, 2020 (www.crisisgroup .org/middle-east-north-africa/gulf-and-arabian-peninsula/yemen/breaking -renewed-conflict-cycle-yemen).

40. Dion Nissenbaum, "Saudi Arabia Agrees to Partial Cease-Fire in War-Shattered Yemen," *Wall Street Journal*, September 27, 2019.

41. See, for example, Peter Salisbury, "The Beginning of the End of Yemen's Civil War?" November 5, 2019 (www.crisisgroup.org/middle-east-north-africa /gulf-and-arabian-peninsula/yemen/beginning-end-yemens-civil-war).

42. International Crisis Group, "Breaking a Renewed Conflict Cycle in Yemen."

43. Stacey Philbrick Yadav, "Fragmentation and Localization in Yemen's War: Challenges and Opportunities for Peace," November 2018 (www.bran deis.edu/crown/publications/meb/MEB123.pdf).

44. Gregory Johnson, "Trump and Counterterrorism in Yemen: The First Two Years," Sana'a Center for Strategic Studies, February 27, 2019 (http:// sanaacenter.org/publications/analysis/7105). (Even the Defense Department admits that "[w]e need a stable, inclusive government in Yemen to provide security to the Yemeni people and reduce, and ultimately eliminate, terrorist safe havens being used by AQAP and ISIS in Yemen.") "What the DOD Says About Its Operations in Yemen," *Frontline*, January 22, 2019 (www.pbs.org/ wgbh/frontline/article/dod-statement-raids-airstrikes-yemen/).

45. Elisabeth Kendall, "Contemporary Jihadi Militancy in Yemen: How Is the Threat Evolving?" Middle East Institute Policy Paper 2018-7, July 2018 (www.mei.edu/sites/default/files/publications/MEI%20Policy%20Paper_ Kendall_7.pdf).

46. Sana'a Center for Strategic Studies, "The Yemen Review: War's Elusive

End," January 2020, 70; Glenn Carey, "Yemen's Fault Lines," Bloomberg, October 1, 2019.

47. Valentin D'Hauthuille, "UAE's Sphere of Influence in Southern Yemen," ACLED, March 9, 2018 (www.acleddata.com/2018/03/09/uaes-sphere-of-influence-in-southern-yemen); Nicholas Heras, " 'Security Belt': The UAE's Tribal Counterterrorism Strategy in Yemen," Jamestown Foundation, June 14, 2018 (https://jamestown.org/program/security-belt-the-uaes-tribal-counterterrorism-strategy-in-yemen); Zachary Laub, "How the UAE Wields Power in Yemen," Council on Foreign Relations, June 22, 2018 (www.cfr.org/interview/how-uae-wields-power-yemen).

48. Nima Elbagir and others, "Sold to an Ally, Lost to an Enemy," CNN, March 2019 (www.cnn.com/interactive/2019/02/middleeast/yemen-lost-us-arms).

49. Elisa Catalano Ewers and Nicholas Heras, "Congressional Action on Yemen Isn't Only About Yemen," Center for a New American Security, February 27, 2019 (www.cnas.org/publications/commentary/h-j-res-37-congressional-action-on-yemen-isnt-only-about-yemen).

50. Farea Al Muslimi, "Iran's Role in Yemen Exaggerated, but Destructive," Century Foundation, May 19, 2017 (https://tcf.org/content/report/irans-role-yemen-exaggerated-destructive); Daniel Byman, "How the U.S. Is Empowering Iran in Yemen," *Foreign Affairs*, July 26, 2018; Gregory D. Johnsen, "No Clean Hands: Reaction and Counterreaction in the Iranian-Saudi Proxy War in Yemen," *Just Security*, November 21, 2018; Becca Wasser and Ariane Tabatabai, "Iran's Network of Fighters in the Middle East Aren't Always Loyal to Iran," *Washington Post*, May 21, 2019.

51. Rawan Shaif, "Saudi Arabia's Self-Fulfilling Houthi Prophecy," *Foreign Policy*, October 2, 2019.

52. Author's interview with a UN official, June 2019.

53. Rauf Mammadov, "Houthi Attack in Strategic Shipping Lane Could Undermine Oil Markets," Middle East Institute, July 27, 2018 (www.mei.edu/publications/houthi-attack-strategic-shipping-lane-could-undermine-oil-markets).

54. See Julian Lee, "Bab al Mandab, an Emerging Chokepoint for Middle East Oil Flows," Bloomberg, July 26, 2018.

55. See Aziz el Yaakoubi, "Yemen's Houthis Threaten to Block Red Sea Shipping Lane," Reuters, January 9, 2018.

56. See, for example, Nima Elbagir and others, "Bomb that Killed Forty Children in Yemen Was Supplied by the U.S.," CNN, August 17, 2018 (https://edition.cnn.com/2018/08/17/middleeast/us-saudi-yemen-bus-strike-intl/index.html); Mwatana for Human Rights, "Day of Judgment: The Role of the U.S. and Europe in Civilian Death, Destruction, and Trauma in Yemen," March 13, 2019 (http://mwatana.org/en/day-of-judgment).

57. Andrew England and Simeon Kerr, "UAE Attacks on Yemen Reveal Fractures in Saudi-Led Coalition," *Financial Times*, August 24, 2019.

58. The early 2019 reporting on the diversion of U.S.-sold armored vehicles and anti-tank missiles from Saudi Arabia and the UAE to AQAP-affili-

ated militias and, in some cases, even the Houthis, makes clear that future arms sales must be limited to those to be physically located in Saudi Arabia and the UAE and incapable of increasing military tensions, if they are to contribute to the de-escalation, rather than escalation, of the conflict in Yemen.

59. Yemen Data Project, "Yemen Air Raids Summary January 2020," January 2020 (https://mailchi.mp/811d6797529d/january2020-yemen-data-project-update-614955).

60. For an excellent overview of the flaws of UN Security Council resolution 2216, see Stephen A. Seche, "Give Peace a Real Chance in Yemen," *New Humanitarian*, April 16, 2018.

61. Annual Gallup polling on U.S. public attitudes toward other countries demonstrates an overwhelming and durably negative perception of Saudi Arabia. Favorable/unfavorable figures for 2019 showed a twelve-point negative shift (to 29 percent favorable/67 percent unfavorable), meaning Saudi Arabia is less popular now than in the poll taken just months after the 9/11 attacks. See Gallup, "Country Ratings" (https://news.gallup.com/poll/1624/perceptions-foreign-countries.aspx).

62. International Crisis Group, "Breaking a Renewed Conflict Cycle in Yemen."

63. A characterization made by an international diplomat familiar with the parties' positions. Author's interview with a UN official, August 2019.

64. Ongoing U.S. military sales or training to Saudi Arabia or the UAE also will need to be sharply ring-fenced and tied to the specific cross-border threat posed by the Houthis, rather than encompassing some broader categorization of "defensive" weapons, given the demonstrable risk that Saudi Arabia and the UAE are willing to ignore U.S. export controls and divert U.S. arms (including those that could be characterized as "defensive," like armored vehicles) to proxies inside Yemen. See CNN, "Sold to an Ally, Lost to an Enemy."

65. To date, arguably the closest the parties have come to peace has been as a result of the diplomatic push by former Secretary of State Kerry in late 2016. It presented the Houthis with a more balanced proposal (not requiring unilateral disarmament and withdrawal before substantive negotiations even began), which they accepted. Hadi's rejection of the plan stemmed from his correct assessment that Trump's election removed any risk of bilateral consequences or pressure from the United States. See "Yemeni President Turns Down UN Peace Deal," *Deutsche Welle*, October 29, 2016 (www.dw.com/en/yemeni-president-turns-down-un-peace-deal/a-36197749); International Crisis Group, "Ending the Yemen Quagmire," 16. Had these steps happened earlier in the Obama administration, with more time before a U.S. presidential transition and thus a clear possibility that a rejection of U.S. diplomatic efforts by Saudi-UAE and Hadi could result in bilateral consequences, it is possible that both sides could have been pressured to sign on.

66. On Houthi humanitarian aid interference, see Peter Beaumont, "Yemen: Houthi Rebels' Food Aid Theft Only Tip of Iceberg, Officials Say," *Guardian*, January 2, 2019.

67. Of course, U.S. diplomacy should be clearly guided by the principle

that it is for Yemenis, and not outside actors, to decide the shape and structure of Yemen's postwar state.

68. UN Office for the Coordination of Humanitarian Affairs, "2019 Yemen Humanitarian Needs Overview."

69. Author's meetings with senior U.S. officials, Spring–Autumn 2019.

70. Radhya Almutawakel, written testimony before the House Foreign Affairs Middle East Subcommittee.

71. Public Law 115-232, sec. 1290 (FY19); Public Law 116-92, sec. 1274 (FY20).

72. Achieving this step forward for accountability likely would require the United States to rejoin the UN Human Rights Council, from which it withdrew under the Trump administration.

73. A. Trevor Thrall, "The False Promises of Trump's Arms Sales," *Defense One*, April 5, 2019; William Hartung, "U.S. Military Support for Saudi Arabia and the War in Yemen," Center for International Policy, November 2018 (https://docs.wixstatic.com/ugd/3ba8a1_5e9019d625e84087af647e6cb91ea3e2.pdf).

74. Josh Rogin, "Trump Has It 'Totally and Completely Backways' on Saudi Arms Sales," *Washington Post*, October 16, 2018.

75. Mwatana for Human Rights, "Day of Judgment: The Role of the U.S. and Europe in Civilians Death, Destruction, and Trauma in Yemen," March 2019 (https://mwatana.org/en/day-of-judgment/); UN Group of International and Regional Eminent Experts on Yemen, "Yemen: Collective Failure, Collective Responsibility," September 3, 2019.

FOUR

Toward a Stable Libya

MEGAN DOHERTY

U.S. Policy in Libya

In Libya, U.S. interests are admittedly limited and primarily indirect. They include the immediate security threat that the instability of the North African country poses to U.S. allies and the potential for terrorist groups such as ISIS to take advantage of a protracted security and governance vacuum. However, a collapsed state two hundred miles from Europe, an ideal sanctuary for terrorists seeking to strike both Europe and the United States, is obviously problematic for U.S. interests. We have also seen in recent years the costs of U.S. disengagement from Libya, including a diplomatic vacuum exploited by Russia and other foreign actors with competing interests, a staging ground for regional rivalries, and a deadly proxy war. Further insecurity in Libya will continue to have a destabilizing effect across the Middle East and North Africa. U.S. diplomatic leadership is needed to mitigate malign foreign meddling and increase the prospects for a durable peace.

While Libya is a country in which the United States should be careful not to overinvest, U.S. foreign policymakers have the potential advantage of sharing costs with European allies who have a more direct stake in Libya. A burden-sharing Libya strategy would put Europe in the lead to address the confluence of insecurity, migration, terrorism, and illicit weapons flows that have destabilized not only Libya but also North Africa and the broader Sahel, notably Mali and Tunisia. Even with more robust European involvement in Libya, the United States still would have a vital, though less resource-intensive role to play, exercising diplomatic leadership to help align the international community in support of UN-led negotiations while guiding European investments to address the challenges posed by Libya's governance vacuum, lawlessness, weapons proliferation, and porous borders. As recent events—including military interventions by Moscow and Ankara—demonstrate, the United States cannot abdicate responsibility for Libya without unleashing additional destabilizing forces.[1] The challenge for the next administration will be to devote enough diplomatic attention to shaping the political process in Libya, as well as the calculations of other external actors seeking to mold it, while protecting against the ever-present risk of escalating commitments.

Though there is a clear opportunity for U.S. diplomacy in Libya, U.S. policy must begin with deep humility born out of a recognition of Libya's myriad internal and external challenges, matched with realistic expectations about what can be accomplished in the short term. Such an approach should begin with acknowledging that the United States and Europe will often have limited influence over the warring factions. Field Marshal Khalifa Haftar, one of the central protagonists in Libya's turmoil, enjoys varying degrees of political and military support from Russia, Egypt, France, the United Arab Emirates (UAE), and Saudi Arabia in his campaign to wrest control of Tripoli from the militias aligned with the internationally recognized Government of National Accord (GNA) and install himself as an Abdel Fattah al Sisi–style authoritarian leader. His backers broadly hope Haftar and his Libyan National Army (LNA) will fight terrorists and defeat Islamist-oriented militias they perceive as threats, and reward their patronage with benefits like military basing rights and favorable oil deals. For their part, the militias aligned with the GNA, a weak unity government established in 2015 by the UN with heavy diplomatic involvement from the United States and other Western governments, enjoy significant material support from Turkey, while the GNA itself has been politically supported by Italy and Qatar.[2]

A future U.S. administration does not need to fix Libya, nor could it even if it wanted to. Given the manifold and multiplying threats to internal stability, seeking a comprehensive solution is simply not a realistic policy objective in the short term. Nor should the United States assume that the right combination of training packages and diplomatic pressure, as undertaken inconsistently by the Obama administration from 2012 until 2016, can cohere disparate localized security actors into a willing or capable national force.[3] It ultimately will be up to the Libyan leaders themselves to negotiate security arrangements that can finally deliver for their beleaguered people. But the next U.S. administration can and should aim in the short term to stop the proxy conflict; degrade the ability of ISIS and extremist groups to use Libya as a staging ground for attacks on our homeland and our allies; prevent a larger-scale civil war that would destabilize the region; and lay the groundwork for Libya's longer-term stabilization, including by introducing accountability and transparency for how oil revenues are used and supporting a civilian-led transition process. Working in concert with the United Kingdom and the EU, modest U.S. investments in diplomacy, security, and development can help mitigate further deterioration and strengthen prospects for longer-term recovery. None of this would necessarily set up the next president for the Nobel Peace Prize in the short term, but it could nevertheless advance core U.S. regional interests in stability and security.

An Uncertain Commitment: Obama's Approach to Libya
The Obama administration's inconsistent investments in Libya reflected the president's overall uncertainty and discomfort regarding military-led state-building in another Middle Eastern country. Obama, who was originally skeptical of a U.S. military intervention in Libya, ultimately sided with those in his administration who argued for the use of force to stop the advance of Muammar Qaddafi's troops amid the Libyan dictator's threats to eliminate the 630,000 residents of the eastern city of Benghazi in March 2011.[4]

Liberal interventionists in the administration were, with much effort, able to persuade Obama that a military intervention authorized by the UN Security Council with limited, short-term objectives, supported by Arab and European allies, represented a very different type of military campaign than those undertaken in the region by Obama's predecessor. In what was deemed a stunning success at the time, the Obama administration worked quickly with allies to pass a UN Security Council resolution authorizing "all necessary measures . . . to protect civilians and civilian-populated areas under threat of attack."[5] The resulting NATO-led military coalition operating under this mandate not only saved Benghazi but also helped to turn the tide in the civil war, which culminated in Qaddafi's death at the hands of Libyan rebels in October 2011.

Unfortunately, neither Libyan nor international actors were able to convert their military success against Qaddafi into a functional political arrangement for the country. Whereas Tunisia and Egypt had some semblance of institutions that endured after their authoritarian rulers were thrown out, Libya's governing bodies were undeveloped and incapable of holding the country together post-Qaddafi. In 2012, the international community focused disproportionately on elections without adequately investing in the capacity of the newly elected bodies. Although the Obama administration and its allies hailed the success of Libya's first post-Qaddafi elections, congratulating the Libyan people on their accomplishment, the reality was that Libyan politicians had no sway over the dozens of well-armed militias holding on to territory gained during the revolution.[6] Some armed groups transformed into black-market profiteers and others carried on local policing functions, while still others surrounded government ministries and the nascent parliament to intimidate the lawmakers.[7] As fighters began to disperse and return from Iraq and Syria in 2014, ISIS took advantage of the lawlessness and established itself in Sirte, Qaddafi's neglected hometown, growing to more than two thousand fighters by 2015.[8]

Part of the blame for Libya's struggles rests with the United States and other international players. The Obama administration, determined to avoid another protracted war in the Middle East, was reluctant to prepare for postconflict scenarios and hoped the Europeans would own the challenge. President Obama later referred to this failure to plan for the aftermath as the "worst mistake" of his presidency.[9] The assumptions underlying the U.S. approach to Libya—that European allies would do more, Libyan oil would pay for costly reconstruction, and the UN would be able to build consensus among the deeply fractured political and tribal factions—proved catastrophically mistaken. While establishing a new political order in Libya was always going to be a challenge, even under the best of circumstances, an uncoordinated international community and a nascent government unable to absorb offers of training and assistance all but ensured a chaotic outcome.

The tragic killing of four Americans, including U.S. Ambassador J. Christopher Stevens, in September 2012 dramatically changed the U.S. government's risk tolerance, both in Libya and for civilians deployed worldwide in insecure environments. This had the direct effect of further limiting U.S. diplomats' ability to engage in the tough work of building governance and institutional capacity. In this more constrained security environment, the Obama administration still tried to support Libya's transition, playing a leading diplomatic role in the 2015 UN-brokered negotiations that formed the internationally recognized GNA. In rushing to reach an agreement on a national unity government, however, the international community, including the United States, gave short shrift to whether the agreement was implementable or sustainable. In the absence of a larger international presence in Libya, there was no enforcement mechanism to ensure compliance with the terms of the new accord, called the Libyan Political Agreement (LPA).

The net effect of the LPA was the opposite of what was intended, further polarizing the country while Haftar—who rejected the LPA—continued his campaign to win territory in the east, supported by Egypt's al-Sisi and the UAE's Mohammed bin Zayed, who felt threatened by Islamist-oriented elements in the new GNA.[10] As these political divisions crystallized into rival parliaments, the United States and the EU made late-stage efforts to mitigate political opponents to the GNA, including imposing sanctions in April 2016.[11] The sanctions did little to change the behavior of actors on the ground, several of whom continued to obstruct efforts for peace. Libya's inchoate bureaucracy and atomized security sector dominated by self-interested militias quashed grand international efforts to build a new national army.[12] The U.S. and European allies shifted course to focus on more discrete partnerships to counter ISIS and al Qaeda. The fractured political landscape and lawlessness had allowed ISIS's presence to grow under the radar to an estimated six thousand in 2016.[13] In August of 2016, the U.S. launched Operation Odyssey Lightning and supported GNA-backed fighters in the four-month campaign that drove ISIS from Sirte. The partnership between the GNA-aligned fighters and AFRICOM (United States Africa Command) provided the GNA a degree of credibility as Libyans saw their new government could request and receive support from the U.S. military. These efforts, however, proved too little too late, as the GNA was unable to parlay a victory against ISIS into meaningful improvements in security, socioeconomic conditions, or national unity.

Trump's Libya Policy Turn

President Trump entered office with very little interest in Libya, notwithstanding his efforts to use the deaths of Americans in Benghazi under then-Secretary of State Hillary Rodham Clinton to weaken his general-election opponent. Making clear his dismissive attitude toward the country, President Trump publicly stated in April 2017 that "I do not see a role in Libya. I think the United States has right now enough roles," though he later qualified this remark by saying, "I do see a role in getting rid of ISIS."[14] Reflecting the president's views, the Trump administration has maintained some counterterrorism efforts, including air strikes against suspected al Qaeda and ISIS targets, but has done little to address the underlying political conditions that continue to generate an opening for ISIS and other extremist organizations to regroup and attract recruits.

Trump's early inattention to Libya posed a dilemma for U.S. policymakers. While his disengagement allowed career U.S. government personnel to continue policies aimed at healing Libya's national divide, U.S. efforts would have been more effective with support and engagement from the White House. The U.S. Department of State and the U.S. Agency for International Development (USAID) proceeded with modest assistance programs to help the GNA access its oil wealth and build local governance capacity, while the U.S. Embassy in Libya—now operating out of neighboring Tunis—helped lead economic dialogues among Libya's fractured economic institutions.[15] Libya began to make some important steps toward longer-term recovery, including restarting oil production, which reached 1.2 million barrels per day in 2018, and preparing for a UN-led national dialogue to negotiate interim power-sharing agreements and a roadmap for elections.[16] But the absence of high-level U.S. diplomatic involvement—and the White House's silence on its strategic objectives—emboldened external actors to play out long-simmering proxy conflicts and created a diplomatic gap that Russia, Egypt, the UAE, Saudi Arabia, and Turkey have exploited.[17]

This dynamic only changed for the worse in April 2019, when days after Haftar launched his assault against the GNA in Tripoli, President Trump called him to discuss a "shared vision" for Libya, implicitly backing the strongman's violent bid for power. Days later, the United States Mission to the UN reportedly blocked a draft UN Security Council Resolution calling for a ceasefire.[18] Haftar, who had long threatened to wage war against the Islamist-oriented militias in Western Libya, many of whom supported the GNA, was likely emboldened by his Egyptian and Emirati backers, who had also interceded with Trump. The LNA's campaign, which started mere days before the planned UN conference to negotiate a peace deal and a transition plan,[19] within a few weeks had killed hundreds, wounded thousands, and led more than 100,000 to flee their homes.[20]

Trump's abrupt reversal of long-standing U.S. policy to support the GNA and a negotiated political solution was predicated on a mistaken belief that Haftar could be a valuable partner for the United States. Contrary to his reputation as a rabid anti-Islamist, Haftar has turned a blind eye to the ISIS and al Qaeda threats in the areas nominally under LNA control. Multiple LNA battalions are, in fact, commanded by Salafists, whose views and activities are often indistinguishable from those of ISIS. In Benghazi, some forces aligned with the LNA have enforced forms of Sharia law and prevented women from gathering in public, restricted community organizations, and killed members of opposing sects.[21] In addition, even if Haftar, emboldened by Russian mercenaries and high-grade weapons, were able to take Tripoli by force, the well-armed tribes in southern and western Libya would continue to violently oppose any of his efforts to rule, prolonging the civil war and preventing stabilization in Libya. Due to Libya's complex security landscape, mitigating terrorist threats emanating from Libya requires an array of partnerships, and prioritizing Haftar as he attacks a civilian population risks other, arguably more valuable partnerships, including with the GNA-aligned Misratans, who helped defeat ISIS in Sirte in 2016. Finally, by validating Haftar instead of prioritizing calls for a negotiated political solution, the United States has burned some of its diplomatic credibility that could have been leveraged to help unite the international community and push for a return to talks.

The Central Policy Questions and Challenges Facing the Next Administration

The next president will inherit this chaotic landscape in Libya, but he or she will also inherit a diminishing but still present opportunity to assert diplomatic leadership to strengthen prospects for stability. By the time there is a new administration, of course, the unpredictable conflict in Libya could have transformed into any number of possible scenarios: one of the two main factions could be in complete control of the capital; the conflict between them could have degenerated into full-blown civil war fueled by foreign patrons; or, most likely, a status quo of instability and political discord could persist. Even if a political agreement is reached in the short term, it will be a fragile one. Whatever the settlement dictates on paper, Libya's weak governing institutions will struggle to build public legitimacy and assert control over disparate security actors. The more than 150 self-interested militias of varying allegiances, capabilities, and ambitions will continue to test the country's stability as they compete for territory and resources.[22] Likewise, external actors with divergent and contradictory agendas, not to mention a willingness to provide weapons and material support to tip the balance in favor of their proxies, will remain a problem for any new government. Finally, violent extremist organizations and transnational criminal networks will continue to find appeal in a weak and lawless state.

Following the confusion created by the Trump administration's combination of inattention and abrupt policy shifts, the next administration will need to quickly rebuild U.S. credibility on Libya with European capitals and Libyan interlocutors if it is to help marshal the international community behind a negotiated political transition. A new president will also need to decide whether he or she is willing to exert pressure on both sides and especially their foreign backers to end the proxy conflict by committing to UN-led negotiations and enforcement of the UN arms embargo. In light of other competing regional priorities, the United States has largely remained silent on the flagrant Russian, Emirati, Turkish, and other violations of the embargo, but a new administration should reexamine this posture, explore trade-offs with foreign powers meddling in Libya, and consider an array of tools, including sanctions. Should Haftar or another strongman establish some nominal control by 2021, a new president will have to decide whether and how to contend with a foreign-backed authoritarian who unabashedly violated international humanitarian law and attacked a civilian population in his quest for power.

The next administration will also confront an atomized and inchoate security sector in Libya, which will necessitate a discussion within the U.S. government about whether, and how, the United States can help to cohere disparate militias into capable local and national forces. Another challenge for the United States, partly the result of Libya's fractured security institutions, will be how to prevent ISIS and other terrorist actors from taking advantage of protracted lawlessness in Libya. In any scenario in which Libya remains mired in conflict, the United States and European allies will struggle to urge Libyan partners fighting each other in a civil war to divert their attention and energy to U.S. counterterrorism priorities.

Beyond these immediate political and security challenges, the next administration will need to consider how much it wants to invest in Libya's broader recovery, including the country's deteriorating humanitarian conditions. In addition to mass displacement and economic disruption, there are thousands of refugees and migrants facing inhumane conditions—arbitrary detention, forced labor, and recurrent human rights violations. The United States will have to make a choice regarding the extent to which it is prepared to mobilize foreign assistance resources and diplomatic leverage to encourage broader development, push back on European counter-migration policies that fund predatory practices that keep refugees and migrants in inhumane detention centers, and address human rights deficits in Libya. Any decision to prioritize stabilization and recovery in Libya will likely require trade-offs in responding to the many other crises around the globe.

Recommended Approach

As Libya will remain a mid-to-low-level priority for the United States, the next administration should adopt a cost-sensitive, though not necessarily cost-averse, strategy to (1) end malign foreign interference; (2) support the achievement of a power-sharing agreement; (3) degrade ISIS and other terrorist actors; and (4) facilitate the development of inclusive governing institutions at the national and subnational levels that are integral to Libya's future political stability and economic recovery. While cost constraints will inevitably limit U.S. influence in Libya, there are considerable burden-sharing opportunities that can be leveraged to advance our priorities. Even when the United States does not take the lead, U.S. leadership still matters, and Libya is no exception. Absent diplomatic attention from the United States, Libya will be dominated by the competition between Russia, Turkey, Italy, the UAE, and France, as well as an EU that largely sees its investments in Libya through a migration-containment lens. Indeed, there is a real opening for the United States to reassert influence to support—but also shape—our European allies, relying on less costly diplomatic engagement and building on the bigger investments they will make. Because it does not share Italy's colonial legacy, Egypt's border concerns, the overt economic interests of Italy, Turkey, or Qatar, and is more distant from the broader Gulf proxy competition for ideological primacy, the United States can arguably play a more constructive leadership role. U.S.-European joint efforts will be viewed with less suspicion than action taken by Europeans on their own. And while they still broadly perceive the United States as self-interested, many Libyans are more inclined to partner with the U.S. government than other international actors.[23]

A cost-effective U.S.-Libya strategy will consist of the following elements:

De-escalate the proxy competition. The UN Special Representative of the Secretary General (SRSG) has repeatedly called for an end to foreign interference in the Libyan conflict, rightly arguing that illicit weapons shipments and mercenaries are prolonging the conflict and causing more civilian deaths.[24] Without a strong diplomatic push from the United States, these calls will continue unheeded and the situation on the ground will further spiral as Russia, the UAE, Turkey, and other actors seek an end state in Libya that favors their interests. The U.S. government should apply high level public and private diplomatic pressure to realign the international community and press the foreign backers to stop transferring weapons and mercenaries. The United States should also demonstrate consequences for countries and companies violating the arms embargo, such as sanctioning Russia's provision of private military contractors or the UAE's use of drones and airpower to commit war crimes via Executive Order 13726—which establishes the basis for sanctions in response to "actions or policies that threaten the peace, security, or stability of Libya, including through the supply of arms or related materiel"—or by joining with European partners on a new multilateral sanctions regime to enforce the UN arms embargo.

Support and shape the UN-led peace process. The UN will continue to be the primary actor leading negotiations to end the conflict and build consensus on a path forward in Libya. But its ability to do so is hampered by the lack of consistent, high-level support from the United States. In the short term, the U.S. government should publicly reaffirm support for the UN-led process and apply diplomatic pressure on warring parties to return to the negotiating table. A coordinated, clarified U.S. policy opposing a military solution would also help prevent Libyan actors from hearing different messages from the White House, State Department, and the Department of Defense, which has had the effect of diluting U.S. influence.

The next administration should help the UN to develop a new strategy for Libya that avoids the well-intentioned but ultimately costly mistakes of the Obama administration. Instead of rushing to hold elections and national conferences as a cure-all that can resolve Libya's many challenges, the United States should work with the UN and other international partners to try and negotiate interim rules of the game among political leaders, tribal powerbrokers, and security actors. Doing so would both expand buy-in and create space for local-level reconciliation and broader government formation talks to take place. The challenge, of course, will remain holding spoilers accountable for violating the agreed-upon rules, but here the United States can play a particularly important role in building support for sanctions designed to deter political spoilers.

Steer European-led humanitarian efforts. Increasing U.S. diplomatic engagement can also bolster important work by our allies, such as Dutch efforts to sanction and prosecute human traffickers. Libya's humanitarian needs are relatively modest compared to those generated by other regional crises in Syria and Yemen. Since 2014, the EU has contributed 338 million Euros to migration-related projects in Libya.[25] These investments, however, have arguably sought to prevent migrants from traversing the Mediterranean and arriving in Europe. For example, EU and Italian funding has built the capacity of the Libyan Coast Guard to intercept migrants and refugees at sea and return them to grisly detention centers in which human rights abuses are well documented.[26] The United States should assert diplomatic pressure on the EU to ensure that funding is not contributing to human rights abuses. While the next administration need not invest at the same level as the EU, it instead should focus on projects in which the United States has extensive experience or can rely on established relationships with local partners, such as providing technical assistance on the closure of detention centers, human rights monitoring, and other cost-sensitive but important investments.

Support thoughtful and limited security sector assistance. Both to bolster efforts to end the current war and limit foreign patrons fueling proxy conflicts, the next administration should work to reinvigorate the UN arms embargo, investigating and publicizing violations. The

United States should incentivize support for a future civilian-led government by offering training, equipment, and access to exchanges or military exercises. This would have the added benefit of countering the attractiveness of Russia, Turkey, and other external actors who are offering training and support to the militias. Militia negotiations need to be coordinated with the formal political negotiations to avoid undermining the ultimate goal, a political agreement supported by security actors on the ground.

The militia challenge is compounded by the longer-term need for Libya to build up functional national security institutions and capable, coherent forces. A future U.S. administration should continue providing technical advice to the ministries of interior and defense to help bolster nascent security-sector reform efforts and improve border security management. Security assistance efforts could build on prior considerable legwork and lessons learned. For example, the United States could offer technical secondments to the European Union Border Assistance Mission (EUBAM) and, once security conditions are permissive, reconsider the 2016 European-led Libyan International Assistance Mission (LIAM).[27]

Defeat ISIS in Libya through an array of partnerships. The next U.S. administration should continue identifying and eliminating ISIS threats in Libya. This will entail sharing intelligence with key European allies, including France and the United Kingdom, each of which has larger-scale operations in the Sahel. This will also include ensuring AFRICOM is appropriately resourced and expanding intelligence collection inside the country. Where possible, the United States should carry out counterterrorism efforts in visible partnership with a future Libyan government. In addition to addressing real threats to our European allies and the homeland, this type of cooperation could help boost the credibility of the GNA with the Libyan public. The United States should also continue to ensure that any counterterrorism partners meet the highest human rights standards, particularly when it comes to avoiding civilian casualties and inhumane or arbitrary detention.

In addition to containing ISIS threats, the next U.S. adminis-

tration should also continue to address the sources of marginaliza-
tion that make people vulnerable to ISIS recruitment. ISIS currently
relies on smuggling networks controlled by disenfranchised tribes in
Libya's restive, underdeveloped southern region. Approximately 33
percent of the population of southern Libya is undocumented and
thus unable to vote or participate in the formal economy.[28] ISIS is
increasingly playing on resource competitions among tribes and recruiting undocumented Libyans with promises of economic returns
and protections. The next administration should continue USAID
investments in local governance in the south to counter the economic
and political grievances exploited by ISIS.

Leverage modest assistance for recovery. To avoid repeated short-term
interventions, U.S. policy will have to cope with Libya's longer-term
stabilization challenges. A future U.S. administration can best address the drivers of instability by continuing modest investments that
help Libya recover and also contribute to longer-term governance.
For nearly a decade, the Libyan people have endured economic dys-
function, deterioration of public services, and inability of repeated
transitional governments to deliver improvements to their quality of
life. The political divisions and physical vulnerability of oil infrastructure to militia capture and shutdown have also prevented the
GNA from being able to harness Libya's vast oil reserves and ensure
resource flows to the municipalities.[29]

Our approach should be to guide and support resource deployment of our allies, especially the EU, which will take on the bigger-
ticket reconstruction efforts. However, the United States will not
be able to credibly steer other donors without being willing to provide some investments in Libya's longer-term recovery. To date, U.S.
development efforts have focused on building the capacity of local
governments, supporting civil society, equipping communities with
conflict-mitigation skills, and providing technical advice to the ministries of justice and interior.[30] These investments, funded predom-
inantly through the Economic Support Fund (ESF), have produced
modest but important returns—for example, strengthening border
security and increasing municipal government capacity to deliver ser-

vices. The next U.S. administration should focus not on mobilizing large amounts of money but instead building on these successful investments to focus on areas where U.S. assistance has unique value to add, including public financial management and border security.

Conclusion

Libya will continue to struggle on its path toward stability. While ultimate responsibility rests with Libyan leaders to negotiate and abide by a political settlement, the United States can play a modest, though important, role to support Libyan recovery and insulate itself and its allies against potential threats. Through targeted investments in diplomacy, security, and development, a new U.S. administration can help mitigate threats, while creating an enabling environment for the difficult work of helping Libya begin to recover from a decade of instability.

Notes

1. Crisis Group Middle East and North Africa, "Stopping the War in Libya" (briefing note), International Crisis Group, May 2019.

2. Tarek Megerisi, "Libya's Global Civil War" (policy brief), European Council on Foreign Relations, June 2019.

3. Missy Ryan, "Libyan Force Was Lesson in Limits of U.S. Power," *Washington Post*, August 5, 2015.

4. Jeffrey Goldberg, "The Obama Doctrine," *The Atlantic*, April 2016.

5. United Nations Security Council Resolution S/RES/1973 (2011).

6. See statement by the president on Libya (White House Press Release, July 2012) and Security Council Press Statement on Libya (SC/10704-AFR-2416, United Nations Security Council, July 2012).

7. As observed by author in Tripoli, in 2012–2014. See also Ghaith Shennib and Jessica Donati, "Gunmen Stage Protest Outside Libyan Parliament," Reuters, April 30, 2013, and Ghaith Shennib and Ulf Leassing, "Libyan Militias Threaten Parliament, Deploy Forces in Tripoli," Reuters, February 18, 2014.

8. Assessments of the ISIS presence in Libya vary. For more information, see "How the Islamic State Rose, Fell, and Could Rise Again in the Maghreb" (briefing), International Crisis Group, July 2017. In 2015, the United Nations estimated from 2,000 to 3,000 fighters (referenced in "Libya a Massive Safe Haven for ISIS Now, U.N. Warns," CBS News, December 1, 2015), while U.S. intelligence agencies estimated from 4,000 to 6,000 (see Department of Defense Briefing by General David M. Rodriguez, April 7, 2016).

9. President Obama Interview with Fox News Sunday, April 10, 2016.

10. Borzou Daragahi, "The Tripoli Offensive: How Did Things Escalate?" Atlantic Council MENASource, May 31, 2019.

11. Executive Order 13726, "Blocking Property and Suspending Entry into the United States of Persons Contributing to the Situation in Libya."

12. See Robin Emmot, "The EU Is Preparing to Deploy Security Mission in Libya if Asked," Reuters, April 15, 2016; and Missy Ryan and Sudarsan Raghavan, "Another Western Intervention in Libya Looms," *Washington Post*, April 3, 2016.

13. See U.S. Department of State *Country Reports on Terrorism 2017* (www.state.gov/reports/country-reports-on-terrorism-2017).

14. Glenn Thrush, "No U.S. Military Role in Libya, Trump Says, Rejecting Italy's Pleas," *New York Times*, April 20, 2017.

15. "Libya Country Profile," United States Agency for International Development, September 1, 2016.

16. "Libyan Oil Production," Crisis Group Analysis/United States Energy Information Administration in "After the Showdown in Libya's Oil Crescent," International Crisis Group, August 2018.

17. "The Libyan Political Agreement: Time for a Reset," International Crisis Group, November 2016.

18. Michelle Nichols, "United States, Russia, Say Cannot Support a U.N. Call for Libya Truce: Diplomats," Reuters, April 18, 2019.

19. Fred Wehrey, "The Conflict in Libya: Testimony before the House of Representatives Foreign Affairs Committee, Subcommittee on Middle East, North Africa, and International Terrorism," May 15, 2019.

20. Libya: Tripoli Clashes—Situation Report #23, U.N. Office for the Coordination of Humanitarian Affairs (UN OCHA), May 10, 2019.

21. "Addressing the Rise of Libya's Madkhali-Salafis," International Crisis Group, April 2019.

22. John R. Allen and others, "Empowered Decentralization: A City-Based Strategy for Rebuilding Libya," Brookings, 2018.

23. Ibid.

24. "Foreign Involvement in Libya Must Be Stopped, Top Official Tells Security Council, Describing 'Race against Time' to Reach Peaceful Solution, Spare Lives," United Nations Security Council Press Release SC/14023, November 18, 2019; and Edith Lederer, "UN Envoy Demands End to All Foreign Interference in Libya," Associated Press, January 6, 2020.

25. "EU Cooperation on Migration in Libya," European Union Trust Fund for Africa—North Africa Window Factsheet (https://ec.europa.eu/neighbour hood-enlargement/sites/near/files/eutf-noa-libya.pdf).

26. See "No Escape from Hell: EU Policies Contribute to Abuse of Migrants in Libya," Human Rights Watch, January 2019.

27. In May 2013, the EU authorized EUBAM Libya under the Common Security and Defense Policy to improve and develop Libyan border security management capacity. In 2016, the United States, several European nations, Canada, and others began planning for the LIAM, which intended to help the GNA protect key government and service installations and train Libyan

forces. The LIAM was unable to get off the ground as it required, and did not receive a formal request from the chaotic and wary GNA.

28. "Lost in Civil Registration: Libyans with Undetermined Legal Status" (policy brief), Mercy Corps, March 2019.

29. "After the Showdown in Libya's Oil Crescent," International Crisis Group, August 2018.

30. U.S. Foreign Assistance Dashboard Libya Country Page (www. foreignassistance.gov/explore/country/Libya).

PART II

Re-Imagining Key U.S. Security Partnerships

FIVE

The U.S.-Israel Relationship and the Israeli-Palestinian Arena

DANIEL B. SHAPIRO

One of the central themes of this volume is that while the Middle East and North Africa (MENA) region has become less important to U.S. foreign policy, it still matters for American interests. U.S. policy toward Israel and the Palestinians embodies both of these realities. Though the Israeli-Palestinian conflict is no longer perceived as the central source of regional instability, outbreaks of violence continue to pose significant challenges for the U.S. position in the Middle East. Should Israel and the Palestinian territories lapse into another paroxysm of terrorism and bloodshed, the conflict would likely rise to the top of the next administration's agenda.

Moreover, strong domestic support in the United States for the U.S.-Israel partnership has helped temper periodic calls for U.S. retrenchment in the Middle East. Successive U.S. administrations, dating back to Israel's founding, have defined American interests in the Middle East to include the existence of Israel as a secure, Jewish state. Part of that calculus was driven by a moral, humanitarian interest, recognizing that centuries of exile and statelessness had led the Jewish people to experience innumerable tragedies, culminating in the Holocaust, and that statehood in the historic homeland of the Jewish people was the logical and appropriate remedy. Israel is also seen as a critical and reliable strategic ally of the United States in an unstable region. That logic persists to this day, supported by a large majority of the American people.[1]

Beyond the domestic political salience of issues relating to Israel and the Israeli-Palestinian conflict, strategic and security interests have also had a prominent place in the U.S.-Israel relationship. Through Israel's first decades, the logic of the Cold War heavily influenced U.S. thinking about the Middle East, leading American administrations to view a U.S. partnership with Israel as a regional counterweight to Soviet alliances with Arab states. In light of Israel's vulnerability to attacks from its Arab neighbors, in time these considerations led to the beginnings of U.S. military assistance to ensure Israel's ability to defend itself. Both considerations dovetailed as well with the long-standing U.S. interest of seeking to promote an end to the Arab-Israeli conflict through negotiated settlements. Doing so was seen as a means of (1) ensuring Israel's security and recognition; (2) promoting greater stability in a war-torn region that was a key source of U.S. energy needs; and (3) moving Arab states from the Soviet to the American orbit, as happened with Egypt upon its signing of a peace treaty with Israel in 1979.

Following the Camp David Accords, the United States and Israel began a process of steadily upgrading their security partnership, which has now reached record dimensions in military assistance, joint training, intelligence sharing, and technology development. This enduring U.S. commitment to Israel's security ensures that Israel can defend itself against the various threats it faces, many unrelated to the Israeli-Palestinian conflict, including Iran, Syria, Lebanese Hezbollah, and others. But the partnership is not a one-way affair. The United States also derives numerous benefits in managing the range of threats—from terrorism to the spread of weapons of mass destruction to the instability of weak neighboring states—that emanate from the Middle East, as well as in improving its own capabilities by incorporating Israeli intelligence, tactics, and technology.

During the same period, the United States devoted extensive efforts to seeking a solution to the Israeli-Palestinian conflict. Since the late 1990s and until the Trump administration, these efforts were defined, generally with Israeli agreement, as pursuing a negotiated, conflict-ending, two-state solution. Despite President Trump's deviation from this norm, this aspiration remains key to U.S. interests in (1) ensuring Israel's security, including against the threat posed by terrorists, and promoting the broader acceptance of its legitimacy in the Middle East; (2) helping maintain Israel's dual identity as a Jewish and democratic state, which is at the heart of the common values shared between the two countries that have enabled their leaders to develop a close security partnership; (3) meeting the legitimate aspirations of the Palestinian people to end life under occupation and achieve self-determination in an independent state of their own; and (4) contributing to broader stability in the region, including through the normalization of relations between Israel and Arab states beyond Egypt and Jordan.

There is an imbalance here: the reality is that the United States is unlikely to ever have anything like the deep, multi-faceted relationship it has with Israel, which affects numerous American interests, with the Palestinians. Moreover, with or without the realization of a two-state solution, the Palestinians will probably never equal Israel's regional influence, and almost certainly will not rival Israel in terms of its salience in domestic U.S. politics and its importance to American voters. The moral, humanitarian interest in helping Palestinians achieve independence is compelling, although not something that has always been achievable for other deserving peoples. The imperative that should drive U.S. attention to the cause is that the Palestinians' unique role in the region means that U.S. interests can certainly be negatively affected by outcomes in which their legitimate aspirations are not met, namely, anything other than a two-state solution.

But the next U.S. administration will be unable to escape the fact that President Trump has walked away from this historic task and taken several damaging steps that have changed the contours of any future negotiation process. To make this observation is not to suggest that Trump enjoyed realistic prospects of achieving a breakthrough agreement. The experience of attempting to negotiate a conflict-ending agreement during the Obama administration was instructive.

In each of his two terms, President Obama appointed a senior official (Special Envoy George Mitchell in the first term and Secretary of State John Kerry in the second) to pursue negotiations toward a conflict-ending, two-state solution. While the goal was clear and the efforts exhaustive, the administration never publicly defined parameters that it hoped to see in a final agreement. Instead of focusing on the core issues of the conflict, it was often stuck dealing with procedural issues like terms of reference for talks, confined to indirect rather than direct negotiations with the two sides, and left simply urging Israelis, Palestinians, and Arab states to take steps that would facilitate talks and avoid those that could hinder them.

At times, the Obama administration's negotiators succumbed to the common temptation to try to deliver requirements or preconditions demanded by one side of the other, producing extended shuttling between the parties on essentially preliminary issues. U.S. negotiators were inconsistent in their demands and criticisms of the parties—at times demanding a full Israeli settlement freeze and at other times letting the issue slide, and not being forthright enough in calling out Palestinian incitement to violence and foot-dragging on coming to talks. Arab states were let off the hook when they failed to step up with gestures to encourage the parties to move. The American ability to engage in a dialogue with the Israeli and Palestinian publics to help them imagine a better future, which might have produced pressure on their leaders to be more forthcoming, was quite limited.

But whatever strengths and weaknesses the Obama effort brought to the table, there was considerable evidence that the Palestinian and Israeli leaderships (and those of many Arab states) were unable or unwilling to make the necessary decisions to reach such an agreement, presenting a nearly insurmountable obstacle for U.S. peacemakers. The record of Palestinian Authority (PA) President Mahmoud Abbas has included both statements of support for negotiating a two-state solution and a frustrating persistence in staying out of, or walking away from, negotiations—first with Israeli prime minister Ehud Olmert at the end of the second Bush administration, and through much of the past decade under both Obama and Trump. He has also shown severe limits on his willingness to tell hard truths to his own people by challenging aspects of the Palestinian narrative in ways that would be necessary to reach an agreement. Abbas has failed repeatedly to denounce acts of terror and educate his people about the illegitimacy of violence, and even glorified perpetrators of violence and refused to end the egregious practice of paying salaries to terrorists who sit in Israeli prisons, essentially rewarding past acts of violence and incentivizing future ones.

Prime Minister of Israel Benjamin Netanyahu, for his part, has demonstrated, at best, an inconsistent commitment to the two-state solution. In 2009, he declared his support for the two-state solution in his Bar-Ilan University speech and participated in peace talks during the Obama administration, discussing two states for two peoples. But he also frequently permitted the continued expansion of West Bank settlements—some in areas that might be accommodated in land swaps in an eventual deal, and some in areas that would dramatically complicate a two-state solution—all of them having the negative political impact that unilateral acts have on prospects for negotiations. From the late 1990s until 2015, Israel was led by prime ministers at least nominally committed to achieving a two-state solution. But since 2015, Netanyahu has led more right-wing governments dominated by voices—in his own Likud party and among his coalition partners—that are openly opposed to a two-state solution, and he has declared that a Palestinian state will not happen on his watch.

Obama also struggled to cope with the legacy of decades of settlement-building. When the Oslo Accords were signed in 1993, 116,300 Israelis lived in West Bank settlements (excluding East Jerusalem). By the time Netanyahu took office in 2009, the number stood at 296,700, and in 2017 had reached 413,400. Perhaps three-quarters of this population live in areas Israel considers the main settlement blocs, the clusters of settlements closer to the 1967 lines that might be most logical for Israel to retain in a land-swap formula.[2] But that still leaves over 100,000 in the territory that in any two-state solution would be likely to become Palestinian. The sheer number of such residents presents an escalating challenge from where it stood as the Oslo era got underway, but so does the current posture of the Israeli government.

While Trump inherited the same unfavorable conditions that bedeviled Obama, he has only compounded them. In January 2020, Trump released his "Vision for Peace, Prosperity, and a Brighter Future for Israel and the Palestinian People," a plan that deviated dramatically from all previous U.S.-led attempts to resolve the conflict. While purporting to envision the creation of a Palestinian state, it did so in name only. The reality of what it proposed was an isolated series of noncontiguous Palestinian self-governed areas, surrounded by extensive Israeli annexation in over 30 percent of the West Bank, and maintaining Israeli settlements under Israeli sovereignty and security protection even within the Palestinian areas. Three disconnected outer East Jerusalem neighborhoods, beyond the security barrier, were identified for a Palestinian capital. The product of extensive consultations with Israel and none with Palestinians, owing to the Palestinian boycott of the Trump administration since December 2017 and Trump's advisers' inability to overcome it, and presented as an ultimatum rather than a basis for negotiations, the Palestinians rejected it immediately. It is unimplementable as an agreed solution, and many have argued that it was never intended to be. Statements by Trump's advisers indicate that if the plan fails, the United States will back Israel in unilaterally annexing the areas it would gain full sovereignty over under the plan. While, as of this writing, the potential timing of such moves to annex West Bank territory was unclear, annexation is a far more likely result than Trump's proposal leading to serious negotiations. The plan represented a major blow to the concept of a two-state solution and placed Israeli, Palestinian, and American interests at further risk.

While far more detailed than earlier Trump administration statements, the plan was consistent with his approach all along. Rather than asserting the U.S. interest in, at a minimum, maintaining the viability of a two-state solution, he has taken a number of steps to accelerate its demise. For three years, Trump refused to define the two-state solution as the goal of U.S. policy, or its achievement as the end of the conflict, and the version that emerged in his plan was unconvincing. Moreover, even while both sides saw benefit in maintaining U.S. assistance programs that supported Palestinian economic development and humanitarian needs, Trump wiped them out—going well beyond the bipartisan consensus to withhold certain accounts to offset Palestinian Authority payments to terrorists and virtually shutting down the USAID mission for the West Bank and Gaza. He downgraded the U.S. diplomatic relationship with the Palestinians by closing the PLO mission in Washington and folding the independent U.S. Consulate General in Jerusalem, which had handled relations with the Palestinian Authority, into the U.S. embassy. His move of the U.S. embassy to Jerusalem included no acknowledgment of Palestinian aspirations in the city. And, most alarming, he stood by as the Anti-Terrorism Clarification Act resulted in the cancellation of U.S. assistance to the PA Security Forces, threatening the capability of those forces and their effective cooperation with Israeli security organs in preventing terrorist attacks.

Finally, Trump's indulgence of maximalist positions, which have been voiced with increasing frequency by the Israeli rightwing, risks emboldening the Israeli government to take steps that could eliminate any remaining prospects for a two-state solution, to the detriment not only of the Palestinians but of Israel and the United States as well. In the run-up to the rollout of his peace plan, Trump signaled—through his silence at growing Israeli calls for annexation of all or parts of the West Bank and through his recognition of Israeli sovereignty in the Golan Heights—that the United States would not object to Israeli annexation moves. When the plan was issued, that prospect became even more realistic. Also left unanswered is the question of how the United States would respond if, under the weight of significant political and economic pressures, the Palestinian Authority would collapse and Israel would be drawn back into the PA-governed areas of the West Bank (Areas A and B). There is scant evidence Trump has considered the dangers that outcomes other than two states would pose to Israel's Jewish and democratic character, or to the stability of Jordan, with its majority Palestinian-origin population. At home, Trump sought to gain partisan advantage on the issue of Israel, contrasting his policies with what he called an "anti-Israel" Democratic Party and making a cause célèbre of the evident animus toward Israel of two Democratic members of Congress, Reps. Ilhan Omar and Rashida Tlaib, despite strong support for Israel among nearly all Democratic officeholders.

Meanwhile, Arab states that had begun a process of cautiously warming their ties with Israel, fueled by exhaustion with the Palestinian issue and by common interests in confronting Iran, have hedged on significant advancement of normalization with Israel while refusing to provide substantial economic support to the Palestinians or political backing to the Trump plan. An "economic workshop" in Bahrain in June 2019 was long on talk of economic benefits to Palestinians, but produced no tangible investments in the absence of any political framework or any meaningful Palestinian participation. The reality is that while Arab states are broadly supportive of Trump's regional policies and open to strategic cooperation with Israel, they still harbor populations deeply sympathetic to the Palestinian cause and maintain at least public fealty to the principles of the Arab Peace Initiative, which calls for two states on the 1967 lines, with a Palestinian capital in East Jerusalem. This position was restated at the Arab League summit on February 1, 2020, following the presentation of the Trump plan. That imposes a low ceiling on what is possible in the area of normalization: occasional visits of Israeli ministers, academics, and athletic teams to Gulf states; quiet business ties in security technologies; the gradual lowering of overflight restrictions for aircraft traveling to and from Israel. These steps are welcome, not insignificant, and may begin to prepare Arab publics for broader normalization in the future. But the odds are very low they will mature into formal diplomatic relations, or open exchanges of embassies, tourism, and trade until Arab leaders can point to significant progress toward a two-state solution.

Trump and his advisers seemed to believe that the Palestinians had arrived at such a weakened state that they would set aside core goals—independence, statehood, citizenship, and a capital in East Jerusalem—in exchange for upgraded economic conditions while remaining under overall Israeli control. They believed that ordinary Palestinians, fed up with their own leaders' fecklessness and inability to deliver, would choose this course, and that Arab states would pressure and incentivize them to do so. But no evidence has emerged of any significant body of Palestinian public opinion that supports this model, and U.S.-Palestinian diplomatic discourse, reduced to nothing more than exchanges of tweets, has offered no opportunities for persuasion.[3]

The next administration will inherit a bleak picture in which Israelis and Palestinians are increasingly skeptical of the two-state solution. For many years, in opinion polls, comfortable majorities of both Israelis and Palestinians expressed support for a two-state solution as their preferred outcome, even while expressing doubt that the other side was a serious partner. Israelis cited past failed negotiations in which their leaders had made what they viewed as generous offers, waves of Palestinian terrorist attacks, including bombings and stabbings, and Hamas's takeover of Gaza after Israel's withdrawal, which the group has used as a platform to fire thousands of rockets at Israeli civilians while digging tunnels under the border. Palestinians spoke of the indignities of living under occupation, the continual expansion of settlements, and the closure and naval blockade imposed on Gaza. The persistence of these conditions over the years has taken its toll. A joint poll conducted by the Palestinian Center for Policy and Survey Research (PCPSR) and the Tami Steinmetz Center for Peace Research at Tel Aviv University, published in August 2018, found only 43 percent of Israeli Jews and 43 percent of Palestinians—both historically low figures—continued to express support for a two-state solution.[4]

The challenge for the next administration will be exacerbated by an impending Palestinian leadership succession—inevitable, given Abbas's advanced age and declining health—with high uncertainty over how it will unfold. In any event, Abbas's eventual successor will face political headwinds against showing more flexibility than he has. But the challenge is heightened by growing interest among Palestinians in abandoning the two-state construct in favor of a unitary democratic state with a one person, one vote principle. Support for this approach reached 24 percent in a 2018 PCPSR survey.[5]

This shift among the Palestinian public comes as growing numbers of Israeli officials in the current coalition now speak of permanent Israeli control of the West Bank with some form of limited Palestinian autonomy, surrounded by annexed settlements—or even more extensive annexation. Indeed, no minister in Netanyahu's recent cabinets has expressed support for Palestinian statehood, reflecting growing skepticism of the two-state solution among the Israeli public at large. Some 47 percent of Israelis believe that a two-state solution is no longer feasible, regardless of whether they support it.[6]

In light of the foregoing, the central question for the next admin-istration will be to determine whether the two-state solution is dead or just on life support. The task of achieving such an outcome is daunting, to be sure, and naysayers abound. But writing it off would be wrong. All surveys show that while support for two states has declined on both sides, it still commands plurality support, and far more than any individual alternative. The history also suggests that public opinion is subject to significant shifts in response to leader-ship initiatives that demonstrate possibility; when negotiations com-mence, optimism generally rises.

Almost any chance of revitalizing prospects for two states re-quires the emergence of new Israeli, Palestinian, and American lead-ers who are able to build trust and take risks. The experience of the Egyptian-Israeli peace treaty is instructive. When Menachem Begin was elected Israeli prime minister in the summer of 1977, neither he nor Egyptian president Anwar Sadat were considered candidates to reach a conflict-ending peace agreement. Both were widely seen as hardliners, immovable on key questions such as Israeli withdrawal from Sinai or Egyptian normalization of relations with Israel. Yet in a remarkably short time, they recalculated their interests, took risks, built imperfect but sufficient trust to support one another in telling hard truths to their own side, and, with a willing American presi-dent accompanying them on the journey, surprised the world (and arguably themselves) by achieving what had previously been deemed impossible, a full peace treaty which has lasted forty years and serves as a pillar of stability in the Middle East. We obviously cannot count on leaders of this quality arising on the Israeli and Palestinian sides, much less simultaneously, but we must do everything in our power to ensure that if and when they do arrive, there is still a path to achieve a two-state solution.

The other reason that we are compelled in this direction is that the alternatives are so much worse. As discussed below, those sce-narios deserve greater study. But in any outcome other than the two-state one, Israelis and Palestinians will be living with a perpetuation of the conflict, not its end. They, their neighbors, and others with interests in the area, like the United States, will need to endure the periodic spasms of violence that the conflict is known for. Israel's ability to maintain both its Jewish and democratic character will face insoluble dilemmas, which will also challenge the values-based partnership with the United States. And in the most likely alternatives, Palestinians will not achieve their legitimate aspirations for independence or genuinely equal rights, with all the humanitarian and security implications that carries, serving as a block on full Israeli-Arab normalization.

The next administration, therefore, will need to try to reinforce the viability of the two-state solution and revive its future prospects. But that cannot be the full extent of U.S. policy. A new policy should serve to buttress American interests in maintaining our strategic partnership with Israel, preserving prospects for a conflict-ending agreement, and contributing to regional stability. That will require sustaining certain policies that have continued into the Trump era, reversing others, moving forward in the new reality that has been created, and exploring a range of alternatives.

Policy Sustainment

Even in a hyper-partisan age, a strong consensus endures about the abiding American commitment to Israel's existence, security, and right and ability to defend itself. President Obama strengthened this commitment with the US$38 billion ten-year Memorandum of Understanding (MOU) on military assistance for Israel signed in 2016, which the Trump administration and Congress commenced implementing in 2019. The hardware supported by this assistance—fighter aircraft, heavy-lift helicopters, multilayered missile defense systems, and the like—is only part of the story. The next administration should continue this aid, which supports Israel's qualitative military edge, as required by U.S. law and policy, and its ability to maintain freedom of action against the many threats it faces from Iran, Syria, Lebanon, and Hamas in Gaza.

Israel, limited in size, maintains a high operational tempo against a heavy volume and wide variety of threats. In so doing, it contains adversaries, such as Iran's attempted military build-up in Syria, and maintains its overall deterrence to prevent major conflicts that could endanger its highly concentrated home front, thus reducing the likelihood of scenarios that might require the United States to intervene and assume additional burden. The United States also benefits directly from its military assistance to Israel. The significant majority—and, by the end of the MOU, 100 percent—of the annual US$3.3 billion allocated for Israel in Foreign Military Financing is spent in the United States, creating jobs in the U.S. defense industry. Through joint development and funding of Israeli missile defense systems (Iron Dome, David's Sling, and Arrow 3), the United States gains access to that technology, helping develop U.S. systems and, in the case of Iron Dome, purchasing it for the U.S. army's own use. These factors make the U.S. contribution to Israel's security a meaningful yet cost-effective and mutually beneficial investment.[7]

In the past year, voices have been heard calling for placing conditions on, or even withholding, U.S. security assistance to Israel to try to shape, or respond to, Israel's policies toward the Palestinians. While the fact of U.S. assistance necessarily provides influence for the United States in discussions with receiving countries—and always has—in the case of Israel, a direct tie or conditionality to other issues is impractical and counterproductive. A weakening of Israel's ability to defend itself from threats posed by Iran, for example, would harm U.S., as well as Israeli, interests. An administration that went down this path would quickly encounter practical, legal, and political hurdles, as well as damage, among others, the critical U.S. interest of ensuring Israel's ability to deter its adversaries. That does not mean the United States should ignore Israeli actions that it may deem damaging to U.S. interests, such as unilateral annexation, but there are many ways for the United States to express its views and use its influence that are not as self-defeating as limiting or conditioning security assistance.

U.S. political support for Israel's right of self-defense, which is still wrongly challenged in international fora, remains critical, and is part of the broader fight against attempts to delegitimize Israel. That fight includes taking on the Boycott, Divestment, and Sanctions (BDS) movement, which can be combated most effectively not through binding legislation that raises constitutional concerns about the protection of free speech but through clear statements of U.S. policy and the deepening of U.S. economic engagement with Israel.

The administration and Congress should educate Americans, in word and deed, how the security partnership, and increasingly the economic synergies fueled by innovation and two-way investment, between the United States and Israel provide the United States with the benefits of training, intelligence, technology, and shared prosperity, and are animated by the bonds of the peoples of two democracies with enduring common values.

Policy Reversals

Reinforcing those bonds, however, requires buttressing the prospects for two states, which Trump's policies have done so much to damage. It is important to note, that means restoring U.S.-led international efforts to support the Palestinian people and the institutions of a future Palestinian state. In 2018, Congress passed the Taylor Force Act (TFA), which appropriately withholds funds from the Palestinian Authority commensurate with payments made by the PA to Palestinian terrorists in Israeli jails. But in the TFA, Congress ensured protection of numerous other streams of assistance to Palestinians that do not touch PA accounts. The Trump administration eliminated them anyway. Building on Congress's partial restoration of humanitarian aid to the Palestinians, the new administration should strengthen U.S. assistance programs that provide economic and humanitarian relief in the West Bank and Gaza, including U.S. contributions to a reformed UN Relief and Works Agency (UNRWA) or a successor body that provides services to its beneficiaries and educates Palestinians for peace; support people-to-people initiatives; and ensure the continued ability of the Palestinian Authority Security Forces to act against terrorism to help sustain the relative stability that has benefited both Israelis and Palestinians and that Trump has jeopardized. Undoing or adjusting other Trump actions that undermine the U.S. commitment to two states—reestablishing a separate diplomatic mission to engage with the Palestinian Authority, for example, and reopening the PLO mission in Washington—will align our diplomatic posture with our central policy goal, signaling clearly to the parties and others that this U.S. commitment has been restored.

Obviously, a critical decision will depend on whether Trump has recognized Israeli sovereignty over unilaterally annexed areas of the West Bank. If those annexations are incompatible with a realistic two-state solution, it may be necessary to withdraw that recognition and consider other steps. If they are not necessarily incompatible, they might be balanced by a parallel U.S. gesture relating to the contours of the Palestinian state it expects to emerge from negotiations. Much depends on the specific details a new administration would encounter.

Some of the Trump administration's decisions, however, either cannot or should not be reversed. For instance, the new administration should keep the U.S. embassy in Jerusalem, acknowledging that recognition of an Israeli capital in the city is fully consistent with a two-state solution. Reversing that decision would do real damage to U.S.-Israel relations and is unnecessary as part of a strategy to fortify prospects for two states. Instead of returning the embassy, which sits in West Jerusalem, to Tel Aviv, the next administration can advance the U.S. goal of two states by articulating clearly that it is the expectation of the United States that the U.S. Embassy to Israel in Jerusalem will eventually be paired with a U.S. Embassy to the state of Palestine in its capital in the Arab neighborhoods of East Jerusalem as part of a final-status agreement reached through negotiations. It should also consider practical steps that will help prepare for the implementation of that aspect of a final status agreement at a later time.

As for Trump's recognition of Israeli sovereignty over the Golan Heights, there is no pressing need for a new administration to make decisions on this issue. The continued instability in Syria makes it unthinkable that any Syrian state will be capable of peace negotiations with Israel for decades, if not longer, or that Israel's security requirements could possibly be met in such a scenario. Israel's own annexation of the Golan Heights in 1981 did not prevent multiple prime ministers from exploring peace agreements that would have required Israeli withdrawal from all or part of the Golan Heights in return for a full peace agreement. If, someday, somehow, that prospect begins to look remotely possible, that would warrant a discussion between U.S. and Israeli leaders. For now, Israeli control of the

Golan Heights—the status quo that pertained before Trump's announcement, which helps ensure Israel can protect itself from the numerous threats in Syria—has not changed in any meaningful respect.

Policy Advancement

But there is no going backward; we can only go forward. Every step
the new administration takes should be measured by the standard
of how it builds on the current reality to keep a two-state solution
viable—not necessarily for immediate achievement if current leaders
remain unable to negotiate, but for future negotiations when new
leaderships emerge. That will require making clear that the new administration is not bound by the Trump plan, which does not envision anything resembling a realistic two-state solution. Regardless of
whether individual elements of the plan could have value, as a whole,
it is not a viable basis for a new administration's approach. That
should be made clear, with no ambiguity, to ensure that all parties
adjust accordingly.

U.S. statements should make clear that our efforts to sustain the
viability of a two-state solution are driven by our interests in (1) ensuring Israel retains its Jewish and democratic character, the essential
characteristics that have enabled the bond of common values that
undergirds the strategic partnership; (2) meeting legitimate Palestinian aspirations for self-determination in an independent state of their
own; and (3) improving the regional environment, including broader
normalization between Israel and Arab states.

The first step is to do something no administration has done: articulate clearly the parameters of a genuine two-states-for-two-peoples
solution that the United States envisions to end the conflict and seek
international support for them. The precedent of the Trump plan,
complete with maps, needs to be considered, but it would be possible
for these parameters to be far less detailed than the Trump plan. While
they would touch on all the core issues of the conflict—territory,
security, Jerusalem, refugees, and mutual recognition—they would
leave many details to be determined by the parties in their talks. Cru-
cially, these parameters should be offered without rancor, and with

no demand or expectation that the parties would accept them or that negotiations would immediately ensue. In fact, the likelihood is that neither party would accept them initially. Rather, they would serve as a new international standard and as the terms of reference for the eventual negotiations the United States would be prepared to sponsor when the parties determine that they are ready. The presentation of such parameters would not produce immediate results, obviously, and may indeed encounter domestic and regional political friction. But they would reassert U.S. leadership, with international support, as the party best positioned to sponsor an eventual resumption of negotiations, and provide clarity on U.S. goals and interests, which will be useful to help traverse a period when negotiations are not possible and steer them when they become possible.

It will be critical for the administration to make clear that it will oppose actions and unilateral measures by either party that are inconsistent with the goal of a two-state solution. Palestinians, including potential successors to Abbas, should be made to understand that the United States will vigorously oppose all one-sided efforts to condemn or isolate Israel internationally, and will expect changes in Palestinian policies and rhetoric that glorify and incite violence or reject Israel's legitimacy as a Jewish state. Trump got this partially right by being clear with Palestinians that these practices must change, but he got it wrong by failing to show Palestinians that if they did change those practices and returned to negotiations, it could lead, with American help, to fulfillment of their legitimate aspirations. At the same time, the United States must make clear that those remain necessary conditions for the Palestinians to achieve statehood.

Similarly, the United States must be clear with Israel that unilateral measures, such as settlement expansion that impedes prospects for two states, and certainly any unilateral annexation moves in the West Bank, will draw strong and vocal American opposition because we see them as damaging our ability to sustain over time the partnership that serves both our countries' interests.

Without any negotiations taking place, there is still much that all parties can do to help sustain prospects for two states. Such measures include curtailing settlement expansion, ending payments to Palestinian terrorists, ceasing incitement and glorification of violence, and expanding and creating contiguity between areas of Palestinian Authority operations in the West Bank.

Addressing the threats Israelis face from Hamas and the appalling humanitarian conditions in Gaza, and taking steps to prepare for Gaza's reintegration into a unified Palestinian polity under leadership that accepts the Quartet Principles—recognition of Israel, renunciation of violence, and adherence to prior diplomatic agreements—will be crucial to preventing the Gaza stalemate from erupting into additional rounds of violence that will set back any efforts to sustain prospects for two states and an eventual resumption of negotiations. The United States should back the easing of restrictions on reconstruction in Gaza while maintaining strong pressure on Hamas, fully support Israel's right of self-defense against its terror campaigns, and create opportunities for the Palestinian Authority to gain a foothold in the territory for eventual displacement of Hamas with Israeli, Egyptian, and international support.[8]

Continued progress on Arab normalization with Israel through visits and exchanges should also be encouraged and welcomed; the United States should do nothing to hold it back while remaining realistic about how far it can proceed before Arab leaders could point to significant progress toward a two-state solution. New U.S. assistance efforts, such as those Congress has proposed in the Palestinian Partnership Fund Act, can support the budding and impressive Palestinian hi-tech sector, linking talented, forward-thinking Palestinian engineers and entrepreneurs with Israeli, Arab, and American partners.[9] The United States and Israel should also resume and update the military-to-military dialogue, formerly led by General John Allen (Ret.), on Israel's security requirements in a two-state solution and the wide range of options—involving technology, intelligence, presence, phase-in timelines, rapid response, training, cooperation with other actors, and a role for international forces, among others—available to political leaders to address them once negotiations resume. A related dialogue should be conducted between the United States and the leadership of the Palestinian security forces.

All of these steps can take place without any attempt to resume negotiations. The experience of the most recent attempts to resume negotiations during the Obama and Trump administrations contains useful lessons. If the next administration immediately tries to drag the parties into those talks, they will almost certainly fail, maybe spectacularly and punctuated by violence. Different leadership dynamics—following a Palestinian transition and almost certainly with a different Israeli coalition—are probably a prerequisite to any attempt at renewed talks. Even then, the United States should conduct a clear-eyed assessment on the prospects for progress before launching an attempt, and avoid overextending itself and its diplomatic resources when there are no chances of success. It remains the case that no outside actor, including the United States, can impose a solution on parties unable or unwilling to make the necessary compromises. *They* should demonstrate to *the United States* that they want *its* help in ending their conflict. It is also worth remembering that every previous major breakthrough in Arab-Israeli peacemaking began in direct back-channel talks in which the United States was not involved. At least in the early phase of the next administration, the goal should merely be to keep the two-state solution alive and viable for the future, leaving space for different leaders to reassess their interests and try again, perhaps initially without direct U.S. involvement. Fortunately, most of the steps this would require are relatively low-cost, both in terms of resources and time.

Direct punishments of either party should be avoided. Proponents of pressure campaigns against Israel and/or the Palestinians have wildly exaggerated their efficacy; they tend to produce very little in the short term and come with a high political cost. Rather, the administration should use reality as a source of pressure, highlighting the inexorable trends at work. For Palestinians, the reality of permanent statelessness if they do not find a way back to talks with a new sense of flexibility and compromise. For Israelis, the reality of losing Israel's Jewish or its democratic character, with the impact that will have on its relationship with the United States in light of U.S. demographic shifts, and the reality of squandering the opportunity for true normalization with the majority of Arab states and full integration into the region. If coercion will not work, highlighting these realities might, including by generating domestic political incentives for the leadership of both sides to try new approaches.

Policy Alternatives

The entire thrust of the next administration's policy should be to extend the life and viability of the two-state solution in the hopes that it can still be achieved if leaders with the vision and daring of Begin and Sadat emerge. But the United States cannot blind itself to the growing likelihood that the preferred outcome will not succeed. At best, the two-state solution is on borrowed time. That reality imposes an obligation to grapple with alternative outcomes. From the perspective of U.S. interests, all of them are worse than a two-state solution. But as the parties may end up in one of them, it is incumbent on the next administration to try to understand how the United States will sustain and protect its key interests should those scenarios come to pass in spite of the best efforts of those committed to two states.

To that end, the new administration should announce that it will conduct a formal policy planning exercise to study alternative outcomes. The results of this study may or may not ever be published; it may simply be a tool to guide internal thinking. Such an announcement comes with some risk: opponents of two states on both sides may embrace it as confirming that they have achieved their goal of killing it. Those claiming the United States is giving up on two states would score a rhetorical point, although not one they have been shy about making anyway. But it could also help to impel other Israelis and Palestinians to redouble their efforts to prove that the two-state solution is not dead.

There is no need, at this stage, to detail the full range of possibilities such a study would examine, but they would include the various versions of a one-state outcome—where West Bank Palestinians are granted full citizenship and where they remain under limited autonomy; options in which Jordan takes on a governance role in portions of the West Bank (including what that means for Jordan's stability); a long-term extension of the status quo (which, in reality, is not static); and a partial, unilateral Israeli withdrawal, either of settlers only or of settlers and the IDF (Israeli Defense Forces), in hopes of reducing the friction of occupation as much as possible, buying time, and hoping for a later effort at a real conflict-ending agreement.

This study must address many complex questions, including: How will each scenario affect Israel's security and its ability to defend itself? What will be the consequences of Israeli annexation in the West Bank for the U.S.-Israel relationship? Is there such a thing as partial annexation, or will it accelerate the collapse of the Palestinian Authority and lead to the full return of Israel to Areas A and B? How will Palestinian humanitarian needs be addressed in a situation of continued occupation and nonindependence? Can the relative stability of recent years be sustained once it is widely acknowledged that the two-state solution is dead? How will Israel's Jewish and democratic character be affected by full annexation with a one-person, one-vote model, or without it? How will different scenarios shape Palestinian succession, and in which outcomes is there the greatest risk of empowering Hamas and a new wave of violence in the West Bank? How will the U.S. interest in sustaining our deep security partnership with Israel be affected if the character of our ties based on the common values we have with Israel as a Jewish and democratic state is altered?

History does not stop. When we think a stable status quo has been achieved, it can change. When we think a door is closed, events can cause it to open again. When we arrive at a given outcome, it sometimes comes with unexpected consequences. And leaders are capable of reassessing their interests and changing direction, making possible what was once impossible.

The goal of the next administration should not be to declare what will happen, or what cannot happen, or what must happen. Rather, it should be to identify U.S. interests, which include ensuring Israel's security and the U.S.-Israel partnership, and achieving a two-state solution that will contribute to that goal by ending the Israeli-Palestinian conflict; make every effort to sustain the viability of achieving it for as long as possible, even through long periods when it cannot be enacted; and prepare for alternative, if clearly less optimal, scenarios. That would restore a level of responsible, values- and interests-based policymaking to this arena.

Even as the United States rationalizes its commitments elsewhere in the Middle East and North Africa, Israel will surely continue to receive high-level attention and resources from the next administration. The U.S. investment in Israel has paid dividends for American taxpayers and U.S. government strategists alike. And, of course, U.S. support is responsive to the enduring sense of obligation that has animated American public opinion toward Israel for decades. Moving forward, U.S. policymakers will nevertheless need to do a better job of injecting some realism into the pursuit of Israeli-Palestinian peace, while creatively exploring ways to improve conditions for the Palestinian people. The next administration's policy toward Israel and the Palestinians is not going to be cost-free, but it can be far more cost-effective.

Notes

1. See Gallup, "Americans, but Not Liberal Democrats, Mostly Pro-Israel," 2019, which finds that 69 percent of U.S. adults view Israel very or mostly favorably, down from 74 percent in 2018, but within the 66 percent to 72 percent range seen between 2010 and 2017 (https://news.gallup.com/poll /247376/americans-not-liberal-democrats-mostly-pro-israel.aspx). See also University of Maryland Critical Issues Poll, "American Attitudes on the Israeli-Palestinian Conflict," 2016, which finds that 76 percent of Americans, across party lines, agree that Israel is a strategic asset to the United States, including 70 percent of Democrats and 68 percent of Independents (www. brookings.edu/wp-content/uploads/2016/12/cmep_20161202_poll_key_ findings_v2.pdf).

2. See Peace Now, "Number of Settlers by Year," 2019, which relies on data from the Israel Central Bureau of Statistics (https://peacenow.org.il/en/ settlements-watch/settlements-data/population).

3. See Palestinian Center for Policy and Survey Research, "Public Opinion Poll No (72) Press Release," 2019, which found 86 percent of Palestinians were pessimistic about the Trump plan, and 85 percent did not think it would lead to the end of the occupation (continuing some version of the status quo) (http://pcpsr.org/en/node/759).

4. See Palestinian Center for Policy and Survey Research, *Palestinian-Israeli Pulse: A Joint Poll (2016–18) Final Report,* 2019 (www.pcpsr.org/en/ node/742).

5. See Palestinian Center for Policy and Survey Research, "Public Opinion Poll No (69)," press release (www.pcpsr.org/sites/default/files/Poll%2069%20 English%20press%20release%20September%202018.pdf).

6. Palestinian Center for Policy and Survey Research, *Palestinian-Israeli Pulse.*

7. See Stockholm International Peace Research Institute, "SIPRI Military Expenditure Database," 2019 (www.sipri.org/databases/milex). Including the U.S. contribution of US$3.1 billion in Foreign Military Financing, the Israeli defense budget stood at US$19 billion in 2018, with the Israeli portion

(US$15.9 billion) accounting for 4.3 percent of GDP, below average for Middle Eastern nations and lower than Jordan, Kuwait, Lebanon, Oman, and Saudi Arabia.

8. For a creative set of proposals to address the overlapping challenges relating to Gaza, see Ilan Goldenberg, Hady Amr, and Natan Sachs, "Ending Gaza's Perpetual Crisis: A New U.S. Approach," 2018 (www.cnas.org/publications/reports/ending-gazas-perpetual-crisis).

9. See "H.R. 3104—Partnership Fund for Peace Act of 2019," 2019 (www.congress.gov/bill/116th-congress/house-bill/3104?q=%7B%22search%22%3A%5B%22Palestinian+partnership+fund+act+of+2019%22%5D%7D&s=1&r=1).

SIX

Why Iraq Matters

JON FINER

In 1982, with the Cold War dominating international headlines, President Ronald Reagan signed a pair of seemingly routine memos that were among the most consequential foreign policy recommendations of their time. Calling for "a review of U.S. strategy" in the Middle East, National Security Study Directive 4-82 led to the abandonment of American neutrality in the two-year-old Iran-Iraq War, in favor of helping Iraq.[1] Thus began the flow of intelligence and, later, materiel to Saddam Hussein's army. Later that summer, CIA officer Thomas Twetten arrived in Baghdad—perhaps the first American security professional deployed to Iraq.

Kept secret in the United States until years later, this intervention immediately ignited in the Iraqi capital a controversy between a global superpower and "a proxy whose leadership was so paranoid about being taken advantage of . . . so internally divided by jealous bureaucrats, and so incompetent in implementation, that the relationship must be understood as deeply adversarial . . ."[2]

Before long, Iraq's thuggish Mukhabarat chief, convinced that his country didn't need America's help, told Twetten to "get the hell out of Iraq."[3] It would not be the last time such a sentiment was expressed, nor the last time it would not come to pass. The Iraqi Army—reeling from a series of Iranian advances and intrigued by the value of American espionage—urged Twetten to stay put. And the United States has been at war in Iraq, in one form or another, virtually ever since.

So began nearly four decades of evolving and interrelated conflicts—including one of the most popular and successful wars in American history (the 1991 Persian Gulf War) and one of the longest and most damaging (the 2003 U.S. invasion of Iraq)—a codependent cycle of intervention, mutual antagonism, and centrifugal pressure to go our separate ways, which continues to this day. Having begun my career writing about the invasion of Iraq; the country's descent into civil war; and the proliferation of terrorism, refugees, and regional instability that resulted, I am drawn to the argument, increasingly common in U.S. policy circles, that it is well past time for the United States to move on. But doing so would also be a mistake. Because regardless of how we got here, Iraq today is where the preponderance of U.S. interests in the region coincide.

Iraq is now, arguably, the most important front in the global fight against terrorism; it is the birthplace of ISIS, the most ruthless and effective terrorist army in history, and it is the most important U.S. partner that is plagued by both Sunni and Shiite terrorist groups.

Iraq is the main fault line in the Middle East's incendiary sectarian divide, still vulnerable to the interreligious conflagration unleashed by the U.S. invasion, but also one of the few places where inter-sectarian cooperation is possible. A Shiite majority country, Iraq has Sunni politicians serving in its cabinet and governing key provinces, and is improving relations with its Sunni Arab neighbors.

Its politics are in perpetual crisis, most evident in the wave of protests that swept the country in 2019 and were met with a bloody crackdown by security forces ill-equipped to address them. But with the exception of Tunisia and perhaps Lebanon, Iraq is also the closest thing that the Arab world has to a pluralistic democracy, albeit a fragile and flawed one. Corruption is rampant, minority groups lack enough political power, and voting tends to break down along ethno-sectarian lines. But elections are, according to international observers, relatively free, fair, and unpredictable. And while Iraqi leaders too often share the autocratic impulses of their counterparts in neighboring states, the political establishment has proved able to eventually check emerging tyrants.[4]

Finally, at a time when several other major oil producers—such as Venezuela, Libya, and Iran—are wracked by instability or crippled by U.S. sanctions, Iraq has some of the world's largest proven reserves, and the potential, with sufficient investment, to dramatically increase exports. By 2030, Iraq's oil production is projected to increase by 1.3 million barrels per day (the third-largest increase globally during that period), making it the planet's fourth-largest oil producer, after the United States, Russia, and Saudi Arabia.[5]

Compare that list of interests to what is at stake for the United States in many other Middle Eastern countries—and particularly those where the U.S. role has been hotly debated in recent years, like Syria, Yemen, and Libya—and it amounts to a strong case for maintaining or even expanding engagement in Iraq, even as the American investment recedes elsewhere in the region.[6] Iraq may never evolve into the type of reliable ally the United States enjoys in other parts of the world—its present challenges and tumultuous recent history, in which the United States has played a leading role, make that unlikely. But in a region where the United States is likely to do less with less than it has in the past, and rightly so,[7] Iraq remains worthy of ongoing investment. So, while no modern president has come to office intending to do more in Iraq—and while the past two have sought, unsuccessfully, to extricate themselves—the next administration should plan to keep Iraq at the center of her or his approach to the Middle East.[8]

An Unlikely Epicenter of American Foreign Policy

Over the past three decades, Iraq has gradually and improbably moved toward the center of the U.S. foreign policy agenda, to varying degrees and in differing ways, and sometimes with devastating effects on both nations. As a result, the American experience in this relatively small and distant nation succeeded World War II and Vietnam as the primary lens through which recent policymakers understood the U.S. role in the world, as well as the extent and limits of our power.

The 1991 Gulf War made Iraq the first battleground of the "unipolar moment," firmly establishing the United States as the world's lone superpower, backed by a global coalition as the Soviet Union disintegrated.[9] The Clinton administration focused its regional strategy on "dual containment" of Iraq and Iran, ordered frequent military strikes on Iraq, and used it as the laboratory for a new tool in the foreign policy arsenal—crippling economic sanctions.[10] The 1998 Iraq Liberation Act made it official U.S. policy to "remove the regime headed by Saddam Hussein from power."[11]

In 2003, President George W. Bush's disastrous invasion of Iraq led to a grinding civil war that cost nearly 4,500 American lives and killed perhaps a hundred times as many Iraqis, while producing both a virulent terrorist threat and what was then the greatest refugee crisis since World War II. The conflict became an emblem of foreign policy foolishness, sowed doubts about American global preeminence, and left the commander in chief with an approval rating just over 20 percent.[12]

Barack Obama's rise to the presidency was fueled in large part by his early opposition to the Iraq invasion, which differentiated him from his main Democratic primary and general election opponents. As he became president, the lessons he drew from Iraq weighed heavily on his foreign policy, including his decisions to draw down U.S. forces from Iraq in 2011, "rebalance" America's foreign policy from the Middle East to East Asia, engage rather than confront Iran, and resist intense pressure from the foreign policy establishment to intervene more forcefully in Syria. But, like his predecessors, he also found himself deepening U.S. involvement in Iraq over time, when the rise of ISIS led to a new round of troop deployments and air strikes.

Like Obama, President Trump came to office professing to oppose Middle Eastern conflicts, which he called "quagmires." In his early years in office, he largely (and successfully) continued Obama's approach to defeating ISIS, and tangled with more hawkish advisers, some of whom had been staunch supporters of the Iraq invasion, over whether to keep U.S. troops in neighboring Syria. In office, Trump has often treated Iraq merely as a subset of other issues, particularly the threat from neighboring Iran. In September 2018 he ordered the closure of the U.S. consulate in Basra after a rocket attack blamed on Iran-backed militias, which produced no U.S. casualties (for its part, Iran, whose consulate was attacked the same day, denied any involvement in the rocketing).[13] In February 2019, Trump explained the United States needed to keep troops in Iraq not to help maintain stability there but to "watch Iran," sparking a predictable movement among pro-Iran factions in Iraq's parliament to evict the American forces. Trump has repeatedly threatened Iraq with sanctions for purchasing Iranian electricity, which supplies 40 percent of Iraq's power grid, even though it lacks a viable alternative. Later that year, the United States withdrew a substantial portion of its diplomats from Baghdad and Irbil, amid saber-rattling about a potential conflict with Iran. And when Israel conducted air strikes against Iran-backed militia targets in August 2019, its first such strikes in Iraq in almost forty years, the United States disclaimed involvement but offered no public objection, despite mounting threats of retaliation against U.S. forces and demands from some Iraqi officials to withdraw them.[14]

Therefore, it should have hardly come as a surprise when Iraq emerged as the primary battlefield in the most provocative escalation in decades between its two primary partners. With tensions mounting after a series of incidents in the Gulf, Iran unleashed its Iraqi militias against U.S. forces stationed on an Iraqi military base and the U.S. embassy in Baghdad, prompting the evacuation of senior diplomats. After Trump authorized an air strike near Baghdad, which killed Iranian Quds Force Commander Qassem Soleimani, Iraq's Council of Representatives, under pressure from Iran, demanded the departure of all five thousand U.S. forces deployed to the country to fight ISIS. While technically nonbinding (and conducted without a quorum, due to the absence of Sunni and Kurdish parties), the vote reflected deep offense at the intrusion on Iraq's sovereignty and a deteriorating relationship that will require deft diplomacy and careful public messaging to rectify.

The Rising Risk of Worst-Case Scenarios

What the next year holds for the United States and Iraq is difficult to predict. The best case is likely a version of the extremely fragile status quo, with the United States maintaining a diplomatic presence that helps Iraq address the legitimate demands of demonstrators and a small military deployment to consolidate the defeat of ISIS.[15] But at least two worst-case scenarios cannot be ruled out.

One would see U.S. forces, and possibly more diplomats, depart the country, either as a result of a U.S. decision or because Iraq throws them out. Such a step would leave Iran as Iraq's main counterterrorism partner and its adviser in dealing with popular unrest (a recipe for more brutality and resistance to reform, since Iranian influence is one of the reform movement's targets).

Avoiding such an outcome will depend on the Trump administration's ability to both navigate Iraqi political sensitivities and persuade the president that an ongoing U.S. presence has value. While the United States reportedly received private assurances from Iraqi leaders that they want U.S. troops to remain, it undermined that support by publicly threatening sanctions against Iraq in response to the legislature's vote. Meanwhile, Trump has made clear his intent to reduce the U.S. troop presence in the region—most dramatically when he shocked his own advisers by declaring he would withdraw from northeastern Syria, though he subsequently scaled back the size of the withdrawal. But his desire to be seen as tough on terrorism, and his criticism of his predecessor's decision to remove U.S. troops from Iraq in 2011,[16] mean that a complete U.S. exit from Iraq may be unlikely. The harder question is whether, with U.S. diplomatic support already diminished by the personnel drawdown and distracted by the dispute over our military presence, the Iraqi government will take steps that are sufficient to meet protesters' demands for a broad overhaul of the political system.[17]

Another worst-case scenario—continued escalation of U.S. conflict with Iran—would be of greater concern indeed. Even short of military conflict, mounting tension between the United States and Iran leaves the Iraqi government torn between its two most important partners. On the one hand, Iraqis have no desire to be dominated, manipulated, or in any way controlled by Iran, with whom they fought in the 1980s an eight-year war that cost up to a million lives. Despite somewhat arbitrary colonial borders, Iraq has forged its own genuine and constructive version of nationalism, fragile but essential both to binding its disparate communities and repelling outside influence.

On the other hand, it is undeniable that Iran wields enormous influence in Iraq.[18] Iran has ingratiated itself into Iraq's security establishment and operates militias beyond the control of the Iraqi government. Iraq and Iran are important trading partners and share a border more than nine hundred miles long, as well as ties of religion, history, and culture. Many of Iraq's Shiite leaders spent years—in some cases, decades—exiled in Iran during the Saddam Hussein era, speak fluent Farsi, and remain very close to Iranian officials.

American pressure to somehow abandon that relationship is both futile and counterproductive, because it strengthens the hand of anti-American factions and plays into the hands of Iran, which has made clear its desire to expel U.S. forces from the region. In other words, while Iraq is far from an Iranian puppet, as it is sometimes portrayed by American analysts, a U.S. administration that asks Iraq to choose between its two most important partners may not like the answer.

A Strategic Partner, If We Can Keep It

If the next U.S. president takes office in the wake of one of the "worst cases" outlined above, she or he may well have an enormous mess to clean up, which will make so much as preserving a constructive relationship with Iraq a significant challenge. But even if the status quo holds, a new administration should make significant changes to how the United States has approached Iraq in the past.

First, the next U.S. administration should resist pressure to wash its hands of Iraq entirely. The 2003 Iraq invasion was a catastrophe. But the debate about Iraq in 2021 should focus on current interests— ours and Iraq's—and not just past transgressions. Those interests, described above, differentiate the debate about Iraq from that over, for example, Syria and Afghanistan, where the rationale for deep, ongoing U.S. engagement, or for our ability to achieve stated objectives, is far more uncertain.

Second, the United States should place a higher priority than it has in the past on improving Iraqi governance, fighting corruption, and upholding human rights. It should do so not simply out of moral obligation, but because inattention to such problems leaves Iraq perpetually on the brink of state failure and destabilizing mass atrocities.[19] Even at the height of U.S. involvement in Iraq, Washington could not dictate outcomes there, nor should it try. But it can, and must, make clear to Iraqi leaders that simply ignoring these issues or responding with excessive force will exacerbate the problems. And among Iraq's few friends and partners, the United States is best positioned to offer advice on political reforms to address these challenges.[20]

Third, the United States should start treating the U.S.-Iraq relationship as strategically important in its own right, not just as a subset of other interests. This means that while Iraq plays a role in countering threats posed by Iran and terrorism, this is not the only argument for engagement. For too long, and to its own detriment, the United States has treated Iraq not as one of the largest, most democratic, most economically viable and pluralistic countries in the Middle East—a nation of 40 million people, with vast natural resources, consequential elections, and a religiously and ethnically diverse population—but rather as an arena for advancing other goals. Not only should the United States avoid treating Iraq as a forum for regional conflicts, it should also not tolerate others—even close partners—doing so.[21] The surest way to squander U.S. influence in Iraq is to disregard Iraqi sovereignty.

Fourth, since a key to stability will be ensuring economic opportunity for as broad as possible a cross-section of Iraqi society, the United States should resume what was once a high priority of encouraging U.S. and other foreign investment in Iraq, particularly in the energy sector, the lifeblood of its economy and an area in dire need of capital to update dilapidated infrastructure. The irony of the long-standing critique of the Iraq invasion as being motivated by economic interests, such as a desire for access to Iraqi oil, is that American companies have engaged relatively lightly in Iraq since 2003. Iraq will also need technical assistance and trading partners to diversify

its economy[22] away from its reliance on hydrocarbons, which provides more than 80 percent of government revenue.[23] More involvement by the U.S. private sector would be good for Iraq and good for
the United States.

Fifth, the United States should continue to support and train the
Iraqi security forces to complete the difficult, long-term project of
either decommissioning or integrating into the Iraqi army the umbrella organization for irregular Shiite militias, the Hashd al Shaabi,
and dismantling designated terrorist organizations like Kata'ib Hezbollah, which are beholden to Iran and threaten the U.S. presence in
Iraq. The United States should encourage like-minded countries—
such as our NATO allies—to stay engaged in this project as well. This
doesn't need to mean perpetual, large-scale U.S. troop deployments,
particularly once the ISIS mission is more definitively completed, but
rather a small and manageable number of uniformed and civilian
personnel whose mission evolves, over time, away from combat operations and toward "training and assisting" Iraqi forces, who must
take the lead in securing their own country.

Sixth, that said, it should be clear at all times that the main U.S.
line of effort in Iraq is diplomatic, led by the American ambassador
and her or his in-country team. A primary diplomatic objective should
be further integrating Iraq in its own region, another way in which the
United States is uniquely able to help. One of the great and unheralded
successes of the recent period in Iraq has been the quiet effort, shaped
by American diplomats, to rebuild ties with the Gulf states, several of
which have reestablished a diplomatic presence in Baghdad in recent
years. Over time, these improved ties between Shiite-majority Iraq
and its Sunni-majority neighbors could help reduce sectarian division
in the region and reduce the risk of regional conflict. And Iraq's own
political and economic success will require constructive relations with
these neighbors, as well as with Turkey and Iran.

Seventh, the United States should avoid framing Iraq's relationships with Tehran and with Washington as zero-sum. The United
States should, of course, pursue its own interests when they are at
odds with Iran's, as American diplomats did successfully during the
formation of the most recent Iraqi governments, resulting in Iraqi
prime ministers and a president with long-standing ties to the United

States. But the United States should also recognize areas of overlapping interest with Iran, inside Iraq, such as basic political stability, countering the terrorist threat, and ensuring Iraq's territorial integrity. While attempts at U.S.-Iran collaboration, or even coordination, would be unwise, confrontation would also be counterproductive for all three countries.[24] An open line of communication between the U.S. and Iranian ambassadors in Baghdad could help clarify intentions and avoid misunderstandings.

Above all, U.S. policymakers should maintain reasonable expectations for Iraq and humility about what can be accomplished there. This does not mean reprising the condescending concept of "Iraq good enough," which characterized some Americans' post-invasion ambitions. But U.S. interests in Iraq, and the benefits from the relationship, should be compared not to some unattainable ideal but to those at stake in other regional relationships. Viewed through that lens, supporting Iraqi efforts to deny a safe haven for terrorists, manage sectarian and inter-ethnic tensions, increase economic diversity, and sustain sovereignty and a credible democracy—while trying to avoid being told, yet again, to "get the hell out," this time for good—remains a worthy agenda.

Decades before the United States first intervened in Iraq, it began what was up to that point the longest and most divisive American conflict since the Civil War, in Vietnam. Today, against long odds, the U.S.-Vietnam partnership is a strategic priority for both countries and a bulwark of security and prosperity in Southeast Asia. U.S. goals in Iraq should be less lofty. But despite the tragedies of our shared history, Iraq and the United States can still forge a relationship that benefits both nations and the broader Middle East.

Notes

1. "U.S. Strategy for the Near East and South Asia," National Security Study Directive Number 4-82, March 19, 1982 (https://fas.org/irp/offdocs/nssd/nssd-4-82.pdf).

2. James Blight and others, *Becoming Enemies: U.S.-Iran Relations and the Iran-Iraq War, 1979–1988* (Lanham, Md.: Rowman & Littlefield, 2012), 119.

3. Blight and others, *Becoming Enemies*, 114.

4. The longest-serving post-invasion prime minister, Nouri al Maliki, who emerged as a Shiite sectarian strongman, was eventually driven from office

through the political process. And after overseeing a crackdown on the recent round of turbulence, one of his successors, Adil Abdul Mahdi, offered his resignation.

5. International Energy Agency, *Iraq's Energy Sector: A Roadmap to a Brighter Future*, April 25, 2019. Investment in Iraq's energy sector peaked at about US$20 billion in 2014 and has since declined to roughly US$12 billion annually.

6. The word "engagement," in this chapter is used to mean the full spectrum of international cooperation, led by civilian and diplomatic efforts, including significant security cooperation, but not necessarily major troop deployments. The November 26, 2007, "Strategic Framework Agreement for a Relationship of Friendship and Cooperation between the United States of America and the Republic of Iraq," to which both countries remain committed, continues to be a sound basis for this diplomacy-first engagement. It lays out general principles for the bilateral relationship and seven discrete areas of cooperation, and establishes a forum for addressing all relevant issues, called the Joint Commission (https://photos.state.gov/libraries/iraq/216651/US-IRAQ/us-iraq-sfa-en.pdf).

7. Mara Karlin and Tamara Cofman Wittes, "America's Middle East Purgatory: The Case for Doing Less," *Foreign Affairs*, January/February 2019.

8. While some senior advisers to George W. Bush had designs on Iraq from the day his administration took office, it is not clear that the president himself had such intentions until after the 9/11 attacks.

9. Charles Krauthammer, "The Unipolar Moment," *Financial Times*, America and the World 1990 (www.foreignaffairs.com/articles/1990-01-01/unipolar-moment).

10. For more on this subject, see Richard Nephew, "Chapter 2: Iraq," in *The Art of Sanctions: A View from the Field* (Columbia University Press, 2017).

11. Iraq Liberation Act of 1998 (www.congress.gov/bill/105th-congress/house-bill/4655).

12. CBS News/*New York Times* poll, January 16, 2009, showing President Bush at 22 percent approval and 73 percent disapproval ("one of the most unpopular departing presidents in history").

13. While the Trump administration cited the threat from Iran in explaining the decision to close the consulate, some administration officials have stated the decision was long-planned and driven by resource considerations. Regardless of the rationale, the message sent was that Iraq was a diminishing priority.

14. Alyssa J. Rubin and Ronen Bergman, "Israeli Air Strike Hits Weapons Depot in Iraq," *New York Times*, August 22, 2019.

15. Maintaining the status quo would also require Baghdad and the Kurdistan Regional Government, with U.S. diplomatic support, continuing to work through the differences that pushed them toward armed conflict after a damaging 2017 independence vote.

16. The wisdom or lack thereof of the Obama administration's decision to remove U.S. forces from Iraq at the end of 2011 remains hotly debated. For

critics, the best evidence that it was a mistake is what happened in Iraq in the years that followed, as ISIS seized a third of Iraqi territory in 2014, threatening key cities like Irbil and even Baghdad. The administration's defenders argue that the relatively small number of residual U.S. forces (in a noncombat role) under discussion between U.S. and Iraqi negotiators would have been unlikely to stem the ISIS onslaught, and the civil war in neighboring Syria played a greater role in the resurgence of terrorism in Iraq than did any U.S. policy decision. Both sides acknowledge that the diminished U.S. presence offered an opportunity for Iran, which rushed military assistance to Iraq during the crisis, months before the United States followed suit. Regardless, the circumstances underlying policy decisions on Iraq today differ markedly and should be assessed on their own terms.

17. The political crisis that began in 2019 is the third near-existential threat Iraq has faced since the fall of Saddam Hussein, after the sectarian civil war and the rise of ISIS (and the first that is primarily political).

18. For the best documentation of Iranian influence in Iraq, see Tim Arango and others, "The Iran Cables: Secret Documents Show How Tehran Wields Power in Iraq," *New York Times*, November 18, 2019. The article provides rare and compelling evidence of close ties between Iranian intelligence and Iraq's security agencies, though it broadly confirms, rather than contests, the prior U.S. assessment. Because the cables consist primarily of Iranian accounts of their own influence, they could be prone to overstatement.

19. Ben Taub, "Iraq's Post-ISIS Campaign of Revenge," *New Yorker*, December 17, 2018.

20. It will be important for the United States to do this while being seen not as siding with the Iraqi government against its own people, but rather as working with the Iraqi government to deliver on the people's demands. This project should distance itself from the discredited concept of nation-building, for which the United States has neither the legitimacy, nor the political will or the resources. Rather, Washington should focus on helping Iraqi officials improve the statecraft on which future stability will depend.

21. In the aftermath of the U.S.-led invasion, interventions in various forms by a range of regional actors—including Turkey, the Gulf states, and, of course, Iran—proved profoundly destabilizing for Iraq. The more recent Israeli strikes, if continued, are an ominous harbinger in this regard.

22. The Iraqi government has significant work to do in order to position the country to effectively receive such assistance, including by improving rule of law to allow for basic contracting, developing its financial system to enable capital flows, establishing a more sophisticated licensing and regulatory framework, and taking further action against corruption.

23. CIA World Factbook, Iraq: Economy—Overview (www.cia.gov/lib rary/publications/the-world-factbook/geos/iz.html).

24. For a well-argued version of this point, see "Iraq: Evading the Gathering Storm," International Crisis Group, Briefing No. 70: Middle East and North Africa, August 29, 2019 (www.crisisgroup.org/middle-east-north-africa/gulf -and-arabian-peninsula/iraq/070-iraq-evading-gathering-storm).

SEVEN

The United States and Egypt

Updating an Obsolete Relationship

AMY HAWTHORNE
ANDREW P. MILLER

In Egypt, as in several other places in the Middle East, the United States is overinvested in a country (1) whose importance to the United States has declined in recent decades, but which Washington cannot afford to ignore; (2) that often is not an effective or willing partner in advancing U.S. priorities; and (3) whose government's repression and poor economic management pose significant threats to stability and thus to U.S. interests. For these reasons, the next U.S. administration should change course and craft a more constructive policy toward Egypt.

A new U.S. president should resist the temptation to keep the relationship on autopilot or even to deepen ties with an Egyptian regime that may be less stable than it seems and, in any event, is unlikely to help advance U.S. regional policies to a degree that justifies condoning its troubling governance record. Instead, the United States should adopt a more conditional and transactional approach to generate more leverage over Egypt than it has at present. Such a policy shift, however, will require overcoming several challenges that have stymied previous U.S. administrations with regard to Egypt.

One such challenge is persuading overburdened and risk-averse policymakers to change course with a country that, compared to other Arab states, is not in immediate crisis. Another is finding ways to reduce and refocus one of the largest U.S. foreign aid packages without risking Egyptian cooperation on U.S. security interests. A third challenge is figuring out how to influence the governance of a regime that depends, to a certain extent, on U.S. support, but often has proven to be resistant to external pressure. This chapter, which assumes that Egyptian president Abdel Fattah al Sisi will still be in power in 2021, describes core American interests in Egypt, reviews recent U.S. policy there, and explains how the United States should recalibrate a relationship that, in its present form, has outlived its usefulness.

Interests

Since the mid-1970s, when Egyptian President Anwar al-Sadat decided to pivot toward the West and pursue peace with Israel, U.S. officials have accorded Egypt a central place in policy toward the Middle East. Egypt's special status has earned it nearly US$80 billion in U.S. military and civilian aid since the late 1970s, regular high-level visits from Washington, and diplomatic support, including effusive rhetoric about the country's importance as a "strategic partner."[1]

The heavy investment in Egypt has been predicated on a belief that U.S.-Egyptian cooperation serves three core national-security interests. One such interest is Arab-Israeli peace. Since brokering the Treaty of Peace between Egypt and Israel in 1979, the United States has urged Egypt to uphold its treaty commitments, as well as sought Egyptian help to achieve a U.S.-led settlement to the broader Arab-Israeli conflict.[2] A second core interest is counterterrorism (CT) cooperation. For decades, Egypt has been a crucial node in the international jihadist movement. Egyptians have played prominent roles in terrorist attacks against local, regional, and U.S. targets—*inter alia*, Egyptian members of al Qaeda were central actors in the 9/11 attacks—leading the United States to prioritize intelligence-sharing and other CT coordination with Egypt.[3] The third main security interest is gaining from Egypt reliable and fast military access through its territory and airspace, specifically for U.S. naval vessels sailing through the Suez Canal and for U.S. military aircraft flying over Egypt (so-called overflight privileges) as they transit to destinations such as East Asia and Afghanistan.[4]

The United States also has sought to bolster stability in Egypt as an overarching goal seen as necessary to protect the security interests described above.[5] Egyptian stability has been considered important because the country has the Middle East and North Africa's largest population (100 million citizens) and its largest armed forces, and because it occupies a strategic location—it borders Israel, has a long Mediterranean coastline, sits across the Red Sea from Saudi Arabia, and is home to the Suez Canal. Because of Egypt's demographic and geographic significance, prolonged instability there could have negative security ramifications not only inside Egypt but also beyond its borders, such as mass migration outflows, weapons proliferation, and empowered militant groups, not to mention destabilizing political effects.

This traditional view of Egypt is not entirely wrong: the U.S. government still has an interest in the country's security and stability. Yet, in continuing to present Cairo as a vital strategic partner, American officials are exaggerating Egypt's current importance to the United States and its contributions to advancing U.S. interests. Egypt is no longer the predominant Arab political player it was in decades past. Its ability to advance U.S. regional goals has diminished, due to changes in the global economy, regional power shifts, and domestic problems that have kept its leaders' attention often focused inward during the past decade.

Over the past decade, Egypt has been outstripped in regional influence by several much smaller and much wealthier Gulf countries. These oil monarchies are eroding Egypt's traditional role as a main go-between with Israel by forging direct (if as yet unofficial) relations with the Jewish state based on a common desire for the aggressive containment of Iran. (Egypt does not share the Gulf states' threat perception on Iran.)[6] The Suez Canal has become somewhat less critical as a global transit route as trade patterns have changed and new means of conveyance, particularly for energy, have been developed.[7] In addition, with the United States winding down its "forever wars" in western Asia, the U.S. military's demand for access to Egyptian airspace is likely to ebb considerably.

Egypt also has proved a difficult partner even in those areas where it retains influence. Egypt has been a less-than-enthusiastic participant in Washington's regional peace initiatives, too preoccupied with its own interests to engage rigorously on the Israeli-Palestinian conflict.[8] In recent years, Egypt has rebuffed U.S. proposals for closer CT cooperation in the Sinai Peninsula, where it faces a persistent jihadist insurgency, and on the border with Libya. It also has rejected Washington's warnings that its CT approach, revolving around mass repression and indiscriminate military tactics that have harmed many civilians, is counterproductive.[9]

And while Egypt wants unconditional support from the United States, it does not always feel a corresponding obligation to cooperate on certain issues important to Washington. Over U.S. protestations, Egypt has pursued closer ties with American adversaries such as China, Russia, and North Korea.[10] It has obstructed U.S.-funded aid programs designed to help Egyptian citizens.[11] Most alarming for a supposed "strategic partner," Egypt under al Sisi has wrongly imprisoned and mistreated numerous U.S. citizens for political reasons, and in January 2020, an unjustly detained American, Mustafa Kassem, even died in custody after Egyptian authorities ignored repeated U.S. requests for his release on humanitarian grounds.[12]

The unfortunate reality of Egypt today is that its regime's approach to political and economic governance, perhaps more than any other factor, is increasing the probability of instability there. Al Sisi's brutally repressive rule has worsened the very problems of widespread disaffection that sparked the 2011 popular uprising against longtime U.S. partner President Hosni Mubarak.[13] On the economic front, the situation is equally bleak for average Egyptians. In accordance with a 2016–19 International Monetary Fund (IMF) program, al Sisi imposed fiscal reforms that, while improving the macroeconomic picture to a certain extent, have severely worsened living conditions for most Egyptians.[14] Today, nearly a third of Egyptians live below the poverty line—even more than before the IMF program began—and some 30 percent (maybe more) of younger working-age Egyptians are unemployed.[15] Al Sisi also has significantly expanded the role of the military in the economy, increasing cronyism and corruption and crowding out the private sector, the most viable source of sustained job creation.[16]

A former minister of defense who seized power through a 2013 coup and then ruthlessly crushed Egypt's nascent pluralistic politics, al Sisi has overseen the unjust detention of tens of thousands of citizens, a sharp rise in state torture and extrajudicial killings, the subordination of all civilian state institutions to his security agencies, and the closing off of space for independent politics and media.[17] This unprecedented violence and repression, carried out in the name of Egypt's "security" and subsidized by U.S. taxpayers, not only deeply offends American values, it may also worsen Egypt's terrorism problem, which is currently serious but manageable, by enlarging the pool of aggrieved citizens susceptible to anti-regime and anti-U.S. radicalization.[18] And separate from fueling the terrorist threat, al Sisi's rule by fear and force may plant the seeds of popular resentment that could lead to an upheaval, possibly violent, against Egypt's power-holders. Without a course correction in governance and economic policy, serious instability could be in store.

To be sure, a sustained period of regime-shaking unrest in Egypt is a low-probability scenario, and the United States has a poor track record anyway of predicting when Arab regimes will go off the rails. But because some key ingredients for instability are present, and because such a scenario would have ramifications for U.S. interests, it should be taken seriously and warrants attention and planning. Indeed, surprise street protests in Egypt in fall 2019, fueled by public anger over economic hardship, revelations of al Sisi's alleged corruption, and mass repression, remind us that the popular support for al Sisi, and the country's stability, may be more precarious than it looks and shakier than what Egyptian officials claim.[19]

Policy Background

While core U.S. security interests in Egypt have remained constant over many decades, other aspects of the relationship have fluctuated, at least since the George W. Bush administration. One such aspect is how large a role the United States has sought for Egypt in regional initiatives such as Israeli-Palestinian negotiations or the campaign against ISIS. Typically, U.S. administrations have started off with ambitious hopes for Egypt to play a pivotal regional role, but as time has gone on, have diminished their expectations in the face of Egypt's lack of interest or capability. Another fluctuating aspect is the degree of importance that the United States has attached to the governance and human rights situation in Egypt and the ways in which it has engaged the Egyptian government on this issue.

Here, there have been two main schools of thought. The first sees giving Egypt's leadership a close embrace—by providing unconditional foreign aid, offering steady public praise and diplomatic attention, and avoiding public (and sometimes also private) criticism—as necessary to support regime stability and to protect security cooperation. Adherents to the second school of thought view authoritarian rule as posing a serious risk to Egypt's stability (as well as conflicting with U.S. values), and believe that playing hardball—by using various forms of U.S. influence to compel Egypt to improve its human rights record and to govern more democratically, as well as by building ties with Egyptians outside regime circles—is the most effective approach to manage this risk. Underlying each approach are different understandings of American influence in Egypt. Does American influence derive from unwavering demonstrations that the United States will always be in the regime's corner, no matter how it behaves domestically, or from incentives for cooperation that Washington can create by providing or withholding aid and other forms of U.S. influence?

President Barack Obama's policy toward Egypt started out with the close-embrace approach, then moved toward a hardball approach, and ended up as an often-confusing mix of both. His policy was shaped, and ultimately defined, by developments inside Egypt that his administration did not anticipate. At the outset of his presidency, Obama sought to repair ties with Mubarak, after bilateral relations had been strained by the preceding administration's Freedom Agenda and invasion of Iraq.[20] In his first two years in office, Obama avoided public criticism of Mubarak's repression, honored Mubarak by choosing Cairo as the venue for his landmark 2009 speech on U.S.-Islamic world relations, and sought to resolve disagreements over aid that had vexed the relationship during the Bush administration.[21] Obama intuitively understood that the Middle East's authoritarian regimes were unsustainable, and in 2010 his national security staff conducted a study on the prospects for political and economic reform in the Arab world. But the Obama administration operated on the assumption that Mubarak's Egypt was largely stable for the time being.

This assumption, of course, was upended by the sudden outbreak in January 2011 of mass protests against Mubarak and for democracy and social justice. Obama's secretaries of state and defense counseled caution in jettisoning a long-standing American partner facing a popular rebellion. But Obama quickly soured on Mubarak's stubborn refusal to meet the protestors' demands and was appalled by his use of violence to quash peaceful demonstrations, leading the U.S. president to vocally back the mostly youthful Egyptians bravely massing in Cairo's Tahrir Square. As Mubarak's hold on power was weakening, Obama sided with those advisers who argued that the United States should be "on the right side of history" and back a democratic opening.[22]

After the Egyptian military forced out Mubarak in February 2011, Obama reset U.S. policy, at least rhetorically, to support a democratic transition and to accept the Egyptian people's electoral choices—so long as any newly elected Egyptian leadership continued to uphold core U.S. security interests.[23] Recognizing that years of deference to Mubarak and erroneous assumptions of regime stability had left the U.S. government with poor contacts among Egyptian opposition forces and civil society, the administration swiftly built relations with the newly legal Muslim Brotherhood and reached out to other ascendant or emerging political movements and civic groups.[24] But concerns that pushing hard on democracy would jeopardize security cooperation with Egypt, skepticism inside the U.S. government about the wisdom of or need for promoting democratic change in Arab countries, and exasperation with Egypt's tumultuous and exhausting post-Mubarak political transition soon dampened U.S. enthusiasm for a genuine pro-democracy policy reorientation. Throughout the first two years of the post-Mubarak transition, the Obama administration largely deferred to both successive Egyptian governments, the first led on a transitional basis by the military and the second by the freely elected Muslim Brotherhood. During this period, the United States did not seek to obstruct democratic change in Egypt. But Obama ultimately was unwilling to exert substantial pressure on Egypt in response to undemocratic moves, such as the military's repeated violence against peaceful protestors, the unjust prosecution of American democracy workers beginning in 2011,[25] or the Brotherhood government's late 2012 attempt to consolidate power amid an outcry by large numbers of Egyptians.[26]

While the Obama White House tried to discourage a military coup against Egypt's first democratically elected president, Morsi of the Brotherhood, other parts of the U.S. government did not give such a clear red light. The administration reluctantly accepted his July 2013 military overthrow, fearing that strongly opposing it would alienate Egypt's military and harm U.S. security interests. This time, the U.S. government sought to be more involved in the details of the transition than it had been after Mubarak's ouster, developing milestones for Egypt's return to a civilian, democratic government, but it was unwilling to apply real pressure in support of these goals. It was not until after Egypt's security forces massacred nearly a thousand Morsi supporters gathered in Cairo in August 2013 that the administration took a punitive step, withholding the delivery of several expensive weapons systems funded by U.S. foreign assistance.[27] The impact of this partial arms suspension, seen by many in Egypt and Washington as a woefully inadequate response to the coup and the killing, was almost immediately undercut by senior administration officials arguing for releasing some or all of these weapons. The Egyptian government appeared to calculate (correctly) that with enough complaining to Washington, and pressure from al Sisi's backers in Israel, Saudi Arabia, and the United Arab Emirates, the United States would blink first.[28]

When Obama eventually decided to release the suspended arms shipments in March 2015, the al Sisi government had fulfilled virtually none of the terms on which the United States had conditioned the delivery of the weapons, including, most important, "credible progress toward an inclusive, democratically elected civilian government," though Obama did announce important changes to the U.S. military aid program at the same time.[29] Bilateral ties, which had been strained because of the arms suspension and the administration's vocal criticism of al Sisi's mass human rights violations, did not recover in the final two years of Obama's presidency. Indeed, the U.S. president kept his distance both from al Sisi, meeting him only once and pointedly never inviting him to the White House, and from Egypt in general. Focused on negotiating a nuclear deal with Iran and fighting ISIS, Obama simply did not regard Egypt as a foreign policy priority.

The Obama administration, in the final analysis, struggled in how to respond to post-Mubarak Egypt. It tended to vacillate between applying modest pressure on the Egyptian government in the service of defending human rights, and accommodating the existing power structure for fear of jeopardizing U.S. security interests. In the span of Obama's tenure, U.S. policy swung from one extreme to the other, from deferring to Egypt's authoritarian government to withholding military aid over human rights violations, and finally caving on its conditions for the resumption of assistance. This approach too often left the United States with the worst of both worlds, doing enough to antagonize the Egyptian leadership, but not persevering with a harder line long enough to apply the degree of pressure that could potentially change its calculus. To be sure, it was always going to be difficult to persuade Egypt to modify its policies on matters it deemed existential—those that it saw as jeopardizing its own grip on power—irrespective of what posture the United States adopted. But there were some moments, such as immediately after the ousters of Mubarak and Morsi, where it seems possible that more could have been done. And, in hindsight, it appears that concerns about losing Egyptian cooperation on core U.S. interests during this period were overblown, suggesting that the Obama administration was too cautious.

President Donald Trump entered office with a completely different attitude toward Egypt and its general-cum-president, reinforced by what seemed to be a compulsion to overturn Obama's policies. It appeared that Trump, who met with the Egyptian president in New York weeks before the 2016 election, admired al Sisi for the very qualities that Obama had disdained: his authoritarianism, brutality, and obsession with power.[30] Senior officials in the Trump administration, including the first national security adviser Michael Flynn and then Secretary of Defense James Mattis, also viewed Egypt as strategically more important than did the Obama administration and regarded al Sisi's mass repression as an effective CT policy—or even as necessary to keep Egypt stable.[31] Adding to Egypt's enhanced reputation in the Trump administration was the view of the Israeli-Palestinian "peace" team, led by Trump's son-in-law Jared Kushner, that Egyptian support for Trump's "deal of the century" was essential to compel the Palestinians to make major concessions.[32] Moreover, Trump's closest regional partners—Israel, Saudi Arabia, and the United Arab Emirates—lobbied hard for strong U.S. backing of al Sisi.

It is, therefore, not surprising that Trump favored an unconditional embrace of al Sisi, likely hoping that blanket U.S. support for the ex-general would guarantee Egyptian cooperation on the administration's agenda and bolster Egypt as a pro-Trump ally. In April 2017, Trump received al Sisi as one of his first foreign counterparts in the Oval Office, the very honor denied to the latter by Obama, and lavished the Egyptian dictator with praise, saying he was doing "a fantastic job" and that "we are very much behind Egypt."[33] The regular public condemnations of al Sisi's rights abuses during the Obama administration were gone, replaced with anodyne praise for Egypt's supposedly pivotal role in the Middle East. Al Sisi apparently believed that the Trump administration would accede to its demands that the Obama administration had refused, such as designating the Brotherhood as a Foreign Terrorist Organization or canceling Obama's 2015 reforms to military aid. Despite the White House's exceedingly warm reception of al Sisi, however, the Trump administration did not immediately grant all Egyptian requests—and even briefly took action on certain human rights issues. Shortly after al Sisi's visit, Trump secured the release of a U.S. citizen unjustly imprisoned in Egypt, humanitarian worker Aya Hijazi, and her husband. Though Trump likely was more interested in one-upping Obama than in promoting civil society freedoms, Hijazi's release was still a notable step. In August 2017, Secretary of State Rex Tillerson made an unusual punitive move by suspending or cutting nearly US$300 million in aid to Egypt. This move was intended to compel Cairo to end its military cooperation with North Korea, to withdraw a law imposing draconian restrictions on nongovernmental organizations (NGOs), and to overturn the 2013 sham convictions of American democracy workers.[34]

The Trump administration's pro-Egypt rhetoric and actions began to converge more closely when Michael Pompeo, who as a member of Congress had been a harsh critic of Obama and the Muslim Brotherhood, replaced Tillerson. In July 2018, Pompeo released the military aid suspended by Tillerson, even though al Sisi had only partly met the attached conditions.[35] In April 2019, Trump once again welcomed the Egyptian president to the White House, and this time al Sisi had a more fruitful visit. At his urging, Trump instructed his administration to explore designating the Brotherhood, launching a process that was continuing as of this writing.[36] Al Sisi's lobbying of Trump on Libya also reportedly was instrumental in persuading the U.S. president to back the renegade warlord and Egyptian ally Khalifa Haftar's April 2019 assault on Tripoli.[37] Perhaps most important, in inviting al Sisi into the Oval Office shortly before his regime staged a phony referendum on authoritarian constitutional amendments that would allow al Sisi to stay in office through at least 2030, Trump provided the Egyptian dictator with a clear endorsement of his power grab.[38]

Yet, Trump's rapprochement with Egypt, hugging al Sisi close while withholding criticism, has largely failed to yield dividends for U.S. interests. Contrary to those who argued that Egypt would reciprocate positive gestures from Washington, Cairo has tended to pocket concessions from the United States. For example, following his 2017 Oval Office meeting, al Sisi proceeded to ratify the aforementioned NGO law, breaking a pledge to Trump's aides to shelve the legislation.[39] Nor has Egypt given the administration fulsome public support for its Israeli-Palestinian peace proposal. And on the eve of al Sisi's 2019 visit to the White House, Cairo even withdrew from Trump's Middle East Strategic Alliance, a regional collective security initiative sponsored by the United States and a cornerstone of the administration's anti-Iran policy.[40]

Making matters worse, the Trump administration's practice of relying on public praise and private diplomacy to address (a very limited number of) human rights concerns has been ineffective. Since Trump took office, al Sisi has tightened his grip and escalated his repression (including arresting several more U.S. citizens). Seemingly buoyed by Trump's effusive, unconditional support, al Sisi is doubling down on the very approaches that risk sowing instability. Underscoring the fundamental flaw in Trump's embrace of al Sisi, it was only when the administration—with a push from key members of Congress—was prepared to apply pressure on Egypt by suspending military aid that al Sisi made a more serious effort to address U.S. priorities, such as by finally exonerating the wrongly convicted democracy workers and reducing some cooperation with the North Korean regime.[41] If the Obama administration's use of military aid as leverage appeared inconclusive, Tillerson's wielding of this tool proved its efficacy. As of this writing, however, Trump seemed determined to go in the opposite direction and draw ever closer to al Sisi, reportedly even calling the Egyptian strongman his "favorite dictator," despite the clear evidence that this approach will not work.[42] A tragic case in point was the January 2020 death in Egyptian custody of Mustafa Kassem, the wrongly imprisoned American citizen. Although Kassem wrote a letter to Trump pleading for the United States to gain his release, and senior U.S. officials did raise his case, the U.S. president apparently failed to intervene personally on Kassem's behalf.[43]

Policy Challenges

After the turmoil in Egypt and the vacillations in U.S. policy over the past decade, the policy questions that will confront the next administration are fundamental and strategic. A new president will have a chance to update U.S. policy toward Egypt to reflect better the reality of that country and the bilateral relationship, an opportunity that must be seized. A new approach will have to grapple with three primary questions.

What role should the United States give Egypt in its broader Middle East strategy? The official U.S. government view of Egypt has not changed much over the last forty-plus years. According to senior U.S. officials, Egypt remains a "key partner" of the United States in the Arab world.[44] But, as argued above, Egypt is no longer the regional power on which the "strategic relationship" was originally premised. And the interests of both countries have begun to diverge in important respects, particularly concerning the role of Russia and the most effective way to counter the spread of violent extremism. Yet, U.S. support for Egypt has remained intact.

Defining Egypt's place in U.S. regional strategy is not just a theoretical exercise. It has direct implications for the U.S. policy agenda in Egypt and the region, for other partnerships, and for resource commitments. Policies that depend on Egypt's ability to rally the Arab world to the U.S. position have become ever more tenuous. A recognition that Egypt is not capable of contributing (or willing to contribute) as much to American interests as it once did also increases the imperative to find more capable partners. And, if Egypt has become less central to U.S. goals in the Middle East, it is harder for the U.S. government to justify providing Egypt with the third-largest U.S. foreign aid package in the world.[45] A new president will need to wrestle with the fact of Egypt's decline and adjust U.S. policies to account for what can be reasonably expected of Cairo in coming years.

What issues should the United States prioritize and how should it manage the tension among priorities? In addition to revisiting Egypt's overall position in U.S. policy, the United States should review which issues in the bilateral relationship should receive the most attention. U.S. security interests traditionally have dominated Egypt policy. There has, moreover, been a tendency to pursue military/security issues and political/human-rights ones on separate tracks, based on a belief that U.S.-Egyptian security relations should be insulated from the political turbulence that pushing on human rights often causes in the larger relationship.

But under this approach, U.S. officials are prevented from addressing human rights and governance issues with the very Egyptian actors who have the most influence on these issues: the military and intelligence chiefs. And it does not account for the interdependence between human rights and security issues, in particular how human rights violations can fuel security threats and contribute to instability.[46] A new administration will be faced with the short-term costs of irritating Egypt by raising the profile of human rights, on the one hand, and the inherent limits of security-centric policies, on the other. In order to navigate these obstacles, the U.S. government will need to weigh these priorities carefully and develop policies that recognize, not deny, the tensions between security cooperation and the promotion of human rights.

Likewise, a new administration will also have to decide which human rights or domestic political issues to prioritize. The Egyptian government's human rights violations are too vast to count, but U.S. influence in Egypt, as in other countries, is not infinite and Washington cannot expect to have an impact on everyone.[47] Rather than diluting U.S. influence by making a full-court press on all matters of concern, it may make more sense for Washington to identify the most important problems—those that the United States believes will be most deleterious to Egyptian stability—and to focus its advocacy and pressure on those concerns.

How much influence should the United States have over Egypt and what approach would maximize U.S. leverage? Like other authoritarian countries, and because it feels entitled to unconditional U.S. support by virtue of having made peace with Israel, Egypt is difficult for the United States to influence under the best of conditions, and particularly in the short term. But contrary to what is sometimes argued, the United States—Egypt's most paramount foreign partner and military supplier—is hardly devoid of leverage.

In the few instances when U.S. officials have tied Egypt's desire for U.S. military aid and diplomatic support to changes in domestic and regional policies, they have succeeded in pushing back on, or even reversing, repressive actions by Cairo, freeing detained American citizens and shaping Egypt's foreign policy in a direction more aligned with U.S. interests.[48] While a new administration should not overstate U.S. influence in Egypt, neither should it operate on the assumption that it has none. The relationship with the United States remains Egypt's most important.

Recommended Policy

The next administration should approach Egypt as a challenge to be managed, not as a strategic asset for which to compete. As argued above, Egypt is no longer a vital U.S. partner in the Middle East. While the United States continues to have security interests there, some of these interests are less significant than in the past and others do not require coddling the regime to achieve. The most important threat to U.S. interests today in Egypt is instability caused by repressive governance and economic mismanagement. Obviously, the United States will not determine Egypt's future trajectory—dynamics inside the country are always paramount—but how the United States engages with Egypt is a factor in what happens there. Too often, U.S. policy toward Egypt unintentionally has served to enable harmful Egyptian domestic policies. Even if we cannot save Egypt from itself, the United States must not make its problems worse and should use what influence it does have more constructively.

Given Egypt's reluctance to address voluntarily the concerns of outside actors and penchant for pocketing U.S. support, the next administration should pursue a more explicitly transactional relationship with Cairo, which avoids tying the United States too closely to al Sisi's authoritarian regime. A new president should calibrate U.S. support, both diplomatic and financial, based on the level of cooperation it receives from the Egyptian government on U.S. interests in security and stability. In practice, this means that the United States should work with and support Egypt to the extent necessary to promote core interests such as CT cooperation, U.S. military transit, and peace with Israel. But where U.S. and Egyptian views diverge, such as over whether al Sisi's repression threatens Egypt's stability, the administration should not hesitate to apply pressure, recognizing that while it will be difficult to modify the regime's behavior, it may be wise to create distance from a regime resented by much of its population and with an uncertain future.

The Egyptian government may perceive such an approach as a deliberate downgrading of the bilateral relationship, but is not likely to respond in ways that cause real damage to U.S. interests in the Middle East. Regarding Israel, for instance, Egypt derives important benefits from the peace treaty, independent of any U.S. action. Indeed, the Egyptian-Israeli relationship has become self-sustaining. Today, as the two neighbors collaborate in unprecedented ways to combat a jihadist insurgency in Sinai and pursue large natural gas deals, Cairo's relations with the Jewish state are probably their strongest ever.[49] On CT cooperation, the Egyptian security services will not cease pursuing terrorists or accepting U.S. intelligence on mutual threats. Jihadists in Egypt who threaten U.S. interests also pose a direct threat to the Egyptian state and the Egyptian authorities must deal with them, irrespective of the standing of the U.S.-Egyptian relationship. Regarding access for U.S. military transit, U.S. military planes cross Egyptian airspace on their way to target common enemies, and the United States actually provides financial compensation to Egypt for each navy ship that goes through the Suez Canal, significant revenue that Egypt is unlikely to forgo.[50]

Similarly, concerns in the national security establishment about "losing" Egypt to Russia or China should the United States recalibrate its support are overblown.[51] While both countries have increased their activities in Egypt under al Sisi, neither represents a credible alternative to the United States. Neither Russia nor China provides military aid to Egypt, as the United States does, and the Egyptian military will remain dependent on U.S.-provided arms, maintenance, and spare parts for decades to come. Egypt will continue to play the United States off Russia and China to maintain some degree of independence, but Cairo has no desire to become a vassal of Moscow or Beijing.

The next administration should reshape U.S. policy toward Egypt by taking the following steps. Congress is a major player in relations with Egypt, and the next administration should engage early and often with Capitol Hill on a reorientation of the U.S. approach.

Reduce Egypt's annual military aid package while leaving open the possibility that this funding could be restored (or even increased) if Cairo begins to make bigger contributions to U.S. interests. There are two compelling reasons to reduce Egypt's military aid. First, the annual US$1.3 billion package, the second-largest in the world behind Israel, has not brought the return on investment envisioned when it began some forty years ago. Egypt's contribution to U.S. security interests has declined, and the aid is more than Egypt needs to address mutual security threats. Some of those resources can be used better elsewhere. In recent years, the U.S. Senate Appropriations Committee has recommended a reduction to US$1 billion in annual military aid for Egypt, a figure that better corresponds with U.S. interests and Egypt's actual security needs.[52] Second, trimming Egypt's aid package would demonstrate the credibility of future U.S. threats to reduce assistance, enhancing Washington's leverage over Cairo.[53] If, as happened during the Obama administration, Egypt does not view U.S. threats to suspend assistance until its conditions are met as credible, it has no reason to adjust its conduct. The only way to shake Egypt from its sense of entitlement is to demonstrate that U.S. military aid is not sacrosanct. Once some aid to Egypt has been cut, the United States can then use the promise of reinstating the lost funding to elicit changes in Egyptian policies.

Resume public criticism of Cairo's human rights record. Private diplomacy with Egypt on human rights issues seldom yields results unless it is paired with public criticism. Public expressions of dissatisfaction signal to Egypt that the United States sincerely cares about an issue and impose a reputational cost on the Egyptian government. The Trump White House's general avoidance of criticizing Egypt in public has sent the message that human rights and governance issues are not U.S. priorities, when in fact they should be seen as critical to Egypt's future and to American interests. It can be argued that the Obama administration was too often public about its human rights concerns, leading the Egyptian government to tune out Washington. But, to the extent this was true, the answer is not to go silent but instead to concentrate public criticism on the rights issues that are most important for Egypt's stability. Such issues include preserving space for Egypt's beleaguered civil society, stopping extrajudicial killings and torture in Egyptian prisons, and releasing political detainees.

Maintain an open channel with al Sisi, but refrain from high-profile, prestige meetings that Egypt could interpret as a U.S. endorsement. Ignoring al Sisi is unlikely to change his behavior, but speaking with him should not be viewed as a reward. Telephone calls are not only appropriate but prudent. Meetings, however, should not take place in the Oval Office, which accords al Sisi the international legitimacy he so desires, and should only happen once Egypt has addressed U.S. policy concerns. In granting al Sisi two White House visits in two years without any prior Egyptian commitments to address U.S. concerns, Trump has needlessly squandered U.S. influence. Egypt deeply values the public embrace of the U.S. government, which along with military aid is the most important source of American leverage over Cairo. The next administration should use Egypt's desire for a U.S. endorsement more strategically, conditioning public signals of support on changes to Egyptian policy.

Redouble efforts to shift U.S.-Egyptian military cooperation away from a heavy focus on equipment transfers and toward professionalization and training of Egyptian forces in modern warfare. Decades of U.S. weapons transfers to Egypt have not substantially improved the capabilities of the Egyptian military, especially in dealing with asymmetric threats such as terrorist groups. This is partly because Egypt has prioritized the acquisition of weapons systems that are inappropriate for its immediate threat environment, such as Abrams tanks, and partly because the Egyptian military tends not to employ U.S.-supplied weapons effectively.[54] While the Obama administration modified U.S. military assistance policy to support the procurement of more appropriate weapons systems, the U.S. military has been unsuccessful in persuading its Egyptian counterpart to reevaluate its strategy and tactics.[55] Since friendly persuasion has not produced the desired results, the next administration should consider conditioning the sale of certain equipment items on Egypt's agreement to participate in U.S. training programs aimed at improving the professionalism of the Egyptian military and its ability to confront terrorist groups.

Boost U.S. diplomatic attention to Egypt's legitimate security challenges, in particular the looming crisis posed by water scarcity in the face of increased population growth. While Egypt's inefficient water-use practices have made the country more vulnerable to a water crisis,

Ethiopia's Grand Ethiopian Renaissance Dam (GERD), which is situated on a tributary of the Nile River (the source of 85 percent of Egypt's fresh water), poses a real danger to Egyptian stability by threatening its share of Nile water flow.[56] If the rate of the fill period for the dam is too rapid, it could reduce Egypt's water supply by up to 20 percent.[57] As discussed above, it is not easy for the United States to address potential sources of instability in Egypt, especially those that stem from the Egyptian government's own actions. Managing water scarcity, however, is one such challenge where the U.S. government may be able to help, and for which the needed U.S. investment— mostly diplomatic attention and technical expertise—is comparatively modest. The Trump administration, commendably, has initiated mediation among Egypt, Ethiopia, and Sudan on the GERD. But even if the conflict over the GERD is resolved, Egypt still faces other serious threats to its water supply, including mismanagement.

Expand U.S. diplomatic outreach to include a wider array of political actors in Egypt. It is a mistake to limit U.S. engagement to the Egyptian regime and its supporters. Egypt is bigger, and more complex, than al Sisi. The United States needs to have relationships and to establish trust with other Egyptian actors. Over Mubarak's thirty years in power, the U.S. government limited interactions with a variety of Mubarak's opponents in deference to the Egyptian leader, which left American officials scrambling after he fell from power.[58] We should not continue this narrow and flawed approach. The next administration should make a strategic decision to engage the widest range of political actors possible, even if doing so antagonizes the Egyptian government. This outreach should mainly take the form of diplomatic outreach rather than aid programs. Certainly, to the extent possible, the United States should look for opportunities to expand civilian (nonmilitary) assistance to reach new sectors of the population, especially in key issue areas such as water management, education, and health. At present, U.S. civilian aid to Egypt is only one-tenth the size of military aid and mostly benefits the Egyptian government and its allies. But the next administration must have modest expectations for what such aid programs can achieve. With tens of billions of aid dollars spent, the U.S. track record on development in Egypt over the past decades is disappointing, and the never very hospitable environment has grown even less permissive under al Sisi. A new U.S. president should also consider creating a special visa category for Egyptian civil society activists, human rights defenders, scholars, journalists, and political figures under threat from al Sisi and seeking to escape Egypt and relocate to the United States or other safe environments. This would be an important humanitarian gesture and a strategic investment to help support influential, pro-democracy Egyptians who could contribute positively to their country in the future. Indeed, helping a pro-democracy contingent of Egyptians survive these very dark times under al Sisi is one of the best investments that the United States could make.

Conclusion

The approach outlined in this chapter will be unsatisfying to those who believe that Egypt is a vital U.S. partner, or that the United States can transform the country. Under present circumstances, the best the United States can do is protect its highest priority interests, stop throwing good money after bad, and begin laying the groundwork for greater influence in the future. Egypt's decline as a regional power and a U.S. partner is regrettable, but it possesses latent potential for regional influence, for economic prosperity, and for better governance that it may be able to harness one day. Should Cairo begin to show signs of tapping into such potential, the United States should be ready to seize on that opportunity to help Egypt chart a new course for its people and for the bilateral relationship. In the meantime, a new president would be wise to accept the limitations of the relationship under Egypt's current leadership and confine cooperation to where it is strictly necessary. Such a policy may not be inspiring, but it would be based on a more circumspect view of today's Egypt and a sounder assessment of U.S. interests, which is more than can be said for the current approach.

Notes

1. Jeremy M. Sharp, "Egypt: Background and U.S. Relations," Congressional Research Service, November 21, 2019 (https://fas.org/sgp/crs/mideast/RL33003.pdf).

2. Ibid.

3. See *inter alia* Lawrence Wright, *The Looming Tower: Al Qaeda and the Road to 9/11* (New York: Random House, 2006).

4. Jim Michaels, "U.S. Military Needs Egypt for Access to Critical Area," *USA Today*, August 17, 2019.

5. Sharp, "Egypt: Background and U.S. Relations."

6. Andrew Miller and Richard Sokolsky, "Actually, Egypt Is a Terrible Ally," *New York Times*, December 18, 2017.

7. Eddy Bekkers, Joseph Francois, and Hugo Rojas-Romagosa, "Melting Ice Caps Will Open the Northern Sea to Commercial Traffic and Change World Trade Patterns," *LSE Business Review*, August 8, 2018 (https://blogs.lse.ac.uk/businessreview/2018/08/08/melting-ice-caps-will-open-the-northern-sea-to-commercial-traffic-and-change-world-trade-patterns/).

8. Aidan Lewis, "Sisi Says Egypt Will Not Accept Anything against Palestinian Wishes," Reuters, June 2, 2019.

9. Miller and Sokolsky, "Actually, Egypt Is a Terrible Ally."

10. Michal Wahid Hanna and Daniel Benaim, "Egypt First," *Foreign Affairs*, January 4, 2018.

11. Amy Hawthorne, "Rethinking U.S. Economic Aid to Egypt," Project on Middle East Democracy, October 2016 (https://pomed.org/wp-content/uploads/2016/11/Rethinking_US_Economic_Aid_Egypt.pdf); Julian Pecquet, "U.S. Shifts Egypt Aid to Other Countries," *Al Monitor*, October 17, 2016 (www.al-monitor.com/pulse/originals/2016/10/us-shift-egypt-aid-other-countries.html).

12. Sudarsan Raghavan, "Egypt Jails American Traveler, Saying She Criticized the Government on Facebook," *Washington Post*, August 8, 2019.

13. Amy Hawthorne and Andrew Miller, "Worse than Mubarak," *Foreign Policy*, February 27, 2019.

14. Andrew Miller, "Egypt: Security, Human Rights, and Reform," Testimony: U.S. House Foreign Affairs Committee Middle East and North Africa Subcommittee Hearing, July 24, 2018 (https://docs.house.gov/meetings/FA/FA13/20180724/108598/HHRG-115-FA13-Wstate-MillerA-20180724.pdf).

15. "Sources: Officials Delayed Survey Results Showing Egyptians Face Highest Poverty Rate since 2000," *Mada Masr*, July 30, 2019 (https://madamasr.com/en/2019/07/30/feature/economy/sources-officials-delayed-survey-results-showing-egyptians-face-highest-poverty-rate-since-2000/); "Unemployment, Youth Total," World Bank, 2018 (https://data.worldbank.org/indicator/SL.UEM.1524.ZS).

16. "From War Room to Boardroom. Military Firms Flourish in Sisi's Egypt," Reuters, May 16, 2018.

17. Miller, "Egypt: Security, Human Rights, and Reform."

18. Amy Woodyatt, "Egypt's Prisons Are Becoming Recruiting Grounds for the Islamic State," *Foreign Policy*, April 8, 2019.

19. Vivian Yee and Nada Rashwan, "In Egypt, Scattered Protests Break Out for Second Week," *New York Times*, September 27, 2019.

20. Peter Grier, "Obama, Mubarak Seek Fresh Start to Strained U.S.-Egypt Ties," *Christian Science Monitor*, August 19, 2009.

21. "The President's Speech in Cairo: A New Beginning," White House, 2009 (https://obamawhitehouse.archives.gov/issues/foreign-policy/presidents-speech-cairo-a-new-beginning).

22. "Obama: U.S. Is 'On Right Side of History' in Mideast," NPR, February 15, 2011.

23. "Clinton Supports 'Full Transition' in Egypt," Al Jazeera, July 14, 2012.

24. Tim Mak, "U.S. Recognizes Muslim Brotherhood," *Politico*, June 30, 2011 (www.politico.com/story/2011/06/us-recognizes-muslim-brotherhood-058094).

25. Josh Levs and Saad Abedine, "Egypt Sentences American NGO Workers to Jail," CNN, June 4, 2012 (www.cnn.com/2013/06/04/world/africa/egypt-ngos/index.html); Amy Hawthorne, "What the United States Should Have Said to Egypt About the NGO Trial," *MENA Source*, Atlantic Council, June 6, 2013 (www.atlanticcouncil.org/blogs/menasource/what-the-united-states-should-have-said-to-egypt-about-the-ngo-trial/).

26. "Morsi 'Power Grab' Angers Egypt Opposition Groups," *Guardian*, November 23, 2012.

27. Elise Labott, "U.S. Suspends Significant Military Aid to Egypt," CNN, October 9, 2013 (www.cnn.com/2013/10/09/world/meast/us-egypt-aid/index.html).

28. David D. Kirkpatrick, *Into the Hands of the Soldiers: Freedom and Chaos in Egypt and the Middle East* (New York: Viking, 2018), 298–330.

29. Peter Baker, "Obama Removes Weapons Freeze Against Egypt," *New York Times*, March 31, 2015.

30. Cristiano Lima, "Trump Praises Egypt's al Sisi: 'He's a Fantastic Guy,'" *Politico*, September 22, 2016 (www.politico.com/story/2016/09/trump-praises-egypts-al-sisi-hes-a-fantastic-guy-228560).

31. David Kirkpatrick, "The White House and the Strongman," *New York Times,* July 27, 2019.

32. Peter Baker and Declan Walsh, "Trump Shifts Course on Egypt, Praising Its Authoritarian Leader," *New York Times*, April 3, 2017.

33. Ibid.

34. Andrew Miller and Todd Ruffner, "President Trump's Second Foreign Affairs Budget," Project on Middle East Democracy, June 2018 (https://pomed.org/wp-content/uploads/2018/06/BudgetReportFY19_Digital.pdf).

35. Andrew Miller, Seth Binder, and Louisa Keeler, "President Trump's Third Foreign Affairs Budget," Project on Middle East Democracy, June 2019 (https://pomed.org/wp-content/uploads/2019/06/BudgetReport_FY20.pdf).

36. Eric Schmitt, Helene Cooper, Edward Wong, and Charlie Savage, "On Muslim Brotherhood, Trump Weighs Siding with Autocrats and Roiling Middle East," *New York Times*, May 6, 2019.

37. Vivian Salama, Jared Maslin, and Summer Said, "Trump Backed Libyan Warlord after Saudi Arabia and Egypt Lobbied Him," *Wall Street Journal*, May 12, 2019.

38. Margaret Talev, "Trump Praises Egypt's al Sisi Amid Efforts to Extend Rule," Bloomberg, April 9, 2019.

39. Noha Elhennawy, "Some Egyptian Rights Activists Dismiss Country's New NGO Law," AP News, August 22, 2019.

40. Stephen Kalin and Jonathan Landay, "Egypt Withdraws from U.S.-Led Anti-Iran Security Initiative," Reuters, April 10, 2019.

41. Andrew Miller, "Trump Blinks and Egypt's Sisi Wins," *Foreign Policy*, August 10, 2018.

42. Nancy A. Youssef, Vivian Salama, and Michael C. Bender, "Trump, Awaiting Egyptian Counterpart at Summit, Called Out for 'My Favorite Dictator,'" *Wall Street Journal*, September 13, 2019 (www.wsj.com/articles/trump-awaiting-egyptian-counterpart-at-summit-called-out-for-my-favorite-dictator-11568403645).

43. Declan Walsh, "American Held in Egypt Prison Dies After a Hunger Strike," *New York Times*, January 13, 2020 (www.nytimes.com/2020/01/13/world/middleeast/egypt-prisoner-moustafa-kassem-dies.html).

44. Jonathan R. Cohen, "Nominee for U.S. Ambassador to the Arab Republic of Egypt," Testimony: U.S. Senate Foreign Relations Committee Nomination Hearing, June 20, 2019 (www.foreign.senate.gov/imo/media/doc/062019_Cohen_Testimony.pdf).

45. Miller, Binder, and Keeler, "President Trump's Third Foreign Affairs Budget."

46. Brian Dooley, "Egypt's President Is Crushing Dissent—and Fueling ISIS," *Defense One*, April 3, 2019.

47. "Egypt: Events of 2018," in *Human Rights Watch World Report 2019* (www.hrw.org/world-report/2019/country-chapters/egypt).

48. Andrew Miller and Seth Binder, "The Case for Arms Embargoes against Uncooperative Partners," *War on the Rocks* (web publication), May 10, 2019.

49. Danny Zaken, "Israel, Egypt Strengthen Energy Ties," *Al-Monitor*, August 1, 2019.

50. Andrew Miller, "Commentary: Five Myths about U.S. Aid to Egypt," Reuters, August 13, 2018.

51. Andrew Miller and Michele Dunne, "Losing Egypt to Russia Isn't the Real Problem—But Collapse Is," *National Interest*, July 20, 2018.

52. Bryant Harris, "Senate Panel Slashes Military Aid to Egypt," *Al-Monitor*, September 6, 2017.

53. Miller and Sokolsky, "Actually, Egypt Is a Terrible Ally."

54. Robert Springborg and F. C. Williams, "The Egyptian Military: A Slumbering Giant Awakes," Carnegie Endowment for International Peace,

February 28, 2019 (https://carnegie-mec.org/2019/02/28/egyptian-military-slumbering-giant-awakes-pub-78238).

55. Jeremy M. Sharp, "Egypt: Background and U.S. Relations," Congressional Research Service, August 12, 2008 (www.everycrsreport.com/files/20080812_RL33003_eb2608abafbafd9c8d5d0e04158f579574bfb7b7.pdf).

56. Tareq Baconi, "The End Is Nile: International Cooperation on Egypt's Water Crisis," European Council on Foreign Relations, July 25, 2018 (www.ecfr.eu/article/commentary_the_end_is_nile_international_cooperation_on_egypts_water_crisis).

57. Michele Dunne and Katherine Pollock, "River of Discontent," Carnegie Middle East Center, October 23, 2017 (https://carnegie-mec.org/diwan/73491).

58. Charles Dunne, "The Right Side of History," *American Interest*, January 31, 2011.

EIGHT

Recalibrating the Terms of U.S.-Saudi Relations

DANIEL BENAIM

As the United States seeks to rationalize its investment in the Middle East and North Africa, its relationship with Saudi Arabia is likely to prove particularly challenging to manage. The U.S.-Saudi relationship, rooted for decades in a foundational bargain of security for oil, has entered a period of turbulence and uncertainty. Ties have whipsawed from the traumas of 9/11 and the Iraq War to profound differences over regional policies under President Barack Obama. Most recently, an unconditional embrace from President Trump has enabled a pattern of aggressive Saudi policies, raising bipartisan objections and all but ensuring the next course correction.

This chapter puts forward a vision for that course correction. It first explores the changes underway on both sides and what they mean for U.S. interests. Then it examines recent challenges in the relationship. Finally, it looks forward to offer a set of policy recommendations for the next U.S. administration. While the U.S.-Saudi relationship will need to change in important ways, the United States still has interests that require cooperating with Riyadh. The dilemma for the next administration will be to navigate these changes without rupturing the bilateral relationship.

Today's uncertainty in the U.S.-Saudi relationship reflects shifts within both countries and within the region as a whole. The United States is less dependent on Middle Eastern energy than at any point in recent memory, and exhausted from recent wars in the region.[1] Many experts wonder if America can afford to "do less" in the region and especially with Saudi Arabia.[2] A disastrous war in Yemen and the killing of journalist Jamal Khashoggi have crystallized bipartisan concerns about Saudi Arabia's behavior and trajectory under the de facto rule of Crown Prince Mohammed bin Salman.[3]

As he consolidates control, bin Salman is transforming Saudi Arabia from a conservative, status quo power into a revisionist, disruptive force in the region.[4] Under the banner of generational change, he is trying to dismantle and remake several pillars of the country's domestic social and political order at once, ranging from reining in the religious police to replacing consensual decisionmaking within the royal family with increasingly coercive one-man rule. Amid widespread perceptions that the United States is pulling back from the Middle East, Saudi foreign policy under bin Salman has become more assertive, confrontational, and risk-tolerant. These dramatic changes have outsized significance for U.S. policy. Accordingly, while referencing broader dynamics among Arab Gulf countries, including the influential expeditionary role of the United Arab Emirates and the Saudis's and Emiratis's vexing dispute with Qatar, this chapter will focus squarely on U.S.-Saudi ties.

Despite fundamental questions about where Saudi Arabia is headed under bin Salman, a working bilateral relationship continues to be in the U.S. national interest. Washington and Riyadh cooperate closely on counterterrorism. Both aim to counter Iran's regional and nuclear goals. Despite its reduced dependence on Middle Eastern energy supplies, the United States retains a substantial interest in ensuring the free flow of energy from the region to the rest of the world, which influences global fuel prices.[5] The fate of Saudi societal and economic changes will have implications for the entire region's future. Saudi Arabia has emerged as one of the leaders in a bloc of U.S.-Arab partners that increasingly work closely with Israel.[6] Saudi economic statecraft, investments in neighbors, and remittances are key to the economic stability of several countries in the Middle East, Pakistan, and far beyond.[7] An unstable Saudi Arabia—whether due to failed reforms, terrorism, or internal strife—could severely damage U.S. interests, disrupting the global economy and creating dangerous openings for adversaries and terrorists alike.

None of these interests require that the U.S.-Saudi relationship be set in stone. And indeed, the baseline of U.S.-Saudi relations has been shifting as President Trump paradoxically both deployed thousands of U.S. troops to Saudi Arabia after a fifteen-year absence and called into question doctrinal U.S. commitments to Gulf security. Meanwhile, Saudi Arabia's actions in recent years have led some U.S. policymakers to question whether the country can or should remain a close U.S. partner.[8] Saudi Arabia's feud with Qatar divided the ranks of U.S. regional allies and distracted from shared endeavors, including the campaign to defeat the Islamic State of Iraq and Syria (ISIS).[9] Its involuntary detention of Lebanon's prime minister was counterproductive and troubling. The war in Yemen, while responding to legitimate threats from a brutal adversary, ensnared the United States in a campaign that has sparked the world's worst humanitarian crisis and empowered U.S. and Saudi adversaries.[10] It remains an open question whether Saudi Arabia under bin Salman's leadership will learn from these episodes and trim its sails to avoid overreach; or whether these are harbingers of a more destabilizing future Saudi foreign policy—a prospect that would necessitate a more profound rethink in relations.

Then there are the fundamental U.S. interests in human rights and universal freedoms. Unlike close U.S. allies in Europe and East Asia, Saudi Arabia does not share these values. Amid important societal reforms, such as allowing women to drive and the welcoming via tourist visas of outsiders into the Kingdom, bin Salman has overseen the kingdom's most aggressive political crackdown in decades.[11] Saudi Arabia has jailed and reportedly tortured royal rivals, dissidents, and even women's rights advocates and business elites.[12] These actions have not only undermined promising economic reforms by scaring off foreign investment.[13] But, as the Khashoggi killing shows, the most egregious cases also reflect a spirit of impunity beyond Saudi Arabia's borders that challenges both core U.S. values and the health of the international system.

These interests and values matter to the United States, both those that Saudi Arabia has helped advance and those its choices have undermined. The challenge for the next U.S. administration will be to enhance American leverage, reassert American expectations for Saudi behavior, and restore a sense of proportion in a bilateral relationship that has been badly damaged by the Trump White House's "blank check."[14] It should aim to foster constructive Saudi behavior, disentangle the United States from dangerous Saudi-led regional adventures, reinsert U.S. values into the dialogue, and build on regionally driven efforts to engage in meaningful dialogue and de-escalation with Iran.

In short, the next administration should present a clear choice to Saudi leaders: the close ties with the United States that you seek will only be possible if you chart a more responsible path forward.[15] It will take careful and deliberate diplomacy to rebalance relations while avoiding a damaging rupture with Saudi leadership that has grown accustomed to President Trump's unbridled rhetorical support and defense from criticism—and cultivated a defiantly nationalistic response to even mild criticism from U.S. allies such as Canada and Germany.[16]

For the United States, outright abandonment of Saudi Arabia would carry significant risks and costs. Seeking relations with other great powers already appears to be a Saudi strategy regardless of the warmth of U.S.-Saudi relations. However, as its recent behavior indicates, if it felt it had little to lose in relations with Washington, Saudi Arabia might well hedge aggressively against American desertion in destabilizing ways—including by pursuing a nuclear deterrent. Hastily unraveling long-standing security arrangements could only increase the risk of conflict. Such steps would likely prove more damaging to Saudi Arabia's own interests than to the United States, a fact that U.S. policymakers should bear in mind. However, that offers no guarantee against aggressive reactions to perceived U.S. betrayal, particularly given bin Salman's well-documented penchant for precipitous action.

An unconditional embrace of Saudi Arabia carries costs as well. As the Trump administration has shown, it enables destructive behavior that deepens regional divides and implicates the United States in policies it would not choose itself. It could even negatively affect the kingdom's own stability. Treating recent excesses as the acceptable cost of reforming Saudi Arabia's hidebound sociopolitical system ignores the risk they also pose to that very cause.

While they increasingly have concerns, complaints, and disenchantments, ranging from Trump's transactional approach to his unsteady investment in their security to worries about losing the rest of Washington, Saudi leaders by and large prefer the Trump administration's approach, as it makes Saudi Arabia a focal point of U.S. regional policy without requiring restraint at home or abroad in return.[17] However, just as the desire to repair relations post-Obama created leverage for Trump—leverage he has misused—so, too, will the desire to preserve close ties create leverage for the next U.S. administration.

From Mutual Disappointment to Blank Check

The terrorist attacks of 9/11, carried out by a terrorist organization led by a Saudi and involving fifteen Saudi hijackers, ushered in a new phase in relations. Alongside the Cold War hallmarks of arms sales, oil exports, and protection from external aggression came the need to cooperate on counterterrorism—and an increasing sense of frustration on both sides. While Saudi rulers came to embrace the fight against al Qaeda once it threatened the kingdom in 2003, Riyadh has yet to shake the widespread U.S. perception that its ultraconservative interpretations of Islam helped lay the ideological groundwork for groups like al Qaeda and ISIS. Still, beginning in 2003, despite some U.S. frustrations regarding Saudi methods, its propagation of Wahhabi ideology, nongovernmental financing, and support for Salafist proxies, U.S.-Saudi cooperation on counterterrorism has been deep, sustained, wide ranging, high level, and significant.[18]

At the same time, Saudi rulers grew increasingly frustrated with America's Middle East policies. Saudi leaders correctly warned President George W. Bush that invading Iraq would empower Iran.[19] They felt his administration ignored the Saudi-authored Arab Peace Initiative, which offered normalized relations with Israel in exchange for a two-state solution, and the Second Intifada nearly led to a rupture in U.S.-Saudi relations.[20, 21] Furthermore, the Saudis objected to the demands of Bush's "Freedom Agenda" for reforms within Saudi Arabia.[22]

The sense of strategic divergence only increased during the Obama administration. Though the Obama administration sought to rectify past mistakes by engaging with King Abdullah's 2002 Arab-Israeli regional peace plan and leaving Iraq, reality intervened in the form of uprisings against the region's authoritarian order and an opportunity for a diplomatic breakthrough with Iran. From 2011 on, Saudi leaders became alienated from an Obama administration that simply had other priorities. Along with other regional leaders, they complained that the policy approach Obama adopted underappreciated America's role in forming and sustaining the Middle Eastern order it came to critique.[23]

First, Riyadh felt betrayed by Washington's cautiously hopeful response to revolutions in Egypt and elsewhere, believing that—when push came to shove—the United States would set aside its calls for reform to actively defend its autocratic partners from domestic challengers. Next came the declared "pivot" or "rebalance" of American resources and attention away from long, costly post-9/11 wars and toward the Asia-Pacific region—which played into long-standing Saudi fears of U.S. abandonment.[24] That was followed by President Obama's decision not to launch military strikes to enforce a U.S. "redline" in Syria, which prompted Saudis to call U.S. credibility into question.[25] Perhaps most contentious of all was Iran. Saudi and other Arab leaders claimed for years that Iran controlled four Arab capitals—Beirut, Damascus, Baghdad, and eventually Sanaa—and needed more aggressive U.S. pushback against Iran's regional ambitions, something they felt never came.[26] Instead, the Saudis' bitter disappointment was cemented when the United States embarked upon secret diplomacy that led to the nuclear agreement with Iran. Even though the Obama administration sought to mollify Saudi criticisms through high-level dialogues, action plans, and record arms sales, the damage was done—and the feeling was mutual. In April 2016, President Obama called Saudi Arabia a "so-called ally" that would eventually have to find a way to "share the neighborhood" in a "cold peace" with Iran.[27] That notion, whatever its merits, remains anathema to Saudi leaders, who pointedly slighted Obama on his visit to Saudi Arabia.[28] These years revealed important policy differences over supporting the region's authoritarians and over the wisdom of military intervention in Syria and Iran. While the Obama administration prized restraint, the Saudi regime came to see itself in existential battle with Iran and increasingly with its small, Islamist-friendly neighbor Qatar as well.[29]

Upon taking office, President Trump saw an opportunity to differentiate himself from his predecessor and seized it wholeheartedly. Where Obama sought at times to bridge regional divides—between Saudi Arabia and Iran, secular autocrats and Islamists, regimes and citizens—the Trump White House has emphatically taken sides. Trump made Riyadh the destination of his first overseas trip—famously photographed alongside the Saudi monarch caressing a glowing orb—and offered initial public defenses of several of the most controversial Saudi actions, including the Qatar blockade, Khashoggi killing, and domestic purges. Trump's approach seems to rest on an assumption that, if given unconditional support, Saudi Arabia can make a decisive difference in advancing core U.S. regional ambitions related to Iran and Israeli-Palestinian peace, as well as domestic job creation in America—and perhaps even provide Washington an eventual ticket out of its intense regional entanglements.

In the meantime, the Trump administration's "maximum pressure" campaign against Iran has spiked tensions across the region, including numerous maritime attacks that the United States has attributed to Iran and an escalation in missile attacks into Saudi Arabia that culminated in the September 14, 2019, attacks on Saudi oil facilities in Abqaiq and Khurais that have been widely attributed to Iran. The U.S. response has been a mix of new military commitments and questioning of older ones: on the one hand, the United States has deployed about three thousand additional troops, B-1 bombers, missile defenses, and other advanced hardware, representing the first time since 2003 that Saudi Arabia has hosted U.S. troops—a shift particularly notable because al Qaeda founder Osama bin Laden used the previous U.S. military presence as a justification for jihad.[30] On the other hand, President Trump did not retaliate kinetically against Iran after the oil refinery attacks, declaring instead that it "was an attack on Saudi Arabia, and that wasn't an attack on us."[31] It was his sharpest statement yet as to the limits of the U.S. willingness to defend Saudi territory even as the maximum pressure campaign pushed Iran, Saudi Arabia, and the region to the brink of war. Moreover, President Trump warned that countries should be "protecting their own ships" in the Strait of Hormuz, where a predominant U.S. security presence protecting shipping lanes has been a cornerstone of U.S. regional policy.[32]

Post-Abqaiq, as the limits of what Trump would do to defend Saudi Arabia from the Iranian blowback to the U.S.-led maximum pressure campaign became clear, Saudi Arabia's leaders appeared to have realized that they were overextended and dangerously exposed.[33] Saudi as well as Emirati leaders undertook a series of regional initiatives to lower tensions. This included significant diplomatic engagement to resolve political disputes in southern Yemen, dialogue with the Houthis, and high-level meetings with Qatari officials in search of an end to the Gulf Cooperation Council (GCC) dispute, as well as reported back-channel dialogue to de-escalate with Iran. It remains to be seen whether these diplomatic efforts will bear fruit and how they will evolve now that the United States has demonstrated its willingness to use force in the killing of Iranian Commander Qassem Soleimani, but they have promise worth exploring.

Overall, despite its unevenness, Trump's approach has earned significant Saudi goodwill, including the creation of a close bilateral channel with the president's son-in-law, Jared Kushner, an endorsement of Trump by bin Salman as "the right person at the right time," and a degree of deference to the administration's top priorities.[34] Saudi Arabia remained quiet as Trump discriminated against Muslims through his travel ban and announced abrupt troop withdrawals from Syria. Even moving the U.S. embassy to Jerusalem was met with an initially muted Saudi response before King Salman—rather than the crown prince—made a pointed statement of opposition at an Arab League summit.[35] Jared Kushner's Mideast peace plan, unveiled in January 2020, was likewise met with a respectful initial Saudi response, though Saudi leaders also joined an Arab League ministerial statement condemning the plan. There is reason to doubt that Riyadh is ready to put its diplomatic weight behind Trump's Mideast peace plan—or, absent progress or in the face of possible Israeli annexation, take dramatic steps in the near term to normalize relations with Israel.

Another notable development in the relationship has been the growing anti-Saudi sentiment on a bipartisan basis among foreign policy experts in Washington and especially in Congress, where few members on either side will publicly defend the U.S. relationship with Saudi Arabia. Such sentiment did not begin with Trump or bin Salman—or even 9/11—although each added fuel to the fire. Indeed, at the end of the Obama administration, Congress overrode a presidential veto to pass a law that limited Saudi Arabia's sovereign immunity from the families of 9/11 victims. On Yemen, President Trump was forced to veto a bill that would have ended all U.S. support to the Saudi-led coalition. Congress also continues to demand a full investigation of the Khashoggi killing, and several of the most prominent foreign policy voices in the Senate from both parties have strongly condemned the crown prince's reported role. While Congress has intermittently opposed Saudi actions, legislators' focus on a single Saudi leader is new. As of early 2020, a raft of legislative proposals with bipartisan support from senior senators have sought to rein in U.S.-Saudi cooperation on issues ranging from the war in Yemen to arms sales to nuclear cooperation to post-Khashoggi investigations and sanctions.[36] While congressional assertiveness is, in part, a rebuke of President Trump's obsequious approach that might wane amid political polarization if a future president takes a firmer tone with Saudi Arabia, this bipartisan trend will probably outlast Trump.

Critics of the Trump approach make five core arguments, each of which has its merits. First, they argue, it unduly cedes U.S. diplomatic leverage in the mistaken belief that America is economically and strategically beholden to Saudi Arabia. Second, critics argue, the relationship often papers over important divergences in interests. Saudi leaders have sought to enlist American support for an open-ended, zero-sum conflict for regional dominance with Iran's regime, only belatedly reckoning with the risks this entails for their own territory given America's limited willingness to go to war to defend them. Saudi Arabia has also sought to draw the United States into its scorched-earth campaign against Qatar and regional groups that do not threaten America and are, in some cases, actually important if checkered U.S. partners. And Saudi Arabia has actively opposed democratic transitions in the region that the United States has sought to support. Third, it remains unclear whether Saudi Arabia will prove able or even willing to deliver on the Trump administration's grand expectations—in pressuring Palestinians to accept Trump's Israeli-Palestinian peace plan and in normalizing relations with Israel; in countering Iran's regional influence; or in making meaningful investments in the U.S. economy. U.S. arms sales, while significant within the defense sector, put Saudi Arabia roughly on par with Switzerland as a U.S. trading partner—and beneath all the hype, there have been few new deals signed.[37] Fourth, detractors argue, unconditional U.S. support creates a moral hazard for Riyadh and implicates the United States in Saudi policies. A fifth critique focuses on Trump's reliance on bin Salman as the seeming linchpin of his Middle East policy—especially in the wake of Khashoggi's murder, critics complain that this relationship is opaque and overly personalized in the hands of Trump, Kushner, and bin Salman.

Supporters of close bilateral relations make several valid points as well. They note that bin Salman could be king for decades and argue that building trust between presidents and kings may matter more than individual policies. They point to Saudi investments, past and future, in U.S. weaponry, business, governmental, and academic ties. Moreover, they note several groundbreaking domestic steps Saudi Arabia has recently taken, steps that outsiders have wanted to see for decades.[38] Attempts to replace Wahhabism with youth-focused nationalism as the legitimizing ideology of the Saudi state appear to be serious and could pay dividends in countering jihadist recruitment. Cooperation and conciliatory rhetoric toward Israel hold the promise of advancing the long-term U.S. aim of bringing its Israeli and Arab partners together despite unfulfilled Palestinian aspirations and rights. Some point to Saudi Arabia's important strategic role supplying oil to East Asia and particularly to America's energy-hungry great power competitor, China. Finally, those opposed to a tougher line point to the difficulty, as demonstrated under the Obama administration, of dissuading Saudi Arabia from policies it considers important to its own security without alienating its rulers.[39]

Recommendations

Taken together, these factors argue for a course correction in the U.S. approach—one that takes seriously opponents' profound and well-founded critiques as well as pragmatic counterarguments. Such an approach would encourage more responsible choices going forward—while continuously testing underlying assumptions and being ready to reevaluate the strategy as new dynamics develop. It would seek to responsibly manage a recalibration of the relationship, making necessary changes to the terms and process of cooperation while seeking to preserve what is valuable and avoid an outright rupture or crisis. The goal would be a more faithful articulation of U.S. interests and values and a renewed effort to shape Saudi choices as both countries' Middle East policies shift.

Reset the terms of cooperation—including a six-month strategic review. The next U.S. president could benefit from Saudi worries about fundamental changes in relations. The right approach is to offer Riyadh a choice: Saudi Arabia can demonstrate its desire to work closely with the United States to craft a more consultative and less confrontational regional policy on issues ranging from its simmering feud with Qatar to its extraterritorial campaigns against dissidents. Or it can expect to see strategic cooperation with Washington grow increasingly limited as cooperation with other nations takes precedence. Under this model, step by step, greater Saudi responsibility begets greater American reassurance. Amid cabinet-level engagement, a leader-level bilateral meeting would likely await significant Saudi progress on confidence-building U.S. priorities. Saudi Arabia may be tempted to forestall this choice. In setting expectations, it will also be crucial—even before a new president takes office—for leaders in Congress and elsewhere to signal on a bipartisan basis draconian costs for any Saudi attempts to interfere in U.S. domestic elections regardless of the outcome.

It is unlikely that the next U.S. administration will define its in-

terests on issues from Iran to human rights in terms quite so close to
Saudi priorities. Such disagreements—and a U.S. refusal to support
certain Saudi initiatives—should be expected in Washington and
Riyadh. To that end, leaders on both sides should commit to a policy
of "no surprises." Saudi leaders were stung by secret negotiations
with Iran. American leaders have reportedly been caught off guard
by Saudi moves, such as the blockade of Qatar. A better approach for
both sides would be to establish an expectation that—while the two
may disagree—they should consult beforehand before taking important or disruptive policy moves.

Certain aspects of the relationship deserve a close reexamination
to reflect Saudi Arabia's more assertive posture. The next administration, working with Congress, should institute a six-month strategic review of various aspects of U.S.-Saudi cooperation. Among the
areas warranting a closer look are arms sales—with a special focus
on foreign military sales and direct commercial sales of potentially
destabilizing offensive weaponry in light of Saudi Arabia's more assertive regional approach; nuclear cooperation; and reforms to govern
the actions of U.S. private intelligence firms that have contributed to
human rights abuses and repression in Riyadh and elsewhere.

As policies diverge on Iran, offer reassurance and consultation. A
policy of "no surprises" means close consultation on the strategy to
confront both Iran's nuclear ambitions and its destabilizing regional
policies. As the United States seeks to establish deterrence and pursue
diplomacy with Iran, close, transparent consultation with regional
partners will be vital. If the next U.S. administration seeks to reenter
or update a nuclear agreement with Iran and the international community, it may also wish to create parallel forums for regional dialogue on key issues, supported by the P5+1 countries (China, France,
Russia, the United Kingdom, and the United States, plus Germany)
that negotiated the 2015 nuclear deal. In returning to a nuclear agreement or undoing other Trump-era policies that Saudi Arabia supports, the United States should make clear that such actions do not
detract from its continued commitment to push back against Iranian
bad behavior—with an emphasis on the kinds of reassurances that
focus on defensive military capabilities, from maritime interdiction

to missile defenses to helping shore up the defense of Saudi critical infrastructure from digital and kinetic threats.

Over time, the United States should seek opportunities to bring Riyadh into dialogue with both Iran and Qatar to lower tensions with Saudi regional rivals. The United States should strongly encourage recent Saudi outreach to Iran, the Houthis, and Qatar to continue. International talks with Iran over nuclear issues may provide a multilateral forum to address some Saudi-Iranian issues. However, flexible formats and groupings—rather than a major new regional institution or dialogue—are most likely to succeed. It could turn out that U.S. facilitation of Saudi talks with Iran raises too many hackles among Saudis wary of abandonment. Another third-party mediator or even direct talks with strong, outside U.S. support could well prove more fertile ground for Saudi-Iranian progress. De-escalatory talks could aim for mutual reassurances to respect each other's sovereignty and cease supporting groups devoted to the overthrow of each other's governments. Over time talks could include maritime crisis prevention and dispute resolution or even missiles, Saudi engagement with the Iran-backed regime in Damascus, or—as the United States separately presses Saudi Arabia and Yemeni parties to end the war— the diminishing of Iran's footprint in Yemen. For the United States, form should matter less than substance.

Ultimately, of course, Washington cannot force adversaries in Tehran or partners in Saudi Arabia to "share the region" when regional leaders see matters so differently and do not respect their neighbors' sovereignty. Nor can Washington dictate an end to rifts between Saudi Arabia and Qatar that have hardened and become personal. Still, it is in the interest of the United States to make it a priority to cultivate and facilitate rapprochement. What the next administration can do is make clear its desire to avoid unneeded escalation, to create opportunities, incentives, and structures for dialogue, and to press all sides to build areas of cooperation.

End U.S. support for the war in Yemen and recommit to help Saudi Arabia defend its territory. The war in Yemen, whatever its original justifications, has created a humanitarian catastrophe and strengthened the U.S. and Saudi Arabia's mutual adversaries. An incoming

administration should encourage Saudi Arabia to deliver a nation-
wide ceasefire with the Houthis as an early sign of progress to uphold.
And the United States should simultaneously prepare its own plans to
end its military support for the Yemen conflict, as explored in detail
by Christopher Le Mon in chapter 3. But the main goal should be to
end the war on the ground, not merely U.S. support. U.S. pullback
could cause both sides to dig in. The United States will need to push
all stakeholders, including Saudi Arabia and its Yemeni partners, to
accept UN peacemaking efforts and make meaningful concessions,
find avenues to pressure the Houthis to do the same, and work with
the international community on humanitarian aid and postconflict
stabilization. An approach that seeks not only to end U.S. support
for the war in Yemen but also the war itself is likely to require deeper
U.S. investments in humanitarian aid, conflict resolution, and certain
defensive capabilities for Saudi Arabia.

Because the goal is to reset and not to rupture U.S.-Saudi relations, U.S. diplomatic efforts to end the Yemen conflict should be
accompanied by renewed public and private assertions of the U.S.
commitment to help Saudi Arabia defend its own territory. Saudi
Arabia faces legitimate security threats from Houthi-held territory
and from Iran, as well as severe limitations in its ability to defend
itself by itself. As part of disengaging from the Yemen military campaign, the United States should sustain and redouble current efforts
to help harden Saudi defenses against Houthi aggression—including
rocket and missile defenses, help countering Houthi unmanned aerial
vehicles (UAVs), and undertake more aggressive maritime patrols and
interdictions of Iranian-supplied weapons to Houthis. As part of a
ceasefire in Yemen, it should also make clear Saudi Arabia's right to
respond to UAV attacks and missile launches into its territory. These
efforts should, moreover, draw a sharp distinction between the war
against the Houthis and efforts to fight al Qaeda and ISIS in Yemen,
which should continue.

**Maintain cooperation in areas of mutual interest and seek opportu-
nities to expand ties.** The United States should continue to maintain
close cooperation with Saudi security and intelligence agencies regarding common threats from al Qaeda and ISIS. U.S. counterter-

rorism cooperation should also try to capitalize on the opportunity presented by bin Salman's frank criticisms of how Saudi Arabia has influenced Islam beyond its borders to address drivers of radicalization. Where Saudi Arabia makes credible efforts to counter extremist ideology—including recent remarkable statements on the Holocaust by Muslim World League Secretary General Mohammed al Issa—the United States should encourage and recognize these positive moves. While it has launched reforms regarding foreign investment, privatized a small share of Saudi Aramco, and implemented several meaningful societal changes that help connect Saudi Arabia with the outside world, bin Salman's broader economic modernization program has been slow out of the gate as measured against its ambitions to remake the Saudi economy. However, it remains in the interest of the United States to help Riyadh meet its professed goal to open up and diversify its economy beyond oil. The country's young population is hungry for greater contact with the outside world, from education to entertainment—creating numerous opportunities to broaden ties beyond oil, arms sales, and counterterrorism.

Another area of importance is regional cooperation. Saudi economic statecraft has become an important economic fiscal backstop for several countries in the Middle East, and far beyond. So long as it remains engaged across the region, the United States will need to continue working with the Saudis as they invest in reconstruction and humanitarian aid in Yemen, support for Syrian refugees, and other shared regional priorities such as the fiscal survival of the Palestinian Authority and Jordan. One particular area of interest—and a potential policy success for the Trump administration—has been Saudi Arabia's intensified engagement with Iraq. At America's urging, Saudi Arabia deepened its ties to Iraqis, reaching beyond traditional Sunni and Kurdish partners to mend relations with a wide spectrum of Shia partners, who in turn expressed hope that such ties could lessen Iraq's dependence on Iran.[40] While the killing of Qassem Soleimani and a nonbinding vote in Iraq's parliament have raised questions about America's own relationship with Iraq, it is in the interest of the United States to see this fragile Saudi-Iraqi rapprochement develop. Another issue with regional implications worth watching closely is Riyadh's declared ambition to begin domestic enrichment of uranium, which the United States should cooperate with other major nuclear suppliers to forestall should Saudi plans to build nuclear reactors advance with international assistance. The United States and Saudi Arabia will bring different interests and priorities to many regional issues, from political transitions in Sudan to repression in Bahrain to relations with Syrian president Bashar al Assad. Open channels for constructive cooperation, quiet pressure, and occasional forthright disapproval will be needed.[41]

Broaden and institutionalize ties. The mode of U.S.-Saudi cooperation should change as well. The next administration should appoint a trusted, empowered U.S. ambassador in Riyadh early on to manage ties. As long as bin Salman remains the preeminent Saudi decision-maker, it will be important to have open channels of direct communication with him and his closest intermediaries. Despite serious concerns, U.S. efforts to dictate who rules Saudi Arabia are unwise and unlikely to end well. Nevertheless, the United States should demand a full accounting of the death of Jamal Khashoggi from the Saudi government, which will forestall an early visit to America to meet the potential incoming U.S. president, as well as a categorical commitment from Saudi Arabia to cease extraterritorial assaults and intimidation of dissidents and other critics, especially, but not exclusively, Americans and those with U.S. ties. The next administration should make clear to Saudi Arabia the damage that the Khashoggi killing has done and—unambiguously, at the highest levels of U.S. political, military, and intelligence leadership—that future similar behavior would be catastrophic and quite possibly fatal for Saudi relations with the U.S. administration and Congress. The dilemma posed by the Khashoggi case only underscores the need for a broader and more institutionalized set of ties between the two countries— that, for example, involves Congress—instead of the opaque contacts between ruling families that exist today.

Reintegrate human rights. America's partnership with Saudi Arabia has never been based on shared democratic values or human rights. But Saudi Arabia's resurgent repression—its campaigns against women's rights activists and overseas dissidents, including Khashoggi—

has raised the costs for U.S. values and interests, especially globally. Saudi Arabia's domestic human rights practices, its brazen and brutal killing of an American resident in Turkey, and other practices have weakened its standing with the U.S. Congress. Past U.S. administrations have raised these issues both privately and publicly with Saudi counterparts, making it clear where America stands. The opposite appears to have unfolded under President Trump, who has defended, outright endorsed, or rationalized away Saudi Arabia's crackdowns. Instead, the next U.S. administration should bring such concerns directly to Saudi leadership and work pragmatically with Congress to apply pressure and uphold U.S. values without rupturing ties.

Under bin Salman, Saudi Arabia is attempting authoritarian economic modernization—opening elements of its society and economy but further closing its political space. Such an approach risks falling prey to its own internal contradictions. The roundup, arrest, and reported abuse of hundreds of prominent Saudis led to a precipitous decline in the foreign direct investment (from US$7.4 billion in 2016 to US$1.4 billion in 2017) needed to finance planned economic reforms.[42] U.S. leaders should make clear that progress on human rights goals—such as the release of jailed women's rights activists and other nonviolent dissidents, especially dual nationals—will not only instill greater confidence in Washington but could also lead to greater international confidence in Saudi Arabia's economic transition. The next administration will need to reestablish the expectation that such issues will be part of the dialogue with the United States going forward, as they are with other countries.

Ideally, the next administration will be able to manage the recalibration of the U.S.-Saudi relationship in a gradual, consultative fashion that minimizes disruptions to mutually beneficial bilateral cooperation. Striking the right balance will require weathering diplomatic pressure and Saudi hedging beyond what is already happening. The next administration will need to implicitly convey its resolve not to be bullied into the old status quo, distinguish posturing from genuinely worrisome steps, and listen carefully for both opportunities for affirmative cooperation and risks of rupture. Saudi Arabia will have its own choices to make and its own nationalist constituency to satisfy. If Saudi Arabia pursues a more conciliatory course,

America should be ready to recognize, assist, and applaud meaningful steps forward. If destabilizing moves, from the Qatar blockade to the Khashoggi murder to demands for domestic enrichment, prove to be a sign of even more aggressive policies on the horizon, then an even deeper rethinking will be required.

The Road Ahead

In the years to come, the U.S.-Saudi relationship will undoubtedly be buffeted by changes in both countries and the region as a whole. Between Presidents George W. Bush and Donald Trump, relations have oscillated from mutual frustration to moral hazard and back again. The next U.S. administration should instead seek a balanced approach—one that creates incentives for constructive Saudi behavior, but also accounts for the fact that the country's internal dynamics and new leadership may push it in a different direction. An initial reset, grounded in clear communication and realistic expectations on both sides, could create more durable terms for cooperation and help to manage the disagreements that will inevitably arise.

Riyadh and its young nationalists will chafe at some of these changes. Some U.S. activists and lawmakers who have condemned the U.S.-Saudi relationship will demand more dramatic disentanglement. Ultimately, even in a more balanced relationship that better reflects U.S. interests and leverage, for all of the disappointments and inconsistencies of America's approach, what is on offer from the United States remains of higher value to Saudi Arabia than what Russia, China, or any other U.S. competitor can match anytime soon: a measure of protection from external aggression, partnership with and deployments from the world's most capable military, and world-class expertise from oil to banking to universities that educate young Saudis.

None of the above is a recipe for bliss in U.S.-Saudi relations. These recommendations constitute a necessary course correction for a relationship—and U.S. regional policies—that have been thrown out of balance.

Notes

1. John Halpin and others, "America Adrift: How the U.S. Foreign Policy Debate Misses What Voters Really Want," *Foreign Policy and Security* (blog), Center for American Progress, May 5, 2019.

2. Mara Karlin and Tamara Cofman Wittes, "America's Middle East Purgatory: The Case for Doing Less," *Foreign Affairs*, December 11, 2018.

3. Colby Itkowitz and Karoun Demirjian, "Senators Introduce Bipartisan Measure to Punish Saudis for Khashoggi Murder," *Washington Post*, July 31, 2019.

4. F. Gregory Gause III, "Is the Saudi Crown Prince Too Disruptive Even for Trump?" *New York Times*, October 12, 2018.

5. Meghan L. O'Sullivan, "U.S. Is Forced to See It Is Far from 'Energy Independent,'" Bloomberg, October 19, 2018.

6. "Arab Quartet Meets in Riyadh to Discuss Regional Developments," *The National*, July 23, 2018.

7. Khalid Abdelaziz, "Saudi Arabia, UAE to Send US$3 Billion in Aid to Sudan," Reuters, April 21, 2019.

8. Susan E. Rice, "A Partner We Can't Depend On," *New York Times*, October 29, 2018.

9. Eric Schmitt, "Senator Puts Hold on Arms Sales to Persian Gulf Nations Over Qatar Feud," *New York Times,* June 26, 2017.

10. "Humanitarian Crisis in Yemen Remains the Worst in the World, Warns U.N.," *U.N. News*, February 14, 2019 (https://news.un.org/en/story /2019/02/1032811).

11. Toby Matthiesen, "A Purge in Riyadh: What Mohammed bin Salman's Crackdown Means for Saudi Arabia and the Middle East," *Foreign Affairs*, November 8, 2017.

12. Mark Mazzetti and Ben Hubbard, "It Wasn't Just Khashoggi: A Saudi Prince's Brutal Drive to Crush Dissent," *New York Times*, March 17, 2019.

13. Rory Jones, Margherita Stancati, and Summer Said, "Saudi Arabia to Spend Billions to Revive Foreign Investment," *Wall Street Journal*, July 22, 2018.

14. Daniel Benaim and Brian Katulis, "Trump's Blank Check for Saudi Arabia," *New Republic*, November 8, 2017.

15. Derek Chollet and Ilan Goldenberg, "The United States Should Give Saudi Arabia a Choice," *Foreign Policy*, November 30, 2018.

16. Eman Alhussein, "Saudi First: How Hyper-Nationalism Is Transforming Saudi Arabia," European Council on Foreign Relations, June 19, 2019 (www. ecfr.eu/publications/summary/saudi_first_how_hyper_nationalism_is_ transforming_saudi_arabia).

17. Interviews with Saudi policymakers, Riyadh, November 2019.

18. Daniel L. Byman, "The U.S.-Saudi Arabia Counterterrorism Relationship," Brookings, March 24, 2016 (www.brookings.edu/testimonies/the-u-s-saudi-arabia-counterterrorism-relationship/).

19. Helene Cooper and Jim Rutenberg, "A Saudi Prince Tied to Bush Is Sounding Off-Key," *New York Times*, April 29, 2017.

20. Marwan Muasher, "The Death of the Arab Peace Initiative?" *The Atlantic*, November 23, 2011.

21. Bruce Riedel, "Why We Have to Get on with the Saudis," *Newsweek*, April 12, 2016.

22. "Freedom Agenda," White House: President George W. Bush, n.d. (https://georgewbush-whitehouse.archives.gov/infocus/freedomagenda/).

23. On background interview with senior UAE diplomatic official, May 2018.

24. Hillary Clinton, "America's Pacific Century," *Foreign Policy*, October 11, 2011.

25. Steven Erlanger, "Saudi Prince Criticizes Obama Administration, Citing Indecision in Mideast," *New York Times*, December 15, 2013.

26. Ian Black, "Iran's Advances Create Alarm in Saudi Arabia and the Gulf," *Guardian*, March 13, 2015.

27. Jeffrey Goldberg, "The Obama Doctrine," *The Atlantic*, April 2016.

28. Ian Black, "Obama's Chilly Reception in Saudi Arabia Hints at Mutual Distrust," *Guardian*, April 20, 2016.

29. Jeffrey Goldberg, "Saudi Crown Prince: Iran's Supreme Leader Makes 'Hitler Look Good,' " *The Atlantic*, April 2, 2018.

30. Ahmed Al Omran, "Saudi Welcome for U.S. Troops Reflects Relations with Mohammed bin Salman," *Financial Times*, July 23, 2019.

31. Steve Holland and Rania El-Gamal, "Trump Says He Does Not Want War after Attack on Saudi Oil Facilities," Reuters, September 16, 2019.

32. Vivian Salama, "Trump Calls on Countries to Protect Own Ships in the Strait of Hormuz," *Wall Street Journal*, June 24, 2019.

33. Benoit Facon, Summer Said, and Warren P. Strobel, "Saudi Arabia Seeks to Ease Tensions with Iran," *Wall Street Journal*, December 12, 2019.

34. Callum Paton, "Saudi Prince Mohammed bin Salman Says Iran Leader Is Like Hitler But Trump Is Right Man for the Job," *Newsweek*, November 24, 2017.

35. Aya Batrawy, "Arab Leaders Meet to Unify Ranks with Eye on Iran, Jerusalem," Associated Press, April 16, 2018.

36. Patricia Zengerle, "U.S. Lawmakers Still Plot to Push Saudi Arabia on Rights, despite Trump," Reuters, August 1, 2019.

37. U.S. Census Bureau, "Foreign Trade," as seen on August 4, 2019 (www.census.gov/foreign-trade/statistics/highlights/top/index.html).

38. Philip Gordon, "To Help Saudi Arabia, Trump Must Offer More than Mere Applause," *Financial Times,* November 14, 2017.

39. Michael Doran and Tony Badran, "Trump Is Crude, But He's Right About Saudi Arabia," *New York Times,* November 21, 2018.

40. Daniel Benaim, "The Next Phase in Iraq's Transition," *Foreign Policy and Security* (blog), Center for American Progress, July 2, 2018 (www.amer icanprogress.org/issues/security/reports/2018/07/02/453034/next-phase-iraqs-transition/).

41. Robbie Gramer, "U.S. Senate Targets Saudi Nuclear Technology," *Foreign Policy*, July 30, 2019.

42. Jones, Stancati, and Said, "Saudi Arabia to Spend Billions."

PART III

Regional Challenges for the United States

NINE

A New Cold War in the Middle East?

ALEXANDER BICK

A decade ago, when former Russian prime minister Yevgeny Prima-kov wrote that "Moscow is very much focused on taking a more active part in resolving Middle East issues," few policymakers in the United States took note.[1] Today, his vision has largely been realized: not only in Syria, but across the region, Russia has reemerged as an important player, building new relationships and competing for influence. This has led some to ask whether we are entering—or have already entered—a "new Cold War" in the Middle East.[2] While the analogy is tempting, it is a poor guide for U.S. policy. There is a greater risk that we will trap ourselves in an unnecessary and costly bidding war with Russia for the fealty of regional states than that Russia will displace the United States in the region. Instead of trying to compete with Russia across the board, the next administration should adopt a policy of "bounded competition," in which the United States vigorously competes with Russia in areas that implicate core U.S. interests, while exercising restraint elsewhere and testing cooperation in areas where U.S. and Russian objectives significantly overlap. Such an approach would help to bring U.S. investment in the Middle East in line with our global priorities without jeopardizing U.S. goals in the region.

Russia Is Back

It is too early to judge with certainty whether President Obama was right or wrong when he predicted in October 2015 that Russia would find itself in a "quagmire" in Syria.[3] But one thing is clear: by inserting itself at the center of a regional vortex, and by adeptly engaging actors on all sides of the war, Russia has leveraged its military intervention to enhance its influence and prestige throughout the Middle East. For the first time in a generation, Moscow has become a key destination for regional heads of state, including those of some of the closest U.S. partners.[4] Russia has deepened cooperation with Iran, its main partner in Syria, while simultaneously forging closer ties to Israel and Turkey. The arrival of Russian mercenaries in Libya has given Moscow leverage in diplomatic negotiations over that country's future. And renewed contacts across the region have facilitated a flurry of deal-making, including new weapons contracts in Egypt, Iraq, and Turkey, as well as significant investments in Russia by Qatar and Saudi Arabia.

Russia's return to the Middle East is, of course, only one facet of its larger resurgence after the collapse of the Soviet Union, and of the transition from an era of U.S. global primacy to one of renewed great power competition. While the Trump administration's 2018 National Defense Strategy articulated this shift with admirable clarity, precisely what it means to compete with Russia (or China) in specific regions is still very much up for debate.[5]

The Cold War offers the most convenient template. But is it the right one? In multiple respects, the differences would appear to outweigh the similarities: the original Cold War was defined by competition within a bipolar system in which there was at least rough parity between the United States and Russia. Today, by contrast, the world looks increasingly multipolar, Russia's economy is less than a tenth the size of that of the United States, and the ideological struggle between capitalism and communism is dead, even in Russia itself.[6] In the Middle East, Russia's objectives are, in key respects, diametrically opposed to those pursued by the Soviet Union: notably, Russia no longer seeks to promote revolutionary change or to bring regional states into a bloc that is exclusively aligned with Moscow.[7] And whereas Cold War competition was typically viewed in zero-sum terms, the United States and Russia, until quite recently, cooperated on key regional initiatives, including the P5+1 process on Iran's nuclear program.

A further difference from the Cold War is presented by the sharp contrast between Russia's desire to deepen its involvement in the Middle East and the imperative for the United States to correct nearly two decades of relative overinvestment in the region in order to free up resources to address other global challenges—especially the rise of China. For Moscow, a reduced U.S. role in the Middle East presents an opportunity both to restore Russia's great power status and to thwart international efforts to isolate Russia over its actions in Ukraine, Europe, and the United States. While our deep relationships with leading Middle Eastern states and our robust military presence make it possible to aggressively push back on Russian designs, the reflexive desire to do so must be weighed against the cost to other global priorities.

In this sense, the fundamental challenge is not determining how to prevent Russian penetration in the Middle East, but rather crafting an approach that right-sizes the U.S. regional posture while still countering Russian actions that threaten core U.S. interests—including preventing terrorist attacks; stopping the spread of nuclear, biological, or chemical weapons; ensuring energy market stability; and promoting governance reform and human rights.

Historical Background

Russia has been involved in the Middle East for centuries, but its motivations, partners, and the scale of its investment in the region have changed markedly over time. Prior to the conclusion of World War II, Russian (and then Soviet) involvement focused primarily on securing access to the Mediterranean Sea, via Turkey, and extending Russian influence in Turkey, Iran, and Afghanistan, the states along its southern border. With the exception of educational and cultural links to the Holy Land, which stemmed from Russia's official status as protector of the Orthodox Christians within the Ottoman Empire, Russia had few ties to the broader Arab Middle East.[8]

The Cold War radically changed this. After Joseph Stalin successively alienated the leaderships of Iran, Turkey, and Israel, the Soviet Union finally found a willing partner in Gamal Abdel Nasser, the charismatic Arab nationalist who overthrew Egypt's pro-Western monarchy in 1952. Over the next two decades, Egypt emerged as the center of Russian influence in the region. The country hosted 15,000 to 20,000 Soviet troops and quickly became the Third World's largest recipient of Soviet military aid.[9] Building on this foundation, the Soviet Union forged closer ties with the leadership of other nationalist, leftist, or anti-Western states, including Algeria, Iraq, Libya, South Yemen, and Syria, as well as the Palestine Liberation Organization (PLO).

During the Cold War, the U.S. presence in the Middle East also grew, largely with the goal of preventing further Soviet penetration. The United States facilitated Turkey's admission into NATO in 1952, helped establish the Central Treaty Organization (CENTO) in 1955, and strengthened ties to Israel, Jordan, and the conservative monarchies of the Persian Gulf, including Iran. By and large, this strategy succeeded.[10] Despite dangerously tense moments during the 1956 Suez Crisis and the 1967 and 1973 Arab-Israeli wars, the United States and Russia never clashed in the Middle East and only once entered directly into a conflict in the region, at least before the Soviet invasion of Afghanistan in 1979.[11]

The Afghan War proved a costly mistake for Moscow, both in terms of lives lost and regional prestige. Together with the completion of Egyptian President Anwar Sadat's slow but decisive pivot toward the West, the Soviet Union found itself with few friends. Those it still had—Iraq, Libya, and Syria—proved difficult to control.[12] When Iraq invaded Kuwait in 1990, the Soviet Union initially sought a negotiated withdrawal but was swiftly reduced to the role of bystander, effectively marking the end of Soviet influence in the Middle East.

Russia's subsequent return to the region did not begin with its military intervention in Syria. Vladimir Putin began working to restore Russian influence in the Middle East shortly after assuming the Russian presidency in 2000.[13] This effort accelerated in the context of the U.S.-led war in Iraq, which Russia opposed—fearing, with reason, that Saddam Hussein's removal would lead to instability and radicalization. These fears were exacerbated by subsequent signals that the United States might next target Iran or Syria.

Putin made his first state visit to Turkey in 2004, followed by visits to Egypt, Israel, and Palestine in 2005 and, over the next two years, to Algeria, Morocco, Saudi Arabia, Qatar, Jordan, the United Arab Emirates (UAE), Iran, and Libya. Russia was granted observer status in the Organization of Islamic Cooperation (OIC) in 2005, and became a founding member of the P5+1 process on Iran's nuclear program, which was established in 2006. In 2008, following the lackluster performance of its military in Georgia, Russia embarked on a ten-year military modernization plan. Notably, this plan included repairs and expansion of the Russian military base at the Syrian port of Tartus.[14] According to a 2009 RAND study, Russia's Middle East and North Africa policy during this period was driven by three factors: enhancing Russia's prestige and influence over regional affairs; increasing trade; and preserving stability.[15]

Given this orientation, it comes as no surprise that Russia showed little enthusiasm for the Arab Spring, which it viewed through the lens of the "color revolutions" of the 2000s and the potential for instability at home, especially following popular opposition to Putin in late 2011. While Russian analysts harbored few illusions about the region's aging and corrupt leadership, they worried that unmanaged political change would destabilize the regional order and empower Islamist groups, with negative consequences for Russia's security. Tellingly, Moscow did not embrace the revolutions in Egypt and Tunisia, even though these toppled pro-Western governments.[16] Under the leadership of President Dmitry Medvedev, Putin's hand-picked successor, Russia abstained in the UN Security Council vote that authorized military intervention to protect civilians in Libya, in the hope that Russia at least would be rewarded for its acquiescence. Instead, Qaddafi's execution and the resulting chaos validated Russian fears and contributed to Putin's decision to return to the presidency after a constitutionally mandated four-year hiatus.[17]

In Syria, Russia acted decisively to prevent the collapse of Bashar al Assad's government, blocking action in the UN Security Council, providing financial and material support, and ultimately intervening militarily when it appeared that Assad might fall. This was Russia's first expeditionary military operation since Afghanistan and its first opportunity to showcase the hardware developed during Russia's military modernization drive. Since the United States had intervened in Syria a year before to target ISIS and other terrorist groups, it was also the first time since World War II that U.S. and Russian combat forces operated in the same theater at the same time. This significantly increased the risk of unintended confrontation, especially in the context of elevated tensions over Russia's role in Ukraine and the closure of bilateral channels of communication that had helped avert and manage crises during the Cold War.

If Russia's earlier efforts to restore its influence in the Middle East amounted to little, the Syria intervention has greatly exceeded Moscow's expectations.[18] At relatively little cost, Russia has succeeded in thwarting the Syrian opposition and stabilizing Assad's government. The Russian military now has two functional bases in the heart of the Levant, at Tartus and Hmeimim. Through its partnership with Iran and Iranian-backed militias, including Hezbollah, Russia has deepened ties with Tehran and demonstrated its ability to manage coalition warfare. At the same time, through its control over access to Syria's western airspace, Russia has made Israel dependent on Russian acquiescence for its own defense. Perhaps most remarkable, despite clearly aligning itself with a minority Alawite government and Iran, the region's only Shia power, Russia has forged closer ties with the leading Sunni states, including Turkey, Jordan, and the Gulf monarchies. In North Africa, Russia has leveraged its steadfast support for a former client to deepen military cooperation with Egypt, while replicating the deployment of Russian mercenary forces to shape Libya's civil war and secure a diplomatic role for Moscow.

Russian Interests in the Middle East

Developing an appropriate policy response requires separating the signal from the noise in this flurry of activity, and offering a clear-eyed assessment of the nature and scope of the threat that Russia poses to U.S. interests in the Middle East.

This is an exercise the Obama administration never systematically undertook. In general, Obama viewed Russia as a declining power that could exercise regional influence and play spoiler, but presented no serious threat to U.S. national security.[19] After initially trying to reset the U.S.-Russian relationship, the administration took an increasingly dim view of Moscow's intentions, but reacted cautiously in the face of growing Russian assertiveness.[20] In the Middle East, the United States continued to work with Moscow in the P5+1 format to address Iran's nuclear program, despite Russia's annexation of Crimea. And although the United States and Russia immediately found themselves on opposite sides of Syria's civil war, Obama was willing to engage Putin on successive peace efforts, as well as on discrete issues where U.S. and Russian objectives aligned. This led, notably, to the 2013 UN-backed deal that removed the majority of Syria's chemical weapons stockpiles. Russia's subsequent military intervention in Syria dramatically increased tensions with the United States, but did not alter this basic dynamic. Obama did not try to prevent Russia from deploying its forces in Syria and was determined to avoid a broader escalatory spiral once they were in theater; instead, the president predicted that Russia would fail and offered U.S. cooperation if Russia focused on fighting ISIS and took steps to renew the political process.[21]

In Syria—as in Libya, Iraq, and Turkey—the Obama administration's policy vis-à-vis Russia in the Middle East largely was determined by country-specific considerations and objectives rather than a coherent regional strategy designed to address increased Russian activity and influence as a distinct challenge in its own right. Obama's October 2, 2015, statement that Syria was "not some superpower chessboard contest" reveals the extent to which the administration underestimated Putin's ability to play a bad hand and failed to anticipate the ways that Russia would leverage its military intervention in Syria to advance its larger geopolitical objectives.

Although the Trump administration has placed great power competition at the center of its national security policy, at least on paper, the administration's single-minded focus on Iran appears to have delayed the development of a strategy for Russia (or China) in the Middle East.[22] The administration argues that "maximum pressure" on Iran has weakened Russia's key regional partner, but it also appears to have pushed Moscow and Tehran closer together, while undermining trust between the United States and its European allies. More broadly, the breakdown of U.S. diplomacy with Iran has enabled Russia to credibly claim it is the only actor who talks to everyone in the Middle East—an important factor in its diplomatic resurgence.

A new U.S. approach must be based on a clear understanding of Russia's regional objectives and their implications for the United States. Russia's objectives include:

- restoring Russia's regional and international prestige;
- reducing Russia's and its neighbors' exposure to Islamist terrorism;
- preserving regional stability;
- maintaining a Russian military presence;
- increasing trade and investment; and
- coordinating energy policy.[23]

This is a less ambitious agenda than during the Cold War, when the Soviet Union sought to create a unified regional bloc hostile to the United States. But in practice, the first objective—restoring Russia's regional and international prestige—has meant working to undermine U.S. leadership, including by engaging or supporting U.S. adversaries, creating fissures in U.S. alliances, spreading disinformation, and blocking U.S. initiatives in the region and in the UN Security Council.

The last two objectives—increasing trade and investment and coordinating energy policy—are also troubling for the United States.

Trade and investment are not strictly zero-sum, and in any event Russian trade with the Middle East represents a fraction of U.S. trade with the region. But arms sales have strategic implications. This is probably less concerning with respect to Egypt, which has declined in regional importance, or Iraq, where U.S.-Iraqi military cooperation is so extensive that Russian sales are unlikely to dent U.S. influence. But Turkey's purchase of the Russian-made S-400 anti-aircraft system is a different matter: the sale poses operational risks for NATO and raises serious questions about Ankara's commitment to the alliance.

With respect to energy policy, in late 2016 Russia was able to negotiate an agreement between Saudi Arabia and Iran, and then with OPEC, to reduce oil exports and support prices.[24] Given that Russia is the world's third largest oil producer, inroads with the Gulf states—especially Saudi Arabia—could enhance Russian influence over global energy markets. However, there are limits to what Russia can achieve, as any rise in prices would increase production and undercut Russia's share of world energy markets.

The implications of Russia's objectives to reduce exposure to Islamist terrorism and preserve regional stability are more ambiguous. The United States and Russia agree that nuclear proliferation poses a threat to regional stability, and both countries are concerned that the fragmentation of Middle Eastern states will breed extremism. At the same time, Russia's aversion to extra-constitutional, grassroots political change is at odds with the U.S. view that the success of popular democratic movements can ultimately enhance regional stability.

Similarly, while at a superficial level counterterrorism appears to be a natural area for cooperation, there are steep challenges: Russia employs a far broader definition of who should be considered a "terrorist"; it is not clear that Russia can be trusted with sensitive intelligence or that it would not exploit cooperation as an opportunity to collect its own intelligence on U.S. platforms, sources, and methods; and Russia's operational approach lacks basic controls—for example, to prevent civilian casualties.[25] These factors do not prevent counterterrorism cooperation with Russia, but they greatly constrain it.

How has Russia sought to advance its objectives? In Syria, Russia doubled down on a former Soviet client state. But this looks more like the exception than the rule. Elsewhere in the Middle East, Russia's approach has been opportunistic and transactional, based on engaging with a wide range of actors across the region's ethnic and sectarian divides, while trying to avoid taking sides in any of the major regional disputes. In Libya, for example, Russia has backed General Khalifa Haftar by printing money for his affiliated government in the eastern city of Tobruk, providing weapons, and facilitating the deployment of several hundred Russian mercenaries. At the same time, Moscow has kept open channels with the UN-recognized government in Tripoli, positioning itself for a diplomatic role but conspicuously stepping back from committing Russian military forces as it did in Syria.

These actions are troublesome for the United States. But they do not indicate that Russia seeks a larger role as the region's primary security guarantor.[26] While clearly intended to diminish U.S. influence, Moscow's outreach to traditional U.S. partners does not appear to be premised on excluding the United States. Quite the contrary: in Iraq, for example, the creation of a Russian-backed intelligence fusion cell was designed specifically to draw the United States into closer counterterrorism cooperation with Russia and its partner, Iran. Rather, Russia has taken advantage of regional states' frustration with the United States to woo new friends. This largely explains both Turkey's rapprochement and the Gulf states' flirtations with Moscow. Russia has made important strides, but there are limits: Turkey does not want to become reliant on Russia, while—in comparison to the United States—Russia has little to offer the Gulf.

Russia also faces systemic challenges. First, resource and demographic constraints will make it difficult to sustain major new investments in the region—though this should not be overstated.[27] Second, while a transactional approach offers flexibility, it inherently limits the depth of Russia's relationships. This problem is likely to be compounded as the military effort in Syria is replaced by the more difficult tasks of political reconciliation and economic reconstruction—areas where Russia has had little success—and as Russia goes from being the new kid on the block to part of the regional diplomatic fabric. In particular, Moscow is likely to find it more and more difficult to span major fault lines dividing Israel and Iran or Turkey and the Kurds.[28] Should a conflict break out between or among its varied partners and interlocutors, Russia may be forced to choose sides, with all the attendant risks; failing to do so would likely weaken Moscow's influence. Finally, Russia—where oil and gas make up 70 percent of total exports—is at a natural economic disadvantage in the world's leading energy-exporting region.

A Policy of Bounded Competition

This does not mean that the United States can simply sit back and wait for Russia to overplay its hand. Strategic patience can be disastrous if an adversary is misjudged, especially in the near to medium term. But it also means that a return to Cold War tactics would be foolish. Doubling down on unreliable and authoritarian partners, or escalating wars in Syria and Yemen, as some have recommended, is more likely to erode U.S. power than to deter Russia.[29]

Instead, the United States should pursue a policy of bounded competition. We should compete vigorously where Russian actions directly threaten core U.S. interests. Most important of these are Russia's efforts to weaken NATO by courting Turkey, and its energy diplomacy with the Gulf states. Elsewhere, we should exercise restraint and take advantage of opportunities as they emerge. This includes cases where our interests or leverage is limited, such as in Egypt and Algeria, or where our relationships are sufficiently robust that Russian engagement is unlikely to undermine our influence, such as in Israel and Jordan. Finally, we should explore limited cooperation with Russia where our interests significantly overlap. This is especially important with respect to regional stability—we should have learned by now that we cannot impose peace on our own at a cost commensurate with our limited interests.

Within this basic framework, the United States should routinely reevaluate countries and issues to ensure that its overall approach preserves U.S. influence vis-à-vis Russia where it matters most, while judiciously balancing our regional investments against U.S. global priorities.

Several recommendations flow from this framework. The next administration should:

Conduct regular assessments of situations Russia could seek to exploit. In Syria, the Obama administration was taken by surprise—both by the scale of Russia's military intervention and by Moscow's ability to leverage it to advance a broader agenda. The next administration should direct the intelligence community to conduct regular assessments of when, where, and how Russia could seek to exploit regional tensions to weaken the United States.

Invest in countering Russian propaganda. Russia's star may be rising, but its influence in the region is greatly exaggerated. The next administration should devote additional resources to countering Russian disinformation and highlighting the deep divisions among Russia's regional partners, the weakness of its economy, and Russia's atrocious human rights record—all actions that are not resource-intensive. At the same time, the United States should be vigilant in the face of regional actors' efforts to play the United States off of Russia.

Seek to reverse Turkey's pivot toward Moscow. U.S.-Turkish relations are at their lowest point in years as a consequence of deep disagreements over Syria, the fate of Turkish dissident Fethullah Gülen, backsliding on democracy and press freedom, and other issues. Notwithstanding these tensions, Turkey remains important to U.S. interests and its pivot toward Russia threatens the NATO alliance. The slow winding down of the U.S.-led campaign to defeat ISIS potentially removes the most significant thorn in the bilateral relationship. While Turkey is likely to remain a difficult partner, a hostile Turkey has the capacity to cause serious damage to U.S. interests in the region and even in Europe. The next administration should therefore continue to work to pull Turkey out of Russia's orbit.

Make clear to Gulf partners that Russian interference in energy markets is a redline. Over the past decade, U.S. reliance on Middle Eastern oil and gas has greatly diminished, but global market stability remains a core U.S. interest. Thanks to its substantial energy reserves and its relationship with Iran, Russia's courtship of the Gulf States could threaten that interest. The United States should make clear to Gulf partners that this is a redline. As Russia cannot offer the Gulf states a viable alternative to the U.S. security guarantee, they are unlikely to risk alienating the United States over an issue of lesser importance to their national interests.

Open new communication channels beyond Syria. Multiple senior U.S. military officials have noted that the United States and Russia no longer have the density of communication channels that helped to prevent escalation during the Cold War.[30] In Syria, the United States and Russia prudently established a dedicated channel at the technical level to deconflict military operations; a separate channel was subsequently opened between the secretary of defense and his Russian counterpart. In light of increased competition throughout the Middle East, a new bilateral channel should be opened, separate from Syria, to discuss regional security issues, including how to respond to the next wave of political unrest.

Engage Russia to help resolve the region's most intractable conflicts. Despite definitions and assumptions that diverge sharply, the United States and Russia share an interest in preventing a further erosion of state authority in the Middle East that would allow extremism to take root. Russia also has a close relationship with Iran, a key player in many of the region's conflicts. In Syria, the United States should continue to engage Russia on a political framework that leads to a durable (if unpalatable) peace that stabilizes the situation and reduces Iran's footprint in Syria. In Yemen, we should seek Russian support for UN diplomatic efforts and ask Moscow to exercise its influence in Tehran to bring the war to a swift conclusion. And in Libya, the United States should accept a Russian diplomatic role and seek a commitment from Moscow to work toward de-escalating the conflict, consistent with the agreement among external parties at the January 2020 Berlin Conference. If engagement with Russia fails to bear fruit, or if engagement is accompanied by Russian actions that directly undermine core U.S. interests—if, for example, Russia continues to pursue an outcome in Libya that threatens NATO's southern flank—the United States should consider more adversarial actions.

————————

This approach will not bring an end to U.S.-Russian tensions in the Middle East. But it could help to focus the U.S. response to Russia's growing regional profile, while avoiding the traps of either inaction or overextension and building on the many strengths we have in the region. The United States will not win the new Cold War with the same tools that won the original one: the world has changed, and so has the balance of power between the United States and Russia within it. Competing with Russia and especially China globally will require being smart about how and where we invest in the Middle East.

Notes

The author wishes to thank the volume editors, along with Salman Ahmed, Chris Blanchard, Eric Ciaramella, Brian Katulis, Matt Rojansky, Lisa Roman, and an anonymous reviewer for comments on earlier drafts of this chapter. All errors are my own.

1. Yevgeny Primakov, *Russia and the Arabs* (New York: Basic Books, 2009), 386.

2. Robert Legvold, *Return to Cold War* (Cambridge: Polity, 2016).

3. "Press Conference by the President," October 2, 2015.

4. Liz Sly, "In the Middle East, Russia Is Back," *Washington Post*, December 5, 2018.

5. Katie Bo Williams, "What's Great Power Competition? No One Really Knows," *Defense One*, May 13, 2019. On China, see Kurt M. Campbell and Jake Sullivan, "Competition Without Catastrophe: How America Can Both Challenge and Coexist with China," *Foreign Affairs*, September 13, 2019.

6. Odd Arne Westad, "Has a New Cold War Really Begun?" *Foreign Affairs*, March 27, 2018; Stephen Walt, "I Knew the Cold War. This Is No Cold War," *Foreign Policy*, March 12, 2018; Michael McFaul, "A Grand Strategy for Confronting Putin," *Foreign Affairs*, June 14, 2018. Hal Brands has argued that the struggle between capitalism and socialism has been replaced by one between democracy and authoritarianism. See Brands, "Democracy vs. Authoritarianism: How Ideology Shapes Great-Power Conflict," *Survival*, vol. 60, no. 5 (2018), 61–114.

7. Mark Katz, "When the Friend of My Friends Is Not My Friend: The United States, U.S. Allies, and Russia in the Middle East," Atlantic Council, May 2019.

8. Dimitri Trenin, *What Is Russia Up to in the Middle East?* (Cambridge: Polity, 2018).

9. Aron Lund, *Russia in the Middle East* (report), Swedish Institute of International Affairs, February 2019.

10. Ray Takeyh and Steven Simon, *The Pragmatic Superpower: Winning the Cold War in the Middle East* (New York: W. W. Norton and Company, 2016).

11. Russian aircraft participated directly in attacks on Israeli forces during the War of Attrition in 1969–70.

12. Trenin, *What Is Russia Up to in the Middle East?* 27.

13. Anna Borshchevskaya, "Russia's Strategic Objectives in the Middle East and North Africa." Testimony submitted to the House Foreign Affairs Subcommittee on the Middle East and North Africa, June 15, 2017.

14. Lund, "Russia in the Middle East," 17.

15. Cited in James Sladden, Becca Wasser, Ben Connable, and Sarah Grand-Clement, "Russian Strategy in the Middle East," RAND Corporation, 2017, 3.

16. Lund, "Russia in the Middle East," 18.

17. Ibid., 19.

18. Samuel Charap, Elina Treyger, and Edward Geist, "Understanding Russia's Intervention in Syria," Rand Corporation, 2019, 8.

19. Angela Stent, *The Limits of Partnership: U.S.-Russian Relations in the Twenty-First Century* (New Jersey: Princeton University Press, 2015).

20. Benjamin Haddad and Alina Polyakova, "Don't Rehabilitate Obama on Russia," Brookings, March 5, 2018.

21. Press Conference by the President, October 2, 2015.

22. The Trump administration has not yet released a new regional strategy for the Middle East. For Africa, see "Remarks by National Security Advisor Ambassador John R. Bolton on the Trump Administration's New Africa Strategy," White House, December 13, 2018.

23. This description of Russian objectives is adapted from Sladden and others, "Russian Strategy in the Middle East"; Brian Katulis, "Assessing the Impact of Russia's Support for Authoritarian State Sponsors of Terrorism in the Middle East and North Africa," testimony before the House Foreign Affairs Subcommittee on the Middle East and North Africa, June 15, 2017; and Dimitri Trenin, "Russia in the Middle East: Moscow's Objectives, Priorities, and Policy Drivers," Carnegie Endowment, March 26, 2016.

24. Trenin, *What Is Russia Up to in the Middle East?*, 126.

25. Legally, counterterrorism cooperation would require the secretary of defense to waive portions of the 2018 National Defense Authorization Act, which stipulates that no funds may be used "for any bilateral military-to-military cooperation between the governments of the United States and the Russian Federation." On the risks of counterterrorism cooperation, see Andrew Exum, testimony before the House Committee on Foreign Affairs on "Chinese and Russian Influence in the Middle East," May 9, 2019.

26. Sladden and others, "Russian Strategy in the Middle East," 7.

27. Stephen Kotkin, "Russia's Perpetual Geopolitics: Putin Returns to the Historical Pattern," *Foreign Affairs*, April 18, 2016. On the dangers of the conventional wisdom of Russia's demographic decline, see Michael Kofman, "Russia's Demographics and Power: Does the Kremlin Have a Long Game?" *War on the Rocks* (web publication), February 4, 2020.

28. Andrey Kortunov, "Russian Foreign Policy in the Middle East: Achievements and Limitations," Russian International Affairs Council, July 22, 2019.

29. Steven Cook, "Russia Is in the Middle East to Stay: Here Is What the United States Should Do About It," *Foreign Policy*, March 16, 2018; Daniel Byman, "Pushing Back Russia in the Middle East: A Thought Experiment," Brookings, April 13, 2018.

30. Dan Lamothe, "U.S. Generals Want Elevated Talks with Russia about Iraq and Syria Operations Because of Aerial Collision Fears," *Washington Post*, February 23, 2017.

TEN

Iran: Leading with Diplomacy

SAHAR NOWROUZZADEH
JANE RHEE

As a significant regional player that presents real threats to U.S. interests, Iran will play a central role in shaping the next president's policies in the Middle East. In seeking to address these threats, the United States risks getting tied down in regional conflagrations that do not lend themselves to quick or easy solutions, can inadvertently exacerbate tensions in a complex environment, and consume a disproportionate share of finite national resources. As this chapter will argue, based in part on the lessons of administrations past, the most effective strategy for achieving our long-term policy goals and securing our interests vis-à-vis Iran will be one that leads with multilateral diplomacy. Clear-eyed direct engagement with Iran can help to resolve our deep differences over time, while the United States leverages international partnerships to deter and contain the threats Iran poses to U.S. interests. By doing so, the next administration can manage the challenges Iran presents to the United States and its partners without squandering unnecessary blood and treasure, increase the prospects for a more stable region, and help lay the foundation for a more constructive relationship between the United States and Iran in the longer term.

U.S. Interests and Iran

The largely adversarial nature of contemporary U.S.-Iranian relations has in many ways shaped U.S. policies across the Middle East over the past four decades. Since Iran's Islamic Revolution in 1979, every U.S. president has shared the objective of addressing the underlying threats and challenges Iran poses to U.S. interests. These include such matters as Iran's nuclear program, ballistic missile development, support for terrorism, destabilizing policies in the region, human rights abuses, and unjust detention of American citizens. Yet today the United States remains in search of credible approaches and sustainable solutions to such challenges.

The nuclear issue has, with good reason, been at the forefront of U.S. policy toward Iran for many years. Iran's nuclear past is checkered with deception, including an organized and covert nuclear weapon design program that, the U.S. intelligence community assesses, was largely halted in 2003[1] and on which a covert Israeli intelligence operation in early 2018 appears to have shed further light.[2] Under the 2015 Joint Comprehensive Plan of Action (JCPOA), reached between Iran and the P5+1 (United States, China, France, Russia, the United Kingdom, plus Germany) and the European Union (EU), Iran explicitly agreed to never seek, develop, or acquire a nuclear weapon[3] and to adhere to strict nuclear limits and intrusive inspections. If Iran were to reverse course and choose to develop a nuclear weapon, it would magnify existing threats to U.S. national security interests, including by undermining global nonproliferation norms, potentially set off a nuclear arms race in an already turbulent region, and possibly embolden Iran to bolster its support to terrorist groups and violent proxies.[4] Such dynamics could seriously threaten U.S. assets, personnel, and partners, and lead to further destabilization of the region.

Across the Middle East and beyond, Iran continues to undermine and challenge the interests of the United States and its partners, primarily by relying on asymmetric means, often to compensate for its conventional military shortcomings.[5] Such means range from support to militant proxies and terrorist organizations like Lebanese Hezbollah to its increasingly sophisticated cyber operations against its adversaries and development of the largest inventory of ballistic missiles in the region.[6] These policies, along with a range of destabilizing policies among other regional players, have contributed to intensified geopolitical competition, increased sectarian tensions, and prolonged proxy conflicts between Iran and its regional rivals. While Iran views such policies as a means to deter its adversaries and pursue vital security interests, its foreign policies and operations often not only undermine U.S. efforts to secure a more prosperous and stable Middle East but are often inherently inimical to U.S. interests.

The last several administrations committed to addressing the dismal human rights record in Iran.[7] Nonetheless, the Iranian government continues to commit gross violations of the fundamental rights and liberties of its citizens under both international and domestic laws. Iran's repressive practices range from discrimination against religious and ethnic minorities and systematic attacks against freedom of expression to the use of torture and a range of due process violations.[8] Tehran's repression often stymies efforts within Iran's constrained yet nevertheless relatively vibrant civil society to foster organic, positive domestic changes over time. Yet despite such oppression, a strategic asset for the United States has been the fact that a majority of the Iranian people have long favored the restoration of diplomatic relations with the United States[9] despite the anti-Americanism that emanates from the current government's core leadership. Iran also continues to unjustly detain U.S. citizens and has yet to provide a full accounting of the fate of Robert Levinson, a former FBI agent who went missing on Iran's Kish Island in 2007 and was presumed dead by his family as of March 2020.[10] Iran's mistreatment of U.S. citizens over the decades has consumed significant U.S. government resources and further complicated the prospects of constructive relations between the United States and Iran.

Shifting U.S. Policy on Iran

When President Barack Obama entered office in 2009, he made clear that he was prepared to pursue all available options, including potential military action, to address the threats posed by Iran. Yet he emphasized that he strongly preferred to resolve the nuclear issue and other differences through diplomacy without preconditions, underscoring that the United States was not seeking regime change and respected the right of the Iranian people to access peaceful nuclear energy. However, Obama's initial outreach to Iran's government in 2009 was quickly complicated by three developments: (1) the Iranian government's violent crackdown on the "Green Movement" protesters and the subsequent legitimacy crisis that followed Iranian president Mahmoud Ahmadinejad's disputed reelection; (2) the public revelation of a previously undeclared uranium enrichment facility, Fordow, buried in a mountain outside the city of Qom; and (3) Iran's decision to renege on its agreement, in principle, to a confidence-building measure, known as the "TRR fuel-swap," with the P5+1, EU, and the International Atomic Energy Agency (IAEA).[11] Even though Iran failed to grasp President Obama's open hand at that time, his willingness to lead with diplomacy shifted much of the blame for the ensuing diplomatic impasse to Iran, enabling the United States to secure broad international buy-in for its approach. Such buy-in was the foundation for a robust global sanctions and diplomatic campaign that eventually provided the United States with significant leverage and helped, along with a range of critical contextual factors, to shift Iran's nuclear decisionmaking over time.

In the interim, however, despite U.S. and international sanctions that exacted a severe toll on Iran's economy, Iran continued to make advances in its nuclear program. The Obama administration explored diplomatic options through both the P5+1 track and through direct engagement with Iran, including through a back channel facilitated by late Omani Sultan Qaboos bin Said Al Said. Over the course of several bilateral meetings in early 2013 in Oman, the United States and Iran discussed various proposals for a diplomatic resolution that could address the threat posed by Iran's nuclear program. The United States signaled that if Iran could take concrete measures to ensure the exclusively peaceful nature of its program as part of a comprehensive understanding, it might be willing to explore the possibility of Iran retaining some form of domestic enrichment—something Iran had long insisted it would never surrender.[12]

The election of Iranian president Hassan Rouhani in June 2013 greatly accelerated the progress of these discussions. A former nuclear negotiator, he campaigned on a platform of constructive engagement in order to end Iran's political and economic isolation,[13] hailing his victory as one "of moderation over extremism."[14] Diplomatic momentum picked up in September, following a bilateral meeting between U.S. Secretary of State John Kerry and Iranian Foreign Minister Mohammad Javad Zarif at the UN General Assembly as well as a phone call between President Obama and Rouhani—the highest level engagement between the United States and Iran since the 1979 revolution. By November, the United States, the P5+1, and the EU reached an interim deal with Iran called the Joint Plan of Action (JPOA), in which Tehran halted its nuclear progress in exchange for a moratorium on new nuclear sanctions to allow time and space for negotiations toward a comprehensive accord.[15] After nearly two years of intense multilateral negotiations and extensive bilateral engagement, the parties reached agreement on the JCPOA, which, in exchange for relief from nuclear-related sanctions, permanently prohibited Iran from acquiring a nuclear weapon and imposed verifiable limits that extended the time it would take Iran to produce enough fissile material to develop one nuclear weapon from two or three months to at least a year, for at least a decade. In order to help prevent a potential covert nuclear breakout, it also secured Iran's commitment to permanent transparency measures and required Iran to comply with what the IAEA has described as "the world's most robust nuclear verification regime."[16]

Beyond constraining Iran's nuclear program, the Obama administration's high-level, sustained engagement with Iran also helped open diplomatic channels that facilitated the 2016 release of five U.S. citizens detained in Iran[17] and the speedy resolution of an incident that same year involving U.S. sailors taken into custody by the IRGC-Navy. President Obama's tenure was also marked by increased outreach to the Iranian people, including through the implementation of such policies as the easing of U.S. visa restrictions for Iranian students and licensing the sale of personal communication devices to increase the free flow of information as well as people-to-people programs, including sports, diplomacy, and environmental and educational exchanges. Such efforts demonstrated a broader U.S. commitment to engagement and proved to hold high public diplomacy value. The Obama administration also spoke out in support of Iranian citizens struggling for their universal rights and took steps to try to hold Iran's government to account, including issuing high-level statements condemning domestic abuses, imposing sanctions on key individuals and institutions responsible for human rights violations, and leading multilateral efforts to establish and maintain a mandate for the first ever United Nations Special Rapporteur on human rights in Iran. In spite of this record, President Obama has been criticized for not speaking out or intervening more forcefully in support of Iranian protesters in the aftermath of Iran's disputed 2009 presidential election. While he strongly and publicly condemned the regime's violence against protesters,[18] his administration took a nuanced approach and refrained from more directly intervening on the ground based on the calculation that such actions would ultimately do more harm than good, given the history of U.S. interference in Iranian affairs and the risk of providing additional fodder to Iran's security forces to crack down even harder.

While the JCPOA succeeded in peacefully constraining Iran's expanding nuclear program and imposing strict verification measures to ensure Iran's compliance, the Obama administration, like administrations prior, was ultimately unable to make significant progress on restraining Iran's ballistic missile development and destabilizing regional policies, or on advancing human rights. Critics argue that prioritizing the threat of a nuclear-armed Iran came at the expense of comprehensively addressing Iran's other problematic policies. However, the critical nature of the nuclear threat combined with the finite nature of U.S. leverage, lack of international unity over Iran's other destabilizing policies, and broader distrust between the United States and Iran, left little time and prospect for similar policy successes on nonnuclear fronts.

Marking a stark shift from Obama's "dual-track" approach of

coupling pressure with diplomacy without preconditions, the Trump administration has sought to compel Tehran to comprehensively address U.S. concerns regarding its policies through its multipronged "maximum pressure" campaign.[19] This approach has thus far been centered on the unilateral withdrawal of the United States from the JCPOA, the ramping up of economic sanctions, and messaging that seeks to expose Iran's problematic policies and government corruption. The campaign has also included steps toward more direct military conflict with Iran, including the January 2020 drone strike in Baghdad that killed one of Iran's most important military leaders, the Quds Force (IRGC-QF) Commander Qassem Soleimani, in addition to high-ranking Iraqi militia officials. A chief architect of many deadly operations in the region over the years, including against U.S. military forces, the Bush and Obama administrations had both reportedly assessed that the risks of killing Soleimani would outweigh the gains.[20]

Although it is difficult to separate the precise impact of sanctions from Iran's own systemic economic challenges, the maximum pressure campaign has clearly imposed significant financial costs on Iran.[21] Sanctions have exacerbated Iran's domestic financial crisis, reducing its oil revenues, undercutting the value of its currency, undermining foreign investment prospects, and complicating its ability to conduct international financial transactions writ large.[22] Indeed, Gallup polling data from June 2019 "paint a picture of a nation where the economy, and people's lives, are getting worse" as a result of U.S. sanctions[23]—so much so that there has been speculation, based in part on statements from senior administration officials alluding to such a desire, that the United States is seeking to spark popular unrest and regime collapse within Iran.[24]

While there is no doubt that it has inflicted greater economic pain on Iran, to date, the Trump administration's campaign has yet to induce its government to negotiate the "better" nuclear deal Trump vowed to secure.[25] The U.S. abrogation of its JCPOA commitments and reimposition of nuclear-related sanctions—including against Iran's Central Bank and oil sales—was initially met with all other parties, including Iran, continuing to abide by the terms of the original accord. Germany, France, and the United Kingdom went so far as to establish a special-purpose vehicle (SPV), called INSTEX, meant to eventually shield financial transactions related to legitimate trade with Iran from U.S. secondary sanctions—a measure symbolic of increased U.S. isolation in its Iran policy.

Nevertheless, decisionmakers in key institutions within Iran, including the Supreme Leader's Office and the IRGC, publicly questioned whether Iran's investment in its full compliance with the JCPOA and broader compromise with the West had reached the point of diminishing strategic returns.[26] Indeed, on the one-year anniversary of the U.S. decision to withdraw from the JCPOA, and following a U.S. decision to revoke waivers that allowed Iran to export uranium and heavy water in excess of JCPOA limits, President Rouhani announced in July 2019 that Iran would cease implementing related nuclear commitments and take additional steps toward reduced compliance, unless the United States lifted sanctions or other JCPOA participants helped Iran secure the economic relief that it asserts was promised as part of the accord. Rouhani claimed that Iran was taking such steps to save the JCPOA and not to end it,[27] citing paragraph 26, which indicates that Iran can treat the re-imposition of sanctions lifted under the JCPOA as grounds to "cease performing its commitments under this JCPOA in whole or in part," as the basis for Iran's decision.[28] Iran continued to take additional incremental steps to reduce its compliance with the deal's terms, which culminated in its January 2020 announcement that it no longer considered itself bound to any remaining operational restrictions within the accord.[29] Importantly, however, Iran simultaneously announced that it would continue to cooperate with the IAEA and the agency has continued to carry out its monitoring and verification mission called for under the JCPOA. Moreover, Tehran's leadership has emphasized the reversible nature of its actions, underscoring that it will return to full compliance if all other parties do so and it obtains the economic benefits it believes it was promised.

Iran's increasing noncompliance with the JCPOA led France, Germany, and the United Kingdom to trigger the agreement's Dispute Resolution Mechanism (DRM) in January 2020, initiating a period of negotiation among parties to resolve outstanding differences. In a joint statement, the foreign ministers of France, Germany, and the

United Kingdom made clear that their objective was to "preserve the JCPOA . . . in the sincere hope of finding a way forward to resolve the impasse through constructive diplomatic dialogue, while preserving the agreement and remaining within its framework."[30] While the process might ultimately allow time for additional efforts aimed at preserving aspects of the accord, it also risks Iran's referral to the UN Security Council and the snapback of multilateral sanctions against Iran that had been lifted under the JCPOA—an outcome reportedly expected by the Trump administration[31] and that would likely kill any prospects for reviving the agreement in its current form. Indeed, Iran has gone so far as to threaten to withdraw from the Non-Proliferation Treaty (NPT) altogether in response to such an outcome.[32]

Judged by whether it has meaningfully deterred Iran's destabilizing policies in the region, Trump's maximum pressure campaign has not been effective. While there have been reports that sanctions are hindering Iran's ability to financially support regional proxies and allies,[33] such financial setbacks appear thus far to be tactical[34] as Iran has continued to soften and mitigate the impact of sanctions through workarounds and circumvention.[35] Critically, Iran has continued to take advantage of the opportunities offered by the region's prolonged conflicts and deterioration of its broader security order to advance its regional objectives[36] in relatively inexpensive ways that have long bedeviled U.S. policymakers. In recent years, this has included its continued provision of logistical, material, and political support to Syrian president Bashar al Assad and Syrian paramilitaries, Hezbollah, Houthi rebels in Yemen, Shia militias in Iraq, and a range of Palestinian militant organizations.[37] Rather than translating financial pressure into a meaningful shift in Iran's strategic calculus or a degradation of its regional capabilities, the Trump administration's overreliance on pressure tools seems to have in certain cases emboldened Tehran to escalate its destabilizing behavior.[38] As compared to the years immediately preceding Trump's inauguration, Iran appears to have ramped up its campaign of directly targeting the interests and assets of the United States and its allies and partners in the region. This dynamic will almost certainly continue following the killing of Soleimani—an action likely to serve as a tactical rather than strategic setback to Iran's proxy networks and its capacity for expeditionary operations in the region.[39] Even prior to its launching of more than a dozen ballistic missiles aimed at U.S. forces stationed at Iraqi military bases as part of its response to Soleimani's killing—the first time Tehran had conducted a direct conventional attack on a U.S. military position in the region[40]—Iran had been ramping up its campaign of targeting U.S. interests. This campaign included attacks on oil tankers in the Persian Gulf allegedly committed by Iran, increased threats against U.S. personnel in Iraq,[41] the transfer of precision-guided missile technology to Hezbollah, and the downing of a U.S. reconnaissance drone that reportedly brought the United States to the cusp of conducting military strikes on Iranian soil.[42] In response to this heightened threat environment, the Trump administration has ordered drawdowns at U.S. diplomatic facilities and deployed additional U.S. troops to the region.[43]

Iran also appears to have continued developing its ballistic missile program amid the maximum pressure campaign, while Iran's human rights situation has only deteriorated further amid heightened threat perceptions as the regime has launched crackdowns across civil society. Indeed, political violence reached new heights in November 2019 with reports that between 300 to more than 1,000 demonstrators had been killed and thousands of others injured,[44] during widespread protests that initially broke out in response to a major hike in fuel prices yet evolved into renewed calls from many for the ouster of Iran's current leadership.[45]

While the Trump administration has expressed its rhetorical support for the protesters, its human rights approach has not diverged significantly from those of recent administrations in practice. Moreover, despite U.S. exemptions for humanitarian trade, there are indications that the maximum pressure campaign has contributed to shortages of medicine and other health supplies, in conjunction with the Iranian government's endemic mismanagement and corruption,[46] as foreign banks steer clear of doing any business with Iran.[47] Indeed, beyond the Iranian government's abject failure in implementing necessary public health measures and its lack of transparency, such dynamics appear to have contributed to Iran's becoming the epicenter of the COVID-19 pandemic in the Middle East, recording nearly 7,000 related deaths and over 100,000 confirmed cases as of mid-May 2020. Experts have cited sanctions and related licensing and banking barriers as one of the factors impeding Iran's ability to procure supplies critical to dealing with the pandemic.[48] Despite calls from senior Iranian, European, and UN officials, as well as select U.S. lawmakers for an easing of U.S. sanctions, to allow Tehran to better battle the virus and limit its spread both domestically and globally, the Trump administration has thus far refused, pointing to Iran's refusal to accept direct U.S. humanitarian assistance and accusing Tehran of using the crisis as a means to secure additional funds to support terrorism.[49]

Further, while the Trump administration has had some success in building on Obama-era authorizations and licensing policies designed to make censorship circumvention technologies from U.S. government-funded companies available to Iranian citizens,[50] the maximum pressure campaign has still led Silicon Valley–based tech companies to block Iranian users from their services in order to comply with U.S. sanctions.[51] The Trump administration's maximalist approach, in sum, has failed to deliver on its stated objectives and contributed to the risk of escalation with the Islamic Republic in a manner unfavorable to U.S. interests. Supporters of the Trump administration's maximum pressure campaign claim Iran is "lashing out" because the campaign has been successful in helping put the regime on edge amid a deteriorating economy and growing grievances among its population,[52] therefore making it more inclined to eventually negotiate and make the concessions the administration is seeking.

Indeed, many of Iran's escalatory actions in 2019 and thus far in 2020 appear to be part of a deliberate strategy to reassert its regional position; test Trump's tolerance for provocation and impose costs on the United States; pressure other parties of the deal to compensate Iran to avoid further escalation; save face domestically; and secure leverage in a future negotiation with the United States, potentially with Trump's successor. Nevertheless, Iran likely assesses it can withstand unilateral U.S. sanctions pressure in the coming years to achieve its core interests. And given the regime's ultimate priority of preserving itself and its legitimacy at all costs, it is highly unlikely to make the broad concessions that the Trump administration is seeking, many of which would undermine much of its fundamental nature.[53]

The net effect of Trump's Iran policy to date has been to limit space for substantive diplomacy and to increase risks to the interests of the United States and its regional partners without securing positive shifts in Iranian policies that are undermining key U.S. security interests.

The Central Policy Questions and Challenges for the Next Administration

The next president will likely inherit an escalatory trajectory between the United States and Iran that will require immediate attention. Among the most pressing and far-reaching challenges this administration will confront is determining the best path forward to ensure the exclusively peaceful nature of Iran's nuclear program, following both the Trump administration's withdrawal from the JCPOA and Iran's decision to breach the accord. The urgency of this dilemma is driven, in part, by the increasingly uncertain status of the JCPOA. Yet even if it remains in place, there will still be a need to plan for (1) the expiration of select restrictions in the accord in coming years (such as those on research and development of advanced centrifuges as well as UN restrictions related to conventional arms transfers and Iran's ballistic missile development); (2) the arrival of key JCPOA milestones (such as Iran's requirement to seek ratification of the Additional Protocol in 2023 simultaneous with the U.S. requirement to seek the termination of nuclear-related sanctions)[54]; and (3) the possibility that Iran will move forward with a separate enrichment and R&D plan it submitted to the IAEA as part of its obligations under the Additional Protocol,[55] which would entail incremental growth of its enrichment capacity beginning in 2025.

At the same time, immediate U.S. options and leverage for addressing concerns regarding Iran's nuclear activities are limited. Diplomacy remains the most viable option to achieving a durable solution, but Trump's withdrawal from the JCPOA and broader maximum pressure campaign have significantly undermined the prospects for reviving a productive political track in the near term. The coercive value of sanctions, already an imperfect and insufficient tool, also has likely decreased in recent years, given not just their overuse but also the U.S. decision to reimpose nuclear-related sanctions on Iran at a time when it was in full compliance with the JCPOA. Moreover, military strikes against Iran's nuclear facilities would likely prompt Iran, directly or through its proxies, to escalate attacks against U.S. targets and increase its motivation to acquire a nuclear weapon. Experts assert that even a successful operation against Iranian nuclear facilities would only set the program back by two years or a maximum of four years.[56]

Any strategy to deal with the Iranian nuclear program must be based on the reality that, as the U.S. intelligence community has long publicly assessed, Iran does not face "any insurmountable technical barriers"[57] to developing a nuclear weapon, making political will the central factor in whether Iran will eventually acquire a nuclear weapon. Ultimately, while preserving technical restrictions on and the transparency of Iran's nuclear program should and must remain a priority, the next administration must also consider how its policies might influence Iran's complex nuclear and broader national security decisionmaking.

A new administration will also be faced with key questions regarding how to curb Iran's decades-long and increasingly indigenous[58] development of short- and medium-range ballistic missiles. UN Security Council Resolution (UNSCR) 2231, which endorsed the JCPOA, does call upon Iran "not to undertake any activity related to ballistic missiles designed to be capable of delivering nuclear weapons,"[59] providing a legal basis for the United States to continue its efforts to disrupt transfers of missile-related technologies to and from Iran. But, importantly, the JCPOA itself did not include concessions from Iran on the ballistic missiles front. During the JCPOA negotiations, some P5+1 partners argued that UN ballistic missile restrictions were meant to be leveraged to achieve a nuclear deal and should therefore be lifted at the outset of JCPOA implementation,[60] but the United States helped forge a consensus that limitations be kept in place until 2023.

Further, the UN arms embargo that prevents states from transferring arms or related material to or from Iran is set to lapse in October 2020 as part of the JCPOA, unless the Trump administration succeeds in convincing the UN Security Council to extend the embargo or the DRM process initiated by the Europeans leads to the snapback of these restrictions. While Iran's ballistic missile program will likely remain focused on indigenous development and illicit procurement of arms, in large part due to the U.S. sanctions and related financial restrictions that remain in place as well as a lack of willing suppliers,[61] the next administration will need to decide whether it will pursue new initiatives to limit both Iran's ballistic missile development and arms transfers to/from Iran. Unlike the nuclear threat, there is a lack of international consensus regarding the threat posed by Iran's ballistic missile program and conventional arms, making widespread international buy-in for any approach a challenge.[62]

When it comes to Iran's regional policies that undermine U.S. interests in the Middle East, the next administration will inherit a complex landscape. Despite the maximum pressure campaign, Iran has continued to exploit security vacuums and political vulnerabilities across the region, many of which arose out of the 2003 Iraq War and the Arab Spring. It has also been seeking to translate battlefield gains into expanded influence across the region. In Syria, this strategy, along with Iran's continued arming of Hezbollah, has prompted a series of Israeli air strikes on Iranian positions,[63] increasing the prospects for escalation and direct conflict between the two countries. As the threat from ISIS continues to decline in Iraq, Iran-linked Shia militias are likely to be well placed to potentially act against U.S. personnel and interests there. Following the U.S. killing of Soleimani, Iran has also indicated that it will enhance its efforts to drive U.S. forces not just out of Iraq but the entire region.

Geopolitical competition between Iran and Saudi Arabia has also reached new heights during the Trump administration—in part due to the administration unequivocally throwing its weight behind the latter[64]—with both sides continuing to fuel the flames of sectarianism and broader conflict in the region. However, Iran and Saudi Arabia have reportedly begun to explore a quiet dialogue to reduce tensions in the region, perhaps influenced by the U.S. failure to respond militarily to the alleged Iranian-sponsored attack on Saudi

Arabia's Aramco facilities in September 2019 along with the abrupt reduction of U.S. troops in Syria.[65] The United Arab Emirates also has recently shown a desire to reduce tensions with Iran,[66] perhaps demonstrating growing interest in regionally led diplomacy by these and other Gulf Cooperation Council (GCC) countries. Yet there is a risk that further U.S. escalation by the Trump administration might destroy the prospects for such dialogue before a new administration even takes office.[67]

A spectrum of unilateral and multilateral options remain available to address Iranian regional activity that threatens core U.S. interests, ranging from diplomatic processes and economic pressure to military and intelligence operations. A new administration must carefully craft its strategy to protect against a variety of risks, including exacerbating regional conflicts, inadvertently disrupting productive regional diplomacy, becoming entrapped in counterproductive proxy battles, or even precipitating a costly war in the region that would distract from global U.S. priorities.

The next administration will also need to decide whether it wants to engage Iran directly to address bilateral points of contention, including, critically, that of unjustly detained and missing Americans, and explore the possibility for cooperation—or at least deconfliction—on shared interests such as the defeat of ISIS or political stability in Iraq and Afghanistan. A new administration will also need to consider whether to engage Iran regarding cooperation on the coronavirus pandemic. However, it remains uncertain how receptive Tehran will be to such engagement, particularly following the Trump years. As such, a new administration may also need to evaluate and pursue trusted third-party interlocutors for these purposes.

The domestic politics on both sides will shape the options available to the next administration. Iranian officials, who previously took a more conciliatory tone, have become more vocal about taking a confrontational approach with the United States, while the Trump administration's bellicose rhetoric has been warmly welcomed by certain factions in Congress and outside groups, despite polls suggesting that a majority of Americans continue to back diplomatic engagement with Iran[68] and oppose the U.S. withdrawal from the JCPOA.[69] Against a backdrop of heated internal debate within Iran, regarding who will succeed not just President Rouhani in 2021 but also who potentially succeeds eighty-one-year-old Supreme Leader Khamenei, the next administration should carefully consider what kind of message it wants to send about the type of future it envisions for U.S.-Iranian relations.

Regardless of the status of relations with Iran's government, the next administration will nevertheless have an opportunity to reinvigorate its engagement with the Iranian people, the majority of whom, as mentioned earlier, have long favored the restoration of diplomatic relations with the United States[70] but are likely to continue to bear the economic brunt of Trump's maximum pressure campaign. Despite the Trump administration's expressions of support for the Iranian people's aspirations for freedom, the cumulative impact of the maximum pressure campaign and other statements from President Trump, such as his threats to bomb sites "important to Iran and the Iranian culture," are likely to have a negative effect on popular views of U.S. intentions among portions of the population. Yet, there is no denying the Iranian public's bravery in continuing to demand government accountability and fundamental change after decades of repression and unaddressed grievances.[71] A new president should consider how best to voice and demonstrate support for human rights in Iran as well as for the broader aspirations of its people, recognizing the limitations of productive U.S. engagement in this area.

Proposed Plan of Action for the Next Administration

While the next administration will encounter a vexing policy environment on Iran, it will have one advantage: the lessons gleaned from the successes and failures of past administrations. Based on these experiences, the next administration should apply the following principles to its Iran policy. First, the U.S. strategy must prioritize both multilateral and bilateral diplomacy with Iran in order to de-escalate tensions, improve the prospects for a more stable region, and lay the foundation for more constructive U.S.-Iranian relations in the longer term. Such engagement with Iran is essential not only for clearly communicating redlines and clarifying intentions, but also for offering credible off-ramps, incentives, and coercive assurances[72] that could shift Iran's strategic calculus and policies over time. Second, the United States must work to rebuild and lead a united international front in support of U.S. aims in Iran. This approach is more likely to yield meaningful engagement with and pressure on Iran to make concessions than is a unilateral effort. Third, the next administration must balance its diplomatic efforts with calibrated coercive measures meant to impose costs on Iran, as well as to deter and contain the threats it poses to core U.S. interests.

Increasing the Prospects for Successful Nuclear Diplomacy
The top priority for the next administration should be to continue to prevent a nuclear-armed Iran. As mentioned earlier in this chapter, an Iran with nuclear weapons would represent a strategic and destabilizing threat to the United States and its partners by amplifying other existing threats from Iran, undermining global nonproliferation norms, and potentially setting off a nuclear arms race in an already turbulent region. Though the prospects of maintaining the JCPOA continue to erode, seeking to reenter the deal under a new administration, if possible, would be the most viable first step for blocking Iran's potential pathways to a nuclear weapon in both the short and long terms.

A "better" deal or even preliminary understandings on the extension of restrictions or broader issues are likely to remain elusive in the near term. This is due not just to diplomatic setbacks under the Trump administration but also to the fact that the JCPOA, which broke a thirteen-year diplomatic stalemate over Iran's nuclear program, was reached amid a unique set of international and domestic circumstances within the United States and Iran that are unlikely to exist in 2021. While the possibility of leveraging a U.S. willingness to rejoin the JCPOA to secure additional concessions or extend key JCPOA provisions at the outset[73] might seem appealing, this approach fails to recognize the damage done to P5+1 unity on Iran and overstates Iran's corresponding incentive to renegotiate already agreed-to terms with the United States. It also places undue emphasis on the provisions within the JCPOA that are set to expire in the short term (the so-called JCPOA sunsets, a feature commonly found in international arms control arrangements)[74] in 2020, 2023, and 2025 as opposed to what are arguably the most critical nuclear restrictions and verification measures that will remain in place until 2031 or indefinitely. Indeed, the verification measures that remain in place will continue to be the best hedge against what would most likely be a covert attempt by Iran to potentially develop a nuclear weapon. An unamended JCPOA still provides for meaningful constraints on Iran's nuclear activity for years to come, providing key time and space to seek follow-on arrangements, while any effort to condition U.S. reentry into the agreement is fraught with risk.[75]

While the next administration should and must make a concerted effort to extend and strengthen nuclear restrictions on Iran, sequencing will be critical. Instead of holding out for immediate agreement on a "better deal," the United States should first seek a return to full compliance with the JCPOA by all parties as the initial step to eventually negotiating a subsequent "more-for-more arrangement." Under this approach, the United States would immediately announce its willingness to return to full implementation of its obligations under the JCPOA if all other parties agree to do likewise. If Iran refuses, then the United States will be in a stronger position to place the onus on it for any ensuing impasse. If all parties do return to compliance, however, that would not only help rebuild unity with the P5+1 and EU and allow time and space for further negotiations, but also begin the process of re-entangling Iran in the international system, incentivizing its adherence to nuclear nonproliferation norms, and increasing the costs of violating those norms in the future.

At the same time, the United States should make clear that it will, in concert with the P5+1, the EU, and Iran, seriously pursue mutually beneficial follow-on arrangements to the JCPOA; lay out a timeline for further negotiations and ideas for what additional steps, nuclear (such as indefinite enrichment level and stockpile caps or an indefinite commitment to refrain from spent fuel reprocessing) or nonnuclear (for example, codifying a limit on the range of its ballistic missiles), the United States would want to pursue; and signal what incentives it and international partners might be willing to offer in order to secure additional concessions from Iran. The U.S. objective should be to make additional diplomatic progress on a follow-on agreement by the JCPOA's Transition Day in October 2023.[76] Further, while the United States should publicly commit to making strong efforts to ensure that Iran benefits from its JCPOA concessions—including by clarifying again for international businesses and banks the scope of both permissible and sanctionable trade with Iran—and to exhausting diplomacy, the United States should also make clear that, absent diplomatic progress, it reserves the right to exercise all available options to address its concerns about Iran's nuclear program in the future. This sequencing of the U.S. strategy would strengthen the U.S. negotiating position and increase the prospects for successful nuclear diplomacy with Iran.

Navigating the Political Complexities of a U.S. Return to the JCPOA

The political complexity of this approach should not be underestimated, either domestically within the United States and Iran or internationally. In the United States, there will be serious opposition within Congress and among interest groups to rejoining the JCPOA and indignation over the administration's perceived failure of not immediately securing a "better deal." Moreover, the next administration might have less flexibility than in the past to ease sanctions in response to cooperative Iranian actions due to efforts during the Trump administration to "build a sanctions wall" to prevent a new administration from rejoining the JCPOA.[77] Significant effort will need to be made to engage members of Congress and the public (which broadly supports diplomacy with Iran) about what is at stake, why a decision to rejoin the JCPOA will be the best approach to secure our strategic interests, and how the United States plans to continue to address both nuclear and nonnuclear threats from Iran. A new administration will have to lay the groundwork to cooperate with Congress, including by keeping members apprised of its diplomatic progress, or lack thereof, across all aspects of the Iran problem set.

Within Iran, which will be ramping up for its own presidential election in the spring of 2021, the Rouhani administration and other pragmatic voices may find it difficult to defend a full return to the JCPOA or broader engagement with the West, absent U.S. concessions to make up for what Iran lost in the intervening years of U.S. noncompliance. Indeed, just as many in the United States believe that we should leverage our return to compliance with our JCPOA commitments to secure more concessions from Iran, some within Iran have advocated that it be paid reparations for the U.S. withdrawal prior to its own return to full compliance with the accord.[78] While a new administration should refuse to entertain the concept of reparations, as it could set a dangerous precedent and would undoubtedly absorb tremendous domestic political capital, it must carefully consider how it carries out and even rhetorically frames a return to the JCPOA, as it will be closely scrutinized within Tehran and could influence the domestic debate within Iran regarding not just the deal but also broader relations with the United States.[79]

With the P5+1 and EU, the United States will need to work to rebuild its reputation as a credible member of the accord that can and will deliver what it promises, even after a decision to return to the JCPOA. Indeed, regardless of the ultimate fate of the JCPOA, a new administration should focus on rebuilding unity with not just our P5+1 and EU partners, but also other key players that hold economic and political leverage vis-à-vis Iran, as their buy-in will be critical to the success and durability of any U.S. approach. In the region, Israel and our Gulf partners will likely oppose a U.S. reentry into the deal absent extensions or modifications. A new administration must engage regional players early on and explain why it views such actions as vital to long-term U.S. interests and the region's security, while laying out its broader strategic vision and plans to deter and contain other nonnuclear-related threats from Iran through targeted diplomatic, economic, intelligence, and military cooperation.

Short of a quick return to the JCPOA, the next administration may also consider modeling an initial understanding of Iran's nuclear program off of the JPOA, the interim deal that effectively froze Iranian nuclear activities in exchange for a freeze on additional nuclear-related sanctions, as part of the step-by-step process to build back up to a more comprehensive deal.

Charting an Alternative to the JCPOA. If there is no plausible path back to either the JCPOA or JPOA or a means by which to use either as an initial foundation for a new understanding, the next administration will have to grapple with identifying an alternative route to its policy objective of preventing Iran from acquiring a nuclear weapon. In this scenario, the U.S. strategy should be guided first and foremost by rebuilding an international coalition with allies and partners both to strengthen the impact of the diplomatic and coercive policy tools at its disposal and to deny Iran the opportunity to divide the members of such a coalition. A new administration should also seek to place the onus on Iran to resume serious engagement regarding its nuclear program by offering both high-level bilateral and multilateral P5+1 talks without preconditions. If Iran refuses to engage, the United States should seek to impose meaningful economic and political costs on Iran in concert with its international allies and partners, while keeping a door open to diplomacy. The history of Iran's nuclear decisionmaking suggests that coercive threats likely need to be coupled with credible coercive assurances to secure meaningful concessions.[80] (As Nobel laureate economist and renowned foreign policy scholar Thomas Schelling stated, ". . . it is not alone the threat that is effective—the threat of pain or loss if he fails to comply—but the corresponding assurance, possibly an implicit one, that he can avoid the pain or loss if he does comply."[81]) Along these lines, the United States must not only continue to offer a diplomatic off-ramp to Tehran that includes potential incentives but also work to rebuild the credibility of its coercive assurances, which was undoubtedly damaged by the Trump administration's decision to withdraw from the deal and reimpose sanctions despite Iran's JCPOA compliance.

Shaping Iran's Decisionmaking on Ballistic Missiles. Regardless of whether the United States is able to convince all parties to return to full compliance with the JCPOA, it is unlikely that a new administration will be immediately well positioned to address the issue of Iran's ballistic missile development, given its central importance to Iran's deterrence strategy and Iran's heightened threat perceptions in recent years. However, the United States can and should take steps to hinder its advancement, strategically shape Iran's decisionmaking regarding the scope of its program, and perhaps seek over time, along with P5+1 partners, to define and codify key parameters and thresholds.

A good place to start might be with Iran's self-imposed limit of two thousand kilometers range for such missiles.[82] A new administration should prioritize engagement but also continue employing economic sanctions, export control restrictions, the thirty-four-country Missile Technology Control Regime (MTCR), and other relevant UN arms embargoes to address missile-related transfers to/from Iran. At the same time, it should consider how broader U.S. policies in the region influence Iran's threat perceptions and corresponding reliance on such technologies for deterrence against perceived outside threats.[83] For example, military experts have recognized that aspects of U.S. efforts to reassure its allies in the region against the threats Iran poses to their interests, including through mass arms sales,[84] could be fueling tensions and ultimately an arms race in the region.[85]

Inheriting Near or Actual War with Iran. It is possible that the next administration could also enter office inheriting a situation in which the United States is on the brink of, or in actual conflict with, Iran, either as an intended or unintended consequence of the Trump administration's maximum pressure campaign.[86] The standoff between the United States and Iran has characteristics of a spiral model of conflict escalation and the classic security dilemma—whereby both sides take defensive measures perceived as threats by the other, and a lack of trust and communication facilitates an escalatory cycle.[87] While it is difficult to predict how such a scenario would unfold, most military experts agree that any direct conflict would be difficult and costly, although the United States maintains a clear military advantage over Iran.[88] If the next administration finds itself in this scenario, it should work to deter attacks from Iran and defend against any aggression by Iran that threatens core U.S. interests, but also immediately lay the groundwork for a return to engagement to de-escalate tensions. It should do so by seeking to establish a high-level diplomatic channel to Iran, either directly or through European or regional partners.

Updating the U.S. Approach to Countering Iran's Destabilizing Policies in the Region. While the next administration should prioritize efforts to prevent Iran from acquiring a nuclear weapon, it should also reevaluate the U.S. approach to countering Iran's regional policies that undermine U.S. interests. Previous administrations of both parties have often pursued less than holistic approaches and perhaps unrealistic objectives regarding these challenges, yielding largely tactical, as opposed to strategic, setbacks for Iran. In recent decades, U.S. policies in the Middle East, as well as missteps by its partners, have at times exacerbated instability and inadvertently increased opportunities for Iran to enhance its regional standing.

The next administration should conduct a comprehensive review of its own objectives for the Middle East, as well as what adjustments it should make to the U.S. presence and to regional partnerships to achieve them without incurring further unnecessary costs or risks to its personnel and partners. As part of that review, it should also evaluate Iran's regional policies in order to develop a new strategy that differentiates between those of Iran's policies that pose a legitimate threat to core U.S. interests and those that have less of an impact on U.S. national security. It should also determine which policies are perceived by Iran to be vital to its national security and therefore are likely to require a more strategic approach to deter over time. Such a review should also identify areas where the objectives of the United States and Iran may actually converge (as they did, to a limited extent, in the campaign to defeat ISIS in Iraq and to achieve political stability in Iraq and Afghanistan).

Rather than make overly broad and ambitious demands of Iran's regional policies, overstate the proportion of its role in regional conflicts, or risk escalation over every undesired action by Iran in the region, the United States should use the findings of the review to guide its priorities and inform its response to Iran's most destabilizing actions. It should do so by building an international campaign to prioritize diplomacy where it can and to impose consequences and limit operational space for such actions where it cannot, which would leverage strategic messaging as well as its combined diplomatic, economic, intelligence, and, when necessary, military resources to disrupt, deter, and push back on Iran.

To start, it should prioritize multilateral diplomacy involving all key stakeholders, including Iran, in order to achieve durable political solutions to the Middle East's underlying conflicts. The region's security environment has not benefited from a lack of dialogue with Iran over the decades. Such dialogue can be used not just to reduce tensions, clarify intentions and redlines, glean insights into Iran's calculus, and potentially deny Iran increased opportunities to exploit conflicts in its favor, but also to test whether Iran might be willing to make some modifications to its regional policies when offered a stake in relevant political processes. As Iran's regional policies are motivated by a complex mixture of threat perceptions, ideology, and competing rational state interests, a credible and informed commitment to engagement toward a more stable regional order will be crucial to potentially shifting how Iran pursues its interests in the region over time. Should Iran refuse to engage or instead seek to undermine political efforts aimed at defusing regional crises, the United States will find it easier to marshal broad opposition to Iran's regional policies and pave the way to increased international pressure aimed at curbing its destabilizing activities if it has exhausted the possibility for constructive engagement.

Iran's support for violent proxies and militias in Lebanon, Syria, and Iraq continues to pose among the most serious and direct regional threats to the interests of the United States. Yet these policies are also likely viewed by Iran as vital to its national security interests. This may explain why a heavy reliance on sanctions, including those reimposed after the U.S. withdrawal from the JCPOA as well as the designation of the IRGC as a foreign terrorist organization, have yet to meaningfully shift Iran's intent or erode its capabilities.[89] As noted earlier, Iran appears determined to protect its key regional interests despite the pressure it is facing.[90] Even as it pursues a regional dialogue to reduce tensions, the next administration should continue to work with Israel, the GCC, and other international partners to utilize the full range of policy tools at its disposal to disrupt, deter, and contain these threats. Such tools should include strategic messaging that exposes Iran's destabilizing actions, sanctions, intelligence sharing, military force posturing, and interdiction operations.

The next administration should also refocus its coordination with our Gulf partners, particularly with Saudi Arabia and the United Arab Emirates, to bolster their defenses against Iran's military, maritime, and cyber activities, while also using its leverage to discourage the kind of counterproductive policies and destabilizing regional adventurism from Gulf states, particularly Saudi Arabia, that in recent years has ultimately yielded strategic advantages for Iran. In particular, the next administration should prioritize reaching a final, diplomatic resolution to the conflict in Yemen—in part, to weaken the Iran-Houthi alliance—and subsequently provide support for its postconflict reconstruction and humanitarian relief. The new administration should also hold close consultations with the GCC on Iran, to include updates on efforts to address Iran's nuclear program and with the goal of having a policy of "no surprises" on issues of shared strategic interest. Relatedly, however, a new administration must be willing to provide clarity to our Gulf partners on the parameters for U.S. actions against Iran, so that it can set expectations about U.S. involvement and engage more effectively about the reality of burdensharing. By doing so, a next administration can potentially help create conditions for engagement between GCC states and Iran, and create room for inclusive political processes that promote regional stability.

The United States should recognize that, while it will not be possible to completely dismantle Iran's networks and influence in the region, it is still both possible and desirable to contain and manage those Iranian actions that undermine core U.S. interests. For example, in Iraq, the United States should leverage its relationship with the Iraqi government to limit Iran's activities inside Iraq that threaten U.S. personnel and partners and work with it to shape and have closer oversight over other facets of Iran's influence. It will be crucial for a new administration to do so without forcing the Iraqi government to choose sides or be drawn into U.S. tensions with Iran, as such developments would ultimately undermine Iraq's tenuous security situation in the post-ISIS period.[91] Similarly, in Lebanon, the next administration should expand its political and economic engagement and invest in the broader stability of the country, given Iran and Hezbollah's demonstrated ability to exploit instability to expand their influence. Protests in both countries in the latter half of 2019 suggest that Iraqi and Lebanese citizens are angered by the often counterproductive role Iran and its proxies have played in recent years, and the

United States should seek to help both governments enact policies to address those grievances and reduce their reliance on Iran.

Toward More Constructive U.S.-Iranian Relations. A new administration should not lose sight of the goal to resolve bilateral issues with Iran's government as part of an effort to build a more constructive relationship over time. Bilateral issues such as the cases of detained or missing American citizens have always required complex and delicate discussions due to the lack of formal diplomatic channels and difficult political dynamics inside both countries. While the Trump administration appears to have, albeit hesitantly according to reports,[92] invested some effort in engaging Iran to seek the return of those unjustly detained or missing in Iran as evidenced by the 2019 prisoner swap, the next administration must ensure a more sustainable and credible channel to Iran, perhaps through a trusted intermediary like Switzerland,[93] to urge the resolution of outstanding cases.

In parallel, the next administration can also take steps to strengthen its relationship with the people of Iran, such as repealing the travel ban; easing visa restrictions more broadly; taking additional steps to ensure the free flow of humanitarian and medical trade, especially that which is most critical to battling the coronavirus crisis in Iran; reinvigorating people-to-people outreach such as State Department–sponsored exchanges on cultural or educational issues; and other actions (either executive or acting in coordination with Congress) to provide support for advancing human rights and civil society capacity in Iran. A new administration should also speak out in favor of human rights inside Iran, while adopting a consistent approach to such matters across the region.

Conclusion

There is little doubt that the next administration will have to prioritize a strategy to deal with the range of threats Iran poses to U.S. interests as part of its broader regional policy. U.S.-Iranian relations have suffered serious setbacks under the current administration, and the history of the relationship since 1979 is littered with missed diplomatic opportunities on both sides. However, the next president will have the opportunity to learn from the mistakes and successes of his or her predecessors and forge a more effective approach to address the challenges Iran poses to U.S. interests by leading with diplomacy. Doing so will require patience, pragmatism, and tremendous political courage, but if progress can be made to resolve our issues with Iran, it will significantly advance our interest in achieving a more stable and peaceful Middle East.

Notes

1. "Iran: Nuclear Intentions and Capabilities," National Intelligence Council, Office of the Director of National Intelligence (November 2007) (https://web.archive.org/web/20101122022043/http:/www.dni.gov/press_releases/20071203_release.pdf).

2. Aaron Arnold and others, "The Iran Nuclear Archive: Impressions and Implications," Belfer Center for Science and International Affairs, Harvard Kennedy School, April 2019 (www.belfercenter.org/publication/iran-nuclear-archive-impressions-and-implications).

3. "Joint Comprehensive Plan of Action," European Parliament, European Union, Vienna, July 14, 2015 (www.europarl.europa.eu/cmsdata/122460/full-text-of-the-iran-nuclear-deal.pdf).

4. Alireza Nader, "Iran After the Bomb: How Would a Nuclear-Armed Tehran Behave?" National Security Research Division, RAND Corporation, 2013 (www.rand.org/pubs/research_reports/RR310.html).

5. J. Matthew McInnis, "The Future of Iran's Security Policy: Inside Tehran's Strategic Thinking," American Enterprise Institute, May 31, 2017 (www.aei.org/press/release-the-future-of-irans-security-policy-inside-tehrans-strategic-thinking/).

6. Daniel R. Coats, "Worldwide Threat Assessment of the U.S. Intelligence Community," Office of the Director of National Intelligence, January 29, 2019 (www.dni.gov/files/ODNI/documents/2019-ATA-SFR---SSCI.pdf).

7. Robert A. Destro, "Bureau of Democracy, Human Rights, and Labor," U.S. Department of State (www.state.gov/bureaus-offices/under-secretary-for-civilian-security-democracy-and-human-rights/bureau-of-democracy-human-rights-and-labor/).

8. "Iran: Events of 2018," Human Rights Watch (www.hrw.org/world-report/2019/country-chapters/iran).

9. "Iranians Favor Diplomatic Relations with U.S. but Have Little Trust in Obama," WorldPublicOpinion.org, September 19, 2009 (http://worldpublicopinion.net/iranians-favor-diplomatic-relations-with-us-but-have-little-trust-in-obama/).

10. "Support for the Family of Robert Levinson," Michael R. Pompeo,

Secretary of State (press statement), March 26, 2020 (www.state.gov/sup port-for-the-family-of-robert-levinson).

11. Ben Rhodes, "Remarks by Deputy National Security Advisor Ben Rhodes at the Iran Project" (https://obamawhitehouse.archives.gov/the-press -office/2016/06/16/remarks-deputy-national-security-advisor-ben-rhodes- iran-project).

12. William J. Burns, *The Back Channel* (New York: Random House, 2019), 356 and 364; and Ben Rhodes, *The World as It Is* (New York: Random House, 2019), 249.

13. Wendy R. Sherman, *Not for the Faint of Heart: Lessons in Courage, Power, and Persistence* (New York: Public Affairs, 2018), 29.

14. "Hassan Rouhani Wins Iran Presidential Election," BBC News, June 15, 2013 (www.bbc.com/news/world-middle-east-22916174).

15. John Kerry, *Every Day Is Extra* (New York: Simon & Schuster, 2018), 500.

16. "Statement by IAEA Director General Yukiya Amano," International Atomic Energy Agency (www.iaea.org/newscenter/statements/statement-by- iaea-director-general-yukiya-amano-9-may-2018).

17. Robin Wright, "Prisoner Swap: Obama's Secret Second Channel to Iran, *The New Yorker*, January 16, 2016 (www.newyorker.com/news/news- desk/prisoner-swap-obamas-secret-second-channel-to-iran).

18. Josh Gerstein, "Obama Toughens Stance on Iran," *Politico*, June 23, 2009 (www.politico.com/story/2009/06/obama-toughens-stance-on-iran-024 087); and Josh Levs, "Fact Check: Was Obama 'Silent' on Iran 2009 Protests?" CNN, October 9, 2012 (www.cnn.com/2012/10/08/politics/fact-check- romney-iran/index.html).

19. Michael R. Pompeo, "After the Deal: A New Iran Strategy" U.S. Department of State (www.state.gov/after-the-deal-a-new-iran-strategy/).

20. Christopher Dickey, Noga Tarnopolsky, Erin Banco, and Betsy Swan, "Why Obama, Bush, and Bibi All Passed on Killing Soleimani," *The Daily Beast*, January 3, 2020 (www.thedailybeast.com/why-obama-bush-and-bibi- all-passed-on-killing-qassem-soleimani).

21. Office of the Spokesperson, "Advancing the U.S. Maximum Pressure Campaign on Iran" (fact sheet), U.S. Department of State, April 22, 2019 (www.state.gov/advancing-the-u-s-maximum-pressure-campaign-on-iran/).

22. Office of the Spokesperson, "Advancing the Maximum Pressure Cam- paign by Restricting Iran's Nuclear Activities" (fact sheet), U.S. Department of State, May 3, 2019 (www.state.gov/advancing-the-maximum-pressure- campaign-by-restricting-irans-nuclear-activities/); and Suzanne Maloney, "As Trump Moves to Cut Off Iran's Oil Revenues, What's His Endgame?" Brookings, April 22, 2019 (www.brookings.edu/blog/order-from-chaos/2019 /04/22/as-trump-moves-to-cut-off-irans-oil-revenues-whats-his-endgame/).

23. Julie Ray, "Inside Iran: Economy, Life Getting Worse," Gallup, June 11, 2019 (https://news.gallup.com/poll/258101/inside-iran-economy-life-get ting-worse.aspx).

24. Kenneth Katzman, Kathleen J. McInnis, and Clayton Thomas, "U.S.-

Iran Tensions and Implications for U.S. Policy," Congressional Research Service, September 23, 2019 (https://fas.org/sgp/crs/mideast/R45795.pdf).

25. "Where's That Better Deal, Mr. Trump?" *New York Times,* May 8, 2018; and Stephen J. Adler, "Iran's Rouhani Says Open to Discuss Small Changes to 2015 Deal If Sanctions Lifted," Reuters, September 24, 2019 (https://www.reuters.com/article/us-iran-usa-un-talks/irans-rouhani-says-open-to-discuss-small-changes-to-2015-deal-if-sanctions-lifted-idUSKBN1 W9267).

26. "How Did Imam Khamenei Predict the Failure of JCPOA?" *Khamenei. ir,* May 19, 2018 (http://english.khamenei.ir/news/5675/How-did-Imam-Kha menei-predict-the-failure-of-JCPOA). Barbara Slavin, "Is Iran Running Out of Patience with Nuclear Agreements?" Atlantic Council, April 29, 2019 (www. atlanticcouncil.org/blogs/iransource/is-iran-running-out-of-patience-with-nuclear-agreements/). Radio Farda, "Rival Camps Point Fingers over JCPOA Failure," Radio Free Europe/Radio Liberty, May 19, 2018 (https://en.radio farda.com/a/iran-factions-in-blame-game-over-jcpoa/29237325.html).

27. Caitlin Oprysko, "Iran Scales Back Commitments under Nuclear Deal, Testing Its Boundaries," *Politico,* May 8, 2019 (www.politico.com/story /2019/05/08/iran-nuclear-deal-commitments-1310448).

28. "Joint Comprehensive Plan of Action," European Parliament, European Union, Vienna, July 14, 2015 (www.europarl.europa.eu/cmsdata/122460/full -text-of-the-iran-nuclear-deal.pdf).

29. As of this writing, Iran is no longer abiding by JCPOA prescribed limitations on the number or type of installed centrifuges at its Natanz enrichment facility; exceeding limitations on its stockpiles of low-enriched uranium (LEU) and heavy water; enriching beyond the 3.67 percent concentration limit; proceeding with prohibited research and development and centrifuge manufacturing activities prohibited by the JCPOA; and injecting uranium gas into centrifuges at its Fordow enrichment facility. For more information, see: Laurel Wamsley and Emily Kwong, "Iran Abandons Nuclear Deal Limitations in Wake of Soleimani Killing," January 5, 2020 (www.npr.org/2020/01/05/793814276/iran-abandons-nuclear-deal-limita tions-in-wake-of-soleimani-killing); "Iran's Nuclear Program: Status," Congressional Research Service, December 19, 2019 (https://crsreports.congress. gov/product/pdf/RL/RL34544); and Michael Wolgelenter and David E. Sanger, "Iran Steps Further from Nuclear Deal with Move on Centrifuges," *New York Times,* November 7, 2019 (www.nytimes.com/2019/11/05/world/ middleeast/iran-nuclear-uranium-centrifuges.html).

30. "Joint Statement by the Foreign Ministers of France, Germany, and the United Kingdom on the Joint Comprehensive Plan of Action," France Ministry for Europe and Foreign Affairs, January 14, 2020 (www.diplomatie.gouv.fr/ en/country-files/iran/news/article/joint-statement-by-the-foreign-ministers-of-france-germany-and-the-united).

31. Steven Erlanger, "Europe's Gamble: Can It Save Iran Deal by Threatening to Kill It?" *New York Times,* January 15, 2020 (www.nytimes.com /2020/01/15/world/europe/europe-iran-nuclear-deal.html).

32. Arsalan Shahla, "Iran Threatens Non-Proliferation Treaty Exit Over European Move," *Bloomberg,* January 20, 2020 (www.bloomberg.com/news /articles/2020-01-20/iran-working-on-final-step-of-reducing-its-nuclear-commitments). Babak Dehghanpisheh, "Iran Lawmakers Call for Debate on Quitting Nuclear Arms Treaty," Reuters, January 28, 2020 (www.reuters.com/article/us-iran-nuclear-npt/motion-for-iran-to-quit-nuclear-prolifer ation-treaty-enters-parliament-idUSKBN1ZR0YQ).

33. Maloney, "As Trump Moves." The leader of Hezbollah, Hassan Nasrallah, has cited the challenges posed by U.S. sanctions and sought to rally increased financial support to his organization. For more information, see Ben Hubbard, "Iran's Allies Feel the Pain of American Sanctions," *New York Times,* March 28, 2019.

34. Dennis Ross and Dana Stroul, "The Flaw in Trump's Maximum Pressure Campaign toward Iran," *Washington Post,* August 29, 2019.

35. Frud Bezhan, " 'Ghost' Tankers, Bartering, and Middlemen: Iran's Playbook for Selling Oil in the Face of U.S. Sanctions," Radio Free Europe/ Radio Liberty, May 7, 2019 (www.rferl.org/a/ghost-tankers-bartering-and-middlemen-iran-s-playbook-for-selling-oil-in-the-face-of-u-s-sanctions/2992 6565.html). Borzou Daragahi, "How Iran Can Evade Sanctions This Time," *The Atlantic,* May 22, 2018.

36. Payam Mohseni and Hussein Kalout, "Iran's Axis of Resistance Rises," *Foreign Affairs,* January 24, 2017.

37. Kenneth Katzman, "Iran's Foreign and Defense Policies," Congressional Research Service, July 23, 2019 (https://fas.org/sgp/crs/mideast/R44017.pdf).

38. Kenneth Katzman, "Under U.S. Sanctions, Iran Regional Influence Grows," Atlantic Council, July 26, 2019 (www.atlanticcouncil.org/blogs/iransource/under-us-sanctions-iran-regional-influence-grows/). "Averting the Middle East's 1914 Moment," International Crisis Group, August 1, 2019 (https://d2071andvip0wj.cloudfront.net/205-averting-the-middle-easts -1914.pdf).

39. William J. Burns and Jake Sullivan, "Soleimani's Ultimate Revenge," *The Atlantic,* January 6, 2020 (www.theatlantic.com/ideas/archive/2020/01/ soleimanis-ultimate-revenge/604471/).

40. Liz Sly and Erin Cunningham, "Iran Took Revenge, No One Died, and the Risk of War Abates, for Now," *Washington Post,* January 8, 2020 (www. washingtonpost.com/world/middle_east/iran-took-revenge-no-one-died-and-the-risk-of-war-abates-for-now/2020/01/08/6d91f048-3227-11ea-971b-43bec3ff9860_story.html).

41. Helene Cooper and Edward Wong, "Skeptical U.S. Allies Resist Trump's New Claims of Threats from Iran," *New York Times,* May 14, 2019.

42. Michael D. Shear and others, "Strikes on Iran Approved by Trump, Then Abruptly Pulled Back," *New York Times,* June 20, 2019.

43. David S. Cloud, "Citing Iran Threat, U.S. to Send up to 1,500 More Troops to Middle East," *Los Angeles Times,* May 24, 2019. Eli Stokols, Chris Megerian, and David S. Cloud, "Amid Conflicting Signals, Trump Sends

More Marines to the Middle East," *Los Angeles Times,* January 6, 2020 (www.latimes.com/politics/story/2020-01-06/trump-iran-war-powers).

44. "Iran: Thousands Arbitrarily Detained and at Risk of Torture in Chilling Post-Protest Crackdown," Amnesty International, December 16, 2019 (www.amnesty.org/en/latest/news/2019/12/iran-thousands-arbitrarily-detained-and-at-risk-of-torture-in-chilling-post-protest-crackdown/). Abigail Williams, Saphora Smith, and Dan De Luce, "U.S. Says Iran May Have Killed Up to 1,000 Protesters," NBC News, December 5, 2019 (www.nbcnews.com/news/world/u-s-says-iran-may-have-killed-1-000-protesters-n1096666).

45. Despite millions of Iranians pouring onto the streets to mourn Soleimani's death in early January 2020 in what appeared to be a surge of national unity, with the IRGC's admission shortly thereafter that it accidentally shot down a civilian airliner when on high alert for an American counterattack in response to Iran's ballistic missile attack against U.S. forces and everyday realities for ordinary Iranian citizens remaining unchanged, antigovernment protests broke out again shortly thereafter and were met with live ammunition, tear gas, and arrests.

46. " 'Maximum Pressure': U.S. Economic Sanctions Harm Iranians' Right to Health," Human Rights Watch, October 29, 2019 (www.hrw.org/report /2019/10/29/maximum-pressure/us-economic-sanctions-harm-iranians-right-health).

47. As a result of related issues, the Trump administration announced the completion of initial financial transactions through a Swiss payment mechanism meant to help facilitate humanitarian exports to Iran in January 2020 (www.bbc.com/news/world-middle-east-51314171).

48. Jarrett Blanc, "Coercion in the Time of the Coronavirus," Carnegie Endowment for International Peace, April 8, 2020 (https://carnegieendow ment.org/2020/04/08/coercion-in-time-of-coronavirus-pub-81495).

49. "Iran's Sanctions Relief Scam," Office of the Spokesperson (fact sheet), U.S. Department of State, April 7, 2020 (www.state.gov/irans-sanctions-re lief-scam).

50. Katrina Manson, "U.S. Boosts Funding of Tech Companies to Help Anti-Tehran Protests," *Financial Times,* January 19, 2020 (www.ft.com/con tent/740a385a-3924-11ea-a6d3-9a26f8c3cba4).

51. Melissa Etehad and Ramin Mostaghim, "When Iran Blocked the Internet, Tech Experts in the U.S. Tried to Hack a Solution. Here's Why They Couldn't," *Los Angeles Times,* December 17, 2019 (www.latimes.com/world-nation/story/2019-12-17/iran-blocked-internet-tech-experts-hack-solution).

52. Richard Goldberg, "Trump Has an Iran Strategy. This Is It," *New York Times,* January 24, 2020 (www.nytimes.com/2020/01/24/opinion/trump -iran.html).

53. Michael R. Pompeo, "After the Deal: A New Iran Strategy," speech delivered at the Heritage Foundation, May 21, 2018 (www.heritage.org/de fense/event/after-the-deal-new-iran-strategy).

54. "Joint Comprehensive Plan of Action."

55. Paul K. Kerr and Kenneth Katzman, "Iran Nuclear Agreement and U.S. Exit," Congressional Research Service, July 20, 2018 (https://fas.org/sgp/crs/nuke/R43333.pdf).

56. "Weighing Benefits and Costs of Military Action against Iran," The Woodrow Wilson International Center for Scholars, September 11, 2012 (www.uscpublicdiplomacy.org/sites/uscpublicdiplomacy.org/files/legacy/media/IranReport_091112_FULL%20FINAL.pdf).

57. James R. Clapper, "Worldwide Threat Assessment of the U.S. Intelligence Community," Office of the Director of National Intelligence, February 9, 2016 (www.dni.gov/files/documents/SASC_Unclassified_2016_ATA_SFR_FINAL.pdf).

58. Robert Einhorn and Vann H. Van Diepen, "Constraining Iran's Missile Capabilities," Brookings, March 2019 (www.brookings.edu/wp-content/uploads/2019/03/FP_20190321_missile_program_WEB.pdf).

59. Security Council Resolution 2231, S/RES/2231, July 20, 2015 (www.undocs.org/S/RES/2231(2015)).

60. Peter Kenyon, "Did Iran's Ballistic Missile Test Violate a U.N. Resolution?" NPR, February 3, 2017.

61. "Full Interview: Javad Zarif on Face the Nation," Face the Nation, CBS News, April 28, 2019.

62. While ballistic missile systems could potentially provide Iran with a nuclear delivery hedge, should it eventually decide to develop a nuclear weapon, Iran views such systems as key to its ability to conventionally deter outside attacks—a view heavily influenced by its experiences during its eight-year war with Iraq in the 1980s—making it a particularly difficult matter to address absent a broader shift in Iran's threat perceptions. See also Einhorn and Vann H. Van Diepen, "Constraining Iran's Missile Capabilities"; and Anthony H. Cordesman, "The Iranian Missile Threat," Center for Strategic and International Studies, January 23, 2020 (www.csis.org/analysis/iranian-missile-threat).

63. Coats, "Worldwide Threat Assessment"; Isabel Kershner, "Israel Is Blamed for Deadly Missile Strikes in Iran," New York Times, July 1, 2019. Zvi Bar'el, "Secret Partner? Behind Iraq's Silence on Alleged Israeli Strikes on Iranian Targets," Haaretz, August 4, 2019.

64. "Trump of Arabia Takes Sides in Sectarian Conflict," Financial Times, May 22, 2017.

65. Farnaz Fassihi and Ben Hubbard, "Saudi Arabia and Iran Make Quiet Openings to Head Off War," New York Times, October 4, 2019 (www.nytimes.com/2019/10/04/world/middleeast/saudi-arabia-iran-talks.html).

66. "UAE Seeks to Reduce Tensions with Iran, Says Media Reports," Radio Farda, October 20, 2019 (https://en.radiofarda.com/a/uae-seeks-to-reduce-tensions-with-iran-say-media-reports/30226264.html).

67. Yaroslav Trofimov, "America's Mideast Allies Want to Sit Out Iranian-U.S. Confrontation," Wall Street Journal, January 7, 2020 (www.wsj.com/articles/u-s-mideast-allies-brace-for-blowback-from-iranian-generals-killing-11578436178).

68. "Iran: Gallup Historical Trends," Gallup, October 21, 2019 (https://news.gallup.com/poll/116236/iran.aspx).

69. "Most Americans Oppose Withdrawing from Iran Deal," *World PublicOpinion.org*, January 6, 2017 (http://worldpublicopinion.net/most-americans-oppose-withdrawing-from-iran-deal/).

70. "Iranians Favor Diplomatic Relations with U.S. but Have Little Trust in Obama," *WorldPublicOpinion.org*, September 19, 2009 (http://worldpublicopinion.net/iranians-favor-diplomatic-relations-with-us-but-have-little-trust-in-obama/).

71. Andrew Miller and Sahar Nowrouzzadeh, "Recognizing the Limitations of American Influence in Iran," *National Interest*, February 14, 2018 (https://nationalinterest.org/feature/why-america-shouldnt-try-influence-irans-future-24504?page=0%2C1). Robin Wright, "The Anger and Anguish Fueling Iran's Protests," *The New Yorker,* January 15, 2020 (www.newyorker.com/news/our-columnists/the-anger-and-anguish-fuelling-irans-protests).

72. A coercive assurance refers to the means by which states pursuing coercion persuade states that are the targets of coercive efforts that punishments will not be carried out if they comply with a coercer's demands. For more information, see Thomas C. Schelling, *Arms and Influence* (Yale University Press, 1967), and Reid B. C. Pauly, "Stop or I'll Shoot, Comply and I Won't: Coercive Assurance in International Politics," PhD dissertation, Massachusetts Institute of Technology, Department of Political Science, 2019.

73. Nahal Toosi, "Democrats Want to Rejoin the Iran Nuclear Deal. It's Not that Simple," *Politico*, July 20, 2019 (www.politico.com/story/2019/07/20/iran-nuclear-deal-democrats-1424113).

74. Richard Nephew, "False Flag: The Bogus Uproar over Iran's Nuclear Sunset," Brookings, March 8, 2015 (www.brookings.edu/blog/markaz/2015/03/08/false-flag-the-bogus-uproar-over-irans-nuclear-sunset/).

75. Sahar Nowrouzzadeh and Katlyn Turner, "How to Ensure Iran Never Resumes Reprocessing," *Bulletin of the Atomic Scientists*, December 13, 2017 (https://thebulletin.org/2017/12/how-to-ensure-iran-never-resumes-reprocessing/#).

76. Transition Day is when U.N. ballistic missiles restrictions are set to be lifted; Iran is to seek formal ratification of the Additional Protocol by its parliament, which will indefinitely allow the IAEA greater access to declared and potentially undeclared facilities if warranted; and the United States and the EU will seek to terminate previously suspended nuclear-related sanctions.

77. Mark Dubowitz, "Build an Iran Sanctions Wall," *Wall Street Journal,* April 2, 2019 (www.wsj.com/articles/build-an-iranian-sanctions-wall-11554246565).

78. Toosi, "Democrats Want to Rejoin the Iran Nuclear Deal."

79. Ariane M. Tabatabai, "Iran's National Security Debate: Implications for Future U.S.-Iran Negotiations," RAND Corporation, October 2019 (www.rand.org/pubs/perspectives/PE344.html).

80. Pauly, "Stop or I'll Shoot."

81. Schelling, *Arms and Influence*, 4.

82. RFE/RL's Radio Farda, "Iran Commanders Say Supreme Leader Limiting Ballistic Missile Range," Radio Free Europe/Radio Liberty, October 31, 2017 (www.rferl.org/a/iran-ballistic-missiles-range-200-km-khamenei/28 826950.html).

83. Farhad Rezaei, "Iran's Ballistic Missile Program: A New Case for Engaging Iran?" *Insight Turkey*, vol. 18, no. 4 (2016), 181–205.

84. Anthony H. Cordesman, "Military Spending and Arms Sales in the Gulf," Center for Strategic and International Studies, April 28, 2015 (www.csis.org/analysis/military-spending-and-arms-sales-gulf).

85. Ellen Laipson, "A New Strategy for U.S.-Iran Relations in Transition," *Atlantic Council Strategy Papers*, Atlantic Council, October 2016 (www.atlanticcouncil.org/wp-content/uploads/2015/08/A_New_Strategy_for_US-Iran_Relations_in_Transition_web_1019.pdf).

86. The manner in which Iran conducted its ballistic missile strikes against U.S. forces in Iraq in response to the U.S. killing of Soleimani appeared to signal a desire to try to manage further, direct escalation as it provided hours of forewarning and appeared to not have sought, even if it was prepared to accept the consequences for, a large number of U.S. fatalities.

87. Michael C. Horowitz and Elizabeth N. Saunders, "War with Iran Is Probably Less Likely than You Think," *Washington Post*, June 17, 2019. Brett McGurk, "A Five-Step Plan to Get Trump out of the Iran Crisis," *Bloomberg*, June 26, 2019.

88. Alex Ward, " 'A Nasty, Brutal Fight': What a U.S.-Iran War Would Look Like," *Vox*, July 8, 2019 (www.vox.com/world/2019/7/8/18693297/us-iran-war-trump-nuclear-iraq). Ilan Goldenberg, "What a War with Iran Would Look Like," *Foreign Affairs*, June 4, 2019.

89. Katzman, "Under U.S. sanctions."

90. David M. Halbfinger, Ben Hubbard, and Ronen Bergman, "The Israel-Iran Shadow War Escalates and Breaks into the Open," *New York Times*, August 28, 2019.

91. "Iraq: Evading the Gathering Storm," International Crisis Group, August 29, 2019 (www.crisisgroup.org/middle-east-north-africa/gulf-and-arabian-peninsula/iraq/070-iraq-evading-gathering-storm).

92. Robin Wright, "The Real Deal Behind the U.S.-Iran Prisoner Swap," *The New Yorker*, December 8, 2019 (www.newyorker.com/news/our-colum nists/the-real-deal-behind-the-us-iran-prisoner-swap).

93. "Freed U.S. Prisoners in Iran Arrive in Geneva," *Swissinfo.ch*, January 16, 2016 (www.swissinfo.ch/eng/us-iran-exchange_freed-american-prisoners -in-iran-flown-to-switzerland/41898544).

ELEVEN

Adapting U.S. Defense Posture in the Middle East for New Priorities

MELISSA DALTON

MARA KARLIN

Substantial U.S. military involvement in the Middle East has been a central and animating feature of U.S. foreign policy in the region for the past thirty years; however, now is the time to recalibrate the U.S. military's regional posture. The United States has been conducting military strikes in Iraq alone across successive military campaigns—spanning Republican and Democratic administrations alike—for nearly all thirty of those years. The U.S. Department of Defense has been authorized to spend US$1.836 trillion (in 2019 nominal dollars) in Overseas Contingency Operations funds from fiscal years 2001 to 2019 to support U.S. forces and activities in Iraq, Afghanistan, Syria, and the broader region.[1]

Over the past fifteen years, and to different degrees, U.S. Presidents Barack Obama and Donald Trump, as well as members of Congress, have sought to decrease U.S. military posture in the Middle East and to increasingly rely on regional states and other actors taking responsibility for their own security. They have attempted to do so for a multiplicity of reasons, among them pressures on the

U.S. defense budget and dwindling support for U.S. military operations in the region. Most compellingly, the demands and limitations of the twenty-first century global security landscape have informed this desire for change, given the threat posed by Iran, interregional dynamics, competition with Russia and China, the imperative to prepare for potential high-end conflict with these two challengers, and counterterrorism imperatives. In some instances, that impulse to draw down U.S. troops has emerged with urgency; for example, in December 2018, President Trump announced that he would immediately withdraw all troops from Syria.[2] Suddenly and unpredictably withdrawing U.S. forces is foolhardy, given ongoing and interlinked conflicts in the region, and the impact it would have on U.S. allies and partners, but there are sound reasons to reduce the U.S. military footprint in the Middle East.

To be sure, the U.S. military will never entirely leave the Middle East, nor is it prudent for it to do so. However, if the Trump administration wants to fulfill its national security strategy and its national defense strategy, which prioritize great power competition with China and Russia, or if a future Democratic administration wishes to scale back military commitments in the region, the U.S. military's posture in the Middle East must get smaller and smarter.[3] Yet the perennial pull of short-term security concerns in the region has complicated the Trump administration's strategy implementation. Escalating tensions with Iran in 2019, culminating in the U.S. killing of IRGC-QF Commander Qassem Soleimani and Iran's retaliatory ballistic missile strikes on Iraqi bases, injuring scores of Iraqi and U.S. forces, saw a parallel buildup of U.S. conventional, special operations, maritime, and missile defense systems in the region in the span of six months.

A meaningful review of U.S. military posture in the Middle East is long overdue, and should include an assessment of what military component will be necessary to deter Iran, in concert with allies and partners and nonmilitary tools.

Moving to a smarter and smaller force posture must include four steps. First, the United States should fundamentally shift the emphasis of its policy focus and budgetary and personnel resourcing to invest more heavily in diplomacy, development, and strategic communication tools. Second, the United States should seek to right-size its military assets and personnel in the Middle East to meet its strategic priorities rather than overinflated threats. Third, the United States should streamline military bases, including reducing the size and staff of its forward headquarters. Finally, as none of these steps come without risks to U.S. interests, the United States must develop mitigation measures to absorb changes to U.S. force posture. Doing so is concomitant with a smaller, smarter approach.

Fluid Future Security Environment

The future security environment in the Middle East will likely remain quite fluid, thereby complicating force planning. The four scenarios forecast below show that there are myriad pathways and drivers of conflict, relationships, and other dynamics that could impede any plans intended to slowly, smartly, and safely reduce the U.S. military footprint in the region. However, despite the risks inherent in these scenarios, continued overreliance on and the maintenance of the current U.S. military footprint in the region will not alone prevent these possible sequences of events from unfolding. U.S. military capabilities and forces present will need to be calibrated to plan for a range of these or similar scenarios.[4]

In the first scenario, the governments of Syria and Iraq fail to effectively stabilize and govern following ISIS's expulsion from key territory in these countries. This fosters a new generation of Salafi fighters, who begin mounting attacks against U.S. and partner interests. With the help of Iran and Russia, President Bashar al Assad's control of the strategically important population centers and coast in Syria's west, center, and east to Deir ez-Zor bifurcates U.S.- and partner-supported zones in the northeast. Meanwhile, Assad's power over much of Syria continues to fuel the Sunni insurgency. Exploiting uneven governance in Syrian opposition-controlled territory, Salafi groups regrow their ranks and tap supply lines stretching across the border with Iraq.

In Iraq, Iranian-backed Popular Mobilization Forces (PMF) militias continue to grow in influence and capability, which, in turn, feed the rising Sunni insurgency. The PMFs bristle at the continuing U.S. force presence in Iraq, yet the United States is compelled to maintain troops there to deter Iran, to counter Sunni insurgents, and to keep an eye on Syria. U.S. leaders find it hard to make or execute plans amid the political uncertainty in Syria and Iraq, and the linkage between the fate of both countries. Moreover, increasing U.S. economic pressure on Iranian-backed networks in the region puts the Iraqi government in a difficult position, with growing calls for the removal of U.S. forces from Iraq, as seen following the assassination of Iran's Qassem Soleimani. This would also undermine any military requirements for pushing back on the ISIS insurgency in western Iraq and northeastern Syria. U.S. plans to slowly and effectively draw down forces would thus be stymied.

The second scenario involves Iran and its pursuit of nuclear and nonnuclear capability development and regional strategy. As the United States pursues its maximum pressure campaign against Iran's destabilizing activities and capability development, following its pull back from the Joint Comprehensive Plan of Action (JCPOA) on Iran's nuclear development, Iran may actually redouble its effort to play a coercive and destabilizing role to reshape the region to its advantage.[5] As European allies diverge from the U.S. assessment on Iran's nuclear development and pledge to uphold the JCPOA, the transatlantic split prevents Washington and its allies from negotiating a follow-on agreement before various provisions of the JCPOA expire, so Iran resumes its nuclear program development and increases its regional destabilizing activities. Israel takes unilateral and preventative action to curtail Iran's capability development in the region, even though the risks to its security have been rising since the last time it pledged to do so (before the JCPOA), given the substantial and sustained presence of the IRGC-QF and militias in Syria and Iraq, and a battle-hardened Lebanese Hezbollah along its northern border. The U.S. military, ordered to boost its efforts to reinforce regional partner security and deter Iran's rogue behavior, draws the necessary resources from the European and Asia theaters, setting back plans for countering Russian and Chinese coercion and for modernizing the future U.S. military force.

Meanwhile, in the absence of an international, unified approach in the waning years of the JCPOA, Iran's supreme leader calculates he can covertly restart additional aspects of Iran's nuclear program without significant blowback. Iran, therefore, clandestinely resumes more nuclear activities as the various JCPOA provisions fall away. Fearful of Iran's moves, Gulf governments and Israel feel more threatened, and they boost efforts to counter Iran's activities in Yemen, Syria, Iraq, and Lebanon. This regional escalation finally compels the United States and European allies to quietly seek patches to extend some provisions of the JPCOA, stopping short of a follow-on comprehensive agreement that will forestall all pathways to a nuclear weapon. Uncertainty lingers about Iran's nuclear future, once again pulling the United States into deeper assurance relationships and deterrence missions with its regional partners. Gulf partners and Israel will likely demand greater U.S. defense investment, depending on the relative success of U.S. Iran policy. More defense investment would likely require the presence of U.S. trainers and advisors, regular deployment of U.S. forces to conduct combined exercises and operations, and the delivery and maintenance of equipment provided by the United States.

In the third scenario, regional competition with Russia, Iran, and China constrains U.S. freedom of action diplomatically, economically, and militarily. Russia solidifies its presence in Syria by reinforcing naval and air bases, rewinds to its tight 1970s relationship with Egypt through arms sales and basing deals, strikes energy agreements with Saudi Arabia and the Iraqi Kurds, and redoubles its military assistance to Iran. Under the Belt and Road Initiative, Chinese economic and infrastructure investments in the Gulf increase, with notable support for Saudi reforms under the Vision 2030 plan. Meanwhile, Iran continues to test the United States and its partners under the threshold of conventional warfare by using proxies in Iraq, Syria, Lebanon, Bahrain, and Yemen; improving its missile, cyber, and maritime capabilities; and colluding with Russia to fill gaps in regional governance and to exploit waning U.S. influence. The robust Russian and Iranian physical presence in the region increases the risk of escalation and constrains U.S. operational choices. Meanwhile, China woos Gulf governments with economic and technological partnerships that carry few strings, weakening perceptions of U.S. relative power in the region.

The United States would have to calibrate its force presence throughout the region to signal, offset, compete, and manage potential escalation with these geopolitical actors. Increased Chinese, Russian, and Iranian capabilities in the information, cyberspace, and electronic warfare areas can confuse, jam, or disrupt U.S. systems, putting U.S. forces and their missions at risk. New U.S. capabilities and operational concepts would be needed to navigate these challenges, requiring adjustments to forces, equipment, infrastructure, and basing over time. In addition, growing Russian and Chinese relationships with traditional U.S. partners and allies in the region may reduce the U.S. negotiating space and diplomatic clout that are important for furthering defense and broader foreign policy goals.

In the fourth scenario, competition among regional U.S. allies and partners compels the United States to bifurcate its regional security planning in ways that contravene its counter-Iran and counterterrorism objectives. Defense relationships and U.S. force presence in countries that are important for countering Iran may not be sustainable over time if differences persist among U.S. regional partners over what amounts to terrorist threats. Brewing regional competitions have complicated the context in which U.S. forces operate in the Middle East. While shared perceptions among Saudi Arabia, the United Arab Emirates (UAE), and Israel have enabled these states to overcome some historical Arab-Israeli animosity, therefore enabling information sharing and planning with the United States, other regional competitions cut against this partnership. Saudi Arabia, the UAE, and Egypt have aligned against Qatar and Turkey, taking steps to politically and economically coerce each other and to back competing proxies in civil wars across Syria, Iraq, and Yemen.

The crisis between Qatar and other Gulf states, fueled by long-simmering tensions over regional competition, is unlikely to abate any time soon. Gulf disunity is unhelpful for several reasons, including impeding efforts to counter ISIS and Iran at both the strategic and operational levels. U.S. Central Command has already indicated that the regional political crisis is undermining its ability to conduct long-term planning. For example, countering Iran's missile threat is best addressed by an integrated air and missile defense approach across the Gulf, which knits together individual systems in each Gulf country, backed by U.S. forces and command and control and intelligence support. Yet, building multinational approaches to integrated air and missile defense has borne superficial returns at best, because of political disputes between and among Qatar and the other Gulf states.

These tensions have been coupled with President Trump's call for U.S. allies and partners to assume greater ownership of the costs of operating shared military bases, including at al Udeid air base in Qatar. The United States is thus unable to develop a comprehensive strategy to address regional security priorities, instead working with individual countries or groups of two to three that share common threat perceptions of Iran and definitions and approaches to violent extremists.

These four scenarios suggest several indicators to watch over the next two to five years. First is Iran's response to an anticipated harder-line U.S. policy, which may show whether Tehran can be deterred in the nuclear, conventional, and unconventional domains. Second, Russia may seek to disrupt U.S. diplomatic and security approaches in the region, which would clarify Moscow's ambitions and intent beyond Syria. Third is the emerging next generation of Salafi fighters; if it thrives, that could be evidence of gaps in local security and governance conditions that Iran and Russia can exploit. Fourth is China's economic investment in the region, which may well help U.S. partners but erode Washington's influence as their preeminent strategic partner. A final indicator is dynamics among and within the Gulf countries. "Unity" in the region is always relative, ebbing and flowing and often more disaggregated. Increasing Gulf propensity for independent and costly military action, combined with assertive Saudi and UAE leaders who seek to move their countries forward, will affect U.S. choices about its force posture in the region.

Some unknowable combination of these possible future scenarios will likely materialize. The United States will need to sharpen its strategy and corresponding posture in the region to adapt to a more agile approach.

Toward a Smaller and Smarter Regional Posture

Given the changing security environment and the increased opportunity cost posed by an overwhelming and disproportionate U.S. focus on the Middle East, a smaller and smarter posture is crucial, but as the previously discussed scenarios underscore, doing so is far from simple. These scenarios offer signposts for how the United States can determine its priorities and weigh tradeoffs that will enable it to move to a smaller and smarter regional posture over time. There are some key ones that exist across scenarios. National security priorities include deterring Iran, countering terrorism, ensuring free and safe access to global waterways, and bolstering allies and partners. The political and financial opportunity costs of defense investments, competition with Russia and China, and perception problems posed by even a gradual U.S. drawdown must be taken into account. The following four-point framework offers guidelines for moving toward a more agile defense approach in the Middle East that still protects U.S. interests and preserves the U.S. military's ability to shift resources if there are indications that one of the above scenarios is materializing.

First, the United States should gradually reshape its "furniture" in the Middle East—that is, its military assets and military personnel—in order to focus on the key objectives of deterring Iran, countering terrorists who threaten U.S. national security interests, securing access to strategic waterways, and broadly supporting allies and partners. This last piece requires a deft approach, since, as one of the other authors argues with Tamara Cofman Wittes, "the United States still has an interest in seeing its main partners—however imperfect they are—stable and secure," but it should not give them a blank check nor indulge their most dangerous and irresponsible tendencies.[6]

This may involve reductions in the U.S. presence, but with an emphasis on smart investments. The goal should be to leave enough for ongoing operations and likely potential contingencies, yet assume some risk in less likely scenarios as prescribed by the 2018 U.S. National Defense Strategy, which calls for "calculated risk-taking" five times in its unclassified summary.[7] For example, U.S. Central Command could relax its requirements for a continuously present carrier strike group, as it has for much of the last three decades—indeed, it often had two carrier strike groups present, consisting of approximately 15,000 U.S. military personnel. Ground forces and the naval presence could be drawn down from Kuwait and Bahrain, respectively, and strike assets could be thinned from the UAE and Qatar. Finally, the proliferation and growth of service and unified command headquarters in the Gulf region should be rolled back through delayering and reducing staff numbers. This last issue will also strengthen U.S. civilian actors in the region by minimizing the viceroy dynamic that has gained steam over the last three decades.[8]

In light of the previously outlined key national security priorities and to better position the U.S. military in the event of likely contingencies, the United States should retain the following elements of its regional posture:

- ballistic missile defense
- adaptable naval and marine configurations that provide littoral, amphibious, lift, strike, maritime domain awareness, and maritime security capabilities
- special operations and counterterrorism capabilities
- intelligence, surveillance, and reconnaissance capabilities
- logistics and enablers required to perform these functions[9]

Second, the United States should streamline its military bases in the region. Research by the RAND Corporation upended a core assumption of the role of bases in securing access for contingencies; a 2014 study found that "the presence of large permanent bases does *not* increase the likelihood of securing contingency access."[10] The array of U.S. bases, primarily situated in the Gulf, which have been sustained and built upon since the 1991 Gulf War, were critical to conducting successive wars in Iraq and remain so for operations in Afghanistan and efforts to fight terrorism and deter Iran. While the latter three missions will remain key features of the U.S. regional approach across a range of possible scenarios, conducting these operations and preparing for the possible crises and contingencies that may emanate from future conflicts do not necessitate keeping all its current bases "hot" in the region. "Hot" bases are continuously manned, operated, and maintained by the primary force user—in this case, the United States—and the host nation. Instead, the United States could shift some of its bases from "hot" to "warm," primarily operated and maintained by the host country rather than by U.S. military personnel under an agreement that permits U.S. forces to surge there when needed either for rotations or in the event of a contingency and, if desired, to preposition equipment.[11]

The criteria for determining which bases should be hot and warm could be focused on the type of capabilities needed in certain parts of the region, where strong security cooperation relationships already exist to burden-share capabilities, and calculations of where the United States could assume some risk. One example to consider is Kuwait, where the U.S. military's long and deep relationship could allow for a transition to warm bases and where a heavy ground-based posture is less relevant for the region's contemporary and future security challenges. Such transitions could be offset by further security cooperation investments to assure critical Gulf partners of U.S. commitment.

Third, the United States must increase the emphasis of nonmilitary tools, which will be vital to enabling regional partners to address long-term challenges of governance and fraying social contracts, and to consolidate counterterrorism and territorial gains into stabilization. Such initiatives will require sustained and accountable funding from both the Department of State and USAID, whose budgets have been slashed by at least 20 percent in every budget request presented by the Trump administration. In addition, the Trump administration has left gaping holes in senior roles focused on the Middle East, including failing to appoint as many as half of its ambassadors to the region. While career foreign, civil, and military service officers can carry forward initiatives quite capably, the absence of the president's representatives in key partner countries limits the political effectiveness of the United States at a time when geopolitical competitors such as Russia and China are deepening their relationships in the region—

and it limits the ability to broker the posture adjustments recommended in this chapter. Without capable and resourced diplomats, the military officials often become the de facto representatives of the United States in the country, which not only does not play to their strengths but represents a real opportunity cost as well.

To this point, the administration must look beyond one commonly used tool—U.S. arms sales—to compete with growing Russian influence in the Middle East. It must strengthen other U.S. diplomatic, economic, intelligence, and strategic communication tools that will be critical to enabling a competitive strategy in the region. It is not a binary choice or substitution of military for nonmilitary tools; rather, diplomatic and development tools and nonmilitary U.S. inducements have been undervalued in this region and should be increased. Leveraging these tools would open opportunities to engage local actors via different communication channels and incentives and enable the United States to help local partners address fundamental drivers of conflict in the region without perennially fighting them. For example, providing stabilization resources to Iraq or encouraging civil society dialogues among various religious groups can deal with the foundational cleavages exploited throughout Saddam Hussein's reign, facilitating security.

Fourth, the United States will need to design a series of mitigation measures to absorb any risks of adjusting its current force posture. These steps should include increasing prepositioned equipment stocks in the region and deepening security partnerships through tailored and targeted advising; institution building; training, exercises, exchanges, and equipping to enable partners to address common security objectives; and a concerted effort to manage partner perceptions. Exercises with several regional militaries, for example, are useful both strategically—deterring Iran; reassuring Gulf partners; and facilitating cooperation among them, given frayed political relationships—and operationally in ensuring the U.S. military maintains readiness for future Middle East conflicts, particularly as it focuses increasingly on other regions. Working with allies such as the United Kingdom and France to pool resources and basing and to synchronize carrier deployments as allied capabilities and regional bases come online would also help offset changes in U.S. posture.

Both countries are increasing their focus on this region; the U.S. military would do well to take advantage of their resurgent interest. Harnessing opportunities to share resources across U.S. combatant commands also provides efficiencies; U.S. Central Command already shares intelligence, surveillance, and reconnaissance (ISR) resources with U.S. Africa Command. Future sharing with U.S. European Command, U.S. Africa Command, and U.S. Indo-Pacific Command could include maritime and strike capabilities. Parallel changes in U.S. force development could also unlock opportunities for adaptation, such as investments in security force assistance brigades and light attack aircraft. Finally, a smaller force may be perceived by partners as reflecting U.S. abandonment of the region. Alleviating these fears requires active engagement by the Department of Defense to outline how, why, and where posture is changing, particularly underscoring that the new posture will be appropriately tailored to future likely threats, which may be appropriately conveyed via wargames or simulations. It should also acknowledge their role in providing regional security in a collaborative manner, and could include a new set of exercises or additional assistance that is rolled out simultaneously. For example, if the United States moves forward with plans to draw down forces in northeastern Syria, it should invest in combined planning and simulations with allies and partners *beforehand* to mitigate risks, share objectives, and work toward a common goal for securing collective interests.

These adjustments should not be taken lightly, as threats and challenges persist in the Middle East. The administration's decision to withdraw the United States from the JCPOA to curb Iran's nuclear program and to seek a more assertive approach to address Iran's destabilizing behavior may trigger escalations that the United States will need to be prepared to address—in close coordination with allies and partners. However, changing realities of the security environment and U.S. political and budgetary dynamics have prompted deep introspection in the Defense Department. It is, therefore, time to make gradual adjustments in the U.S. Central Command theater to reflect it.

The Trump administration and Congress should examine the implications for future force posture in the Middle East. These assessments should include an explanation of how the Department of Defense plans to apply its global operating model and dynamic force employment concepts outlined in the national defense strategy in the Middle East context, and how war plans will necessarily also change with posture adjustments. The region will continue to pose considerable and evolving challenges to U.S. national security. U.S. policymakers should aim to shape U.S. posture to be flexible, adaptive, and responsive to meet requirements in the Middle East theater, but also in the context of global priorities.

The findings in this chapter are adapted from Mara Karlin and Melissa Dalton's article series for *Defense One*: "It's Long Past Time to Rethink U.S. Military Posture in the Middle East," August 7, 2017; "How Should the Pentagon Reshape Its Mideast Posture? Four Indicators to Watch," January 20, 2018; and "Toward a Smaller, Smarter Force Posture in the Middle East," August 28, 2018.

Notes

1. Brendan W. McGarry and Susan B. Epstein, "Overseas Contingency Operations and Funding: Background and Status," Congressional Research Service, January 15, 2019 (https://fas.org/sgp/crs/natsec/R44519.pdf), 2.

2. Donald Trump, "After Historic Victories against ISIS, It's Time to Bring Our Great Young People Home," December 19, 2018 (https://twitter.com/realdonaldtrump/status/1075528854402256896?lang=en).

3. The National Defense Strategy explicitly notes that "Inter-state strategic competition, not terrorism, is now the primary concern in U.S. national security," indicating a shift to focusing on state-based competitors, primarily China and Russia, as the national security priority. Summary of the 2018 National Defense Strategy of the United States of America (https://dod.defense.gov/Portals/1/Documents/pubs/2018-National-Defense-Strategy-Summary.pdf).

4. For additional background reading on the use (and misuse) of scenarios for defense planning, see Andrew Krepinevich, *7 Deadly Scenarios: A Military Futurist Explores the Changing Face of War in the 21st Century* (New York: Random House, 2009); and Michael Fitzsimmons, *Scenario Planning and Strategy in the Pentagon* (Carlisle, PA: U.S. Army War College Press, 2019).

5. As of January 2020, the Trump administration's "maximum pressure" strategy seemingly had failed to halt the prevailing trend of Iranian destabilizing activities or use of proxy forces in the region. See Seth Jones, "Containing Tehran: Understanding Iran's Power and Exploiting Its Vulnerabilities," Center for Strategic and International Studies, January 2020 (www.csis.org/analysis/containing-tehran-understanding-irans-power-and-exploiting-its-

vulnerabilities); and Michael R. Pompeo, "Confronting Iran: The Trump Administration's Strategy," *Foreign Affairs,* October 15, 2018.

6. Mara Karlin and Tamara Cofman Wittes, "America's Middle East Purgatory: The Case for Doing Less," *Foreign Affairs*, December 11, 2018.

7. "Summary of the 2018 National Defense Strategy of the United States of America."

8. Two books detail this dynamic effectively and from very different perspectives. Dana Priest, *The Mission* (New York: W. W. Norton & Company, 2004), and Ronan Farrow, *War on Peace: The End of Diplomacy and the Decline of American Influence* (New York: W. W. Norton & Company, 2018).

9. Readers interested in learning more about this issue would do well to peruse Joshua Rovner and Caitlin Talmadge, "Less Is More: The Future of the U.S. Military in the Persian Gulf," *Washington Quarterly*, vol. 37, no. 3 (Fall 2014), 47–60.

10. Stacie Pettyjohn and Jennifer Kavanaugh, *Access Granted: Political Challenges to the U.S. Overseas Military Presence, 1945–2014*, RAND Corporation, 2016 (www.rand.org/pubs/research_reports/RR1339.html).

11. For example, the air base at Agadez, Niger, is a "warm site."

TWELVE

The Use and Misuse of Security Assistance in the Middle East and North Africa

STEPHEN TANKEL

The Middle East and North Africa region still matters to the United States, but less so than in the past. As the United States reorients its priorities and approach in keeping with the recommendations made by other chapters in this book, it will also need to realign its security assistance to the region and use of such assistance in the region. The coronavirus pandemic and its aftereffects are likely to reinforce the need for the United States to reconsider its national security priorities, and how it uses instruments of national power such as security assistance to achieve them. Currently, the United States is overcommitted to its security partners in the Middle East in terms of the security assistance it provides. Countries in the region received approximately 45 percent of all such assistance since 2002 and 50 percent of foreign military sales during the same period.[1] Moreover, too often, the United States has gotten a poor return on this investment. In some cases, this assistance has helped achieve mutual security goals. In too many other instances, however, security assistance has failed to yield desired results for various reasons, including because U.S. objectives for such assistance were either unrealistic or in tension with one another. The U.S. government's focus on security assistance, as compared to other forms of foreign assistance, sometimes also has hindered its pursuit of long-term goals in the region, particularly the promotion of stable and accountable political institutions in governments that make steady improvements in the areas of democratic development, governance, and rule of law.

This chapter argues that as the United States seeks to reduce the extent of its commitments to the Middle East, maximizing its resources and investments requires it to reduce and realign security assistance to the region and ensure that remaining assistance is used more efficaciously. This means improving accountability for all assistance, sales, and training programs to ensure they are being used to confront threats to and advance the interests of the United States. Increasing the dividends from U.S. security assistance also requires a greater emphasis in the Middle East on improving the professionalism, transparency, and accountability of a partner's security forces and institutions. Perhaps most importantly, the United States must approach security assistance with a clear-eyed understanding of its partners' priorities, as well as their capabilities. There is often a misalignment of threat perceptions and priorities between the United States and recipient Middle Eastern countries. No matter how vast the training, the assistance, or arms the United States provides, assistance will rarely be enough on its own to change a partner's threat perceptions or security priorities.

All of this requires the U.S. government to be more rigorous in its planning and prioritization of security assistance in ways that are direct and frank about U.S. interests, partner objectives, and the ways in which such assistance might affect power dynamics in the recipient country as well as the region. Any such process will need to include a rigorous assessment, monitoring and evaluation program, and greater synchronicity between U.S. security assistance and civilian assistance tools, which is the topic of the next chapter. It must also identify policy redlines when the U.S. government will reduce or end assistance or cease arms sales based on partner behavior, such as the indiscriminate slaughter of civilians in a conflict zone, extreme domestic repression, or the diversion of U.S. weapons to terrorist organizations. The

United States must not only identify potential redlines, but communicate them clearly to partners and then enforce them. Enforcement is crucial and requires political will, which U.S. policymakers should begin to exercise before a crisis hits, by building redlines into agreements with risky partners. Recipients of assistance also should be encouraged to enter into multiyear compacts with the United States that link assistance to jointly agreed upon benchmarks regarding political reforms and reforms to national security institutions.

The Use and Misuse of Security Assistance

Security assistance has been a vital component of American statecraft for decades. It encompasses a range of activities, including training and education, advising, institution building, and, of course, the provision of defense articles. The Departments of State and Defense are the principal agencies responsible for implementing security assistance.[2] State Department security-sector assistance has represented approximately 20 percent of the total foreign assistance budget since 2002. This number jumps to approximately 45 percent if Department of Defense security assistance programs, which are not formally part of the foreign assistance budget, are included.[3] Assistance administered by the Pentagon falls under the umbrella of broader security cooperation, which encompasses all Department of Defense interactions with foreign defense establishments and includes joint military exercises, intelligence cooperation, and logistics support, among other activities.

The United States provides security assistance to civilian and military forces, agencies, and institutions ranging from local law enforcement and judicial systems on one end to standing militaries on the other end. The State Department implements assistance across the entire security sector, whereas the Department of Defense mainly provides assistance to partner militaries.[4] Security assistance is vast. Some of the most notable programs include foreign military financing (FMF); international military education and training (IMET); international narcotics control and law enforcement programs; nonproliferation, anti-terrorism, demining, and related programs; Section 333 building partner capacity programs; the provision of Excess

Defense Articles (EDA); and support for peacekeeping operations (PKO). In addition to providing assistance, the United States also conducts foreign military sales (FMS) and other arms transfers, as well as licensing direct commercial sales. I differentiate between traditional assistance—grants, loans, credits, and other transfers—and arms sales where relevant.

The United States has provided roughly US$140 billion in security assistance and executed almost as much in FMS deliveries to countries in the Middle East since 2002.[5] It has done so in pursuit of various objectives: building partner nations' military or civilian security capacity to contribute to efforts that address common security challenges; increasing partner militaries' interoperability with the U.S. military; building or maintaining relationships in order to secure access and cultivate influence; shaping the policies and actions of partner governments in general or elements of their security sector specifically; and promoting the purchase of U.S. arms and other security-related goods.

These are global objectives, however, and do not account for why such a large amount of assistance and arms sales has flowed into the Middle East and North Africa. Two additional factors contribute to the disproportionate emphasis on the region. Each of these factors helps to explain why this region receives so much in the way of assistance and arms sales, and hints at why the United States is not realizing an adequate return on its investment.

First, the United States still uses assistance to sustain the peace treaty between Israel and Egypt, providing them with approximately US$3.3 billion and US$1.3 billion in FMF, respectively, every year. This accounts for almost two-thirds of total global FMF annual funding, despite the fact that security assistance is no longer critical for keeping either Israel or Egypt committed to the peace treaty. Indeed, Israeli-Egyptian security cooperation has increased in recent years without U.S. inducements, particularly with regard to counterterrorism collaboration in the Sinai.[6] Israel has also lobbied the U.S. government on Egypt's behalf, including pressing the Obama administration to deliver ten Apache helicopters that were withheld from Egypt after the suspension of some U.S. military aid following its 2013 coup.[7]

Military aid for Israel still enjoys strong, and reasonably bipartisan, support for all of the reasons Daniel Shapiro identifies in chapter 5. It is worth reiterating that Israel is considered a reliable U.S. ally in an unstable region and that the benefits of the bilateral relationship flow both ways, even if Israel is the larger beneficiary. The bipartisan consensus that undergirds the relationship has been strained in recent years, partly as a result of Israeli Prime Minister Benjamin Netanyahu's attempts to curry favor with the Republican party and his political alliance with President Donald Trump. Growing concerns among some Democrats about Israeli settlements, treatment of Palestinians, and the fate of the two-state solution could imperil bipartisan support for the U.S.-Israel relationship in the future. Yet, as Shapiro observes, even in today's hyperpartisan age, "a strong consensus endures about the abiding American commitment to Israel's existence, security, and right and ability to defend itself."

The U.S. government is committed, by law, to maintain Israel's qualitative military edge (QME) over other regional countries. This legal provision informs the levels of security assistance provided to Israel as well as to other countries in the Middle East and North Africa. It is highly unlikely that the United States will abandon its commitment to maintaining Israel's QME in the near term, though it is possible that if U.S. security assistance and arms sales to Israel's neighbors declined, aid to Israel also could be reduced. This presumes, however, that the technological and tactical capabilities of Arab militaries in the region would decline proportionately with reductions in U.S. assistance and arms. In any event, of the two largest recipients of security assistance in the region, reductions to Egypt are considerably more likely than to Israel.

U.S. assistance to the Egyptian Armed Forces may facilitate preferential treatment for U.S. military traffic through the Suez Canal and incentivize the Egyptians to enable U.S. military overflight of its territory, which was important during the Iraq War of 2003, when other Arab states closed their airspace. But at approximately US$1.3 billion annually, the United States is overpaying for these benefits, especially when one considers the various ways in which Egypt has increasingly undermined U.S. interests in the region and beyond, as discussed in chapter 7. In addition, it is clear that the over US$50 billion in security assistance that the United States has given to Egypt since 1978 (the first year in which such assistance was provided) may have unintentionally bolstered authoritarian control—increasing the military's capacity to curtail universal rights and limit economic reform prospects.[8]

Egyptian leaders believe, or at least promote the perception that they believe, such assistance is an entitlement. As mentioned above, the Obama administration suspended some U.S. military aid following the 2013 coup.[9] This assistance was withheld "pending credible progress toward an inclusive, democratically elected civilian government through free and fair elections."[10] Egyptian leaders responded by portraying these reasonable conditions as shortsighted cuts in assistance.[11] U.S. concerns about jihadist violence in Egypt, Cairo's willingness to cooperate on counterterrorism, and the desire for Egyptian support for the anti-ISIS coalition ultimately convinced policymakers that a return to the status quo was a priority.[12] This anxiety about Egyptian counterterrorism cooperation highlights the second factor that explains the disproportionate amount of security assistance provided to countries in the Middle East.

Since September 11, 2001, the U.S. government has increasingly relied on security assistance to promote counterterrorism cooperation and build the capacity of local partners to fight shared threats from non-state actors. This effort began in earnest with the use of assistance to rebuild the military in Iraq (as well as Afghanistan). In recent years, efforts to build capacity and interoperability have spread throughout the region and beyond, as the United States has sought to get other countries to carry more of the burden in terms of the costs and risks of counterterrorism in order to conserve its own resources and military strength. Congress created numerous new authorities after 9/11, many of which were vested under the Department of Defense instead of the State Department. Congress consolidated many of these authorities under Section 333 building partner capacity programs in 2017.

Capacity building efforts have expanded beyond training and equipping partner forces to include advising, assisting, and accompanying them on missions. This robust approach to working "by, with, and through" partners goes beyond the traditional conception of assistance and increasingly blurs the lines between security cooperation and combat. It has had some operational successes, most notably in the counter-ISIS campaign, partnering with the Iraqi Security Forces and the Syrian Democratic Forces. As this experience illustrated, train-and-equip efforts were insufficient on their own. In addition to supporting the development of local security actors, U.S. special operations forces (SOF) were embedded in combat units and operated with indigenous forces closer to the front lines. SOF bring with them critical "operational enablers," which is the term for things like close air support to protect forces on the ground and airlifts to deploy, evacuate, and sustain them. It also includes the provision of intelligence, surveillance, and reconnaissance, often via unmanned drones, and other logistical support. When combined with the tactical advice SOF provides, these enablers can make partner forces much more effective. But this approach is not in line with the traditional concept of security assistance. And it is not without risks.

Getting the most out of U.S. military advisers requires placing them close to operations, which increases the likelihood of U.S. casualties. There are also real security risks to putting U.S. troops in a position where they are aware of, or complicit in, abuses that could expose them to legal jeopardy, stain America's reputation, and provide U.S. adversaries with propaganda victories. Yet their exposure to such abuses has increased, because many local forces do not share the U.S. military's commitment to the Law of Armed Conflict.

In addition to these immediate costs, some of the benefits of working by, with, and through may be more limited or finite than they appear. The U.S. special-operations community is relatively small. If relying on local partners is partly intended to free up U.S. forces for other missions, then its effectiveness is arguably undermined by the dependence on one of the most overstretched elements of the American military for operational success.[13] Moreover, "by, with, and through" is intended to improve partners' capabilities and give them "ownership" over the aftermath of military operations that involve the United States. Too often, however, advise-and-assist missions temporarily make a partner more effective, but fail to improve that partner's ability to manage its own security challenges. This suggests the need for a much longer and deeper commitment.

The by, with, and through approach is predicated on the assumption that local partners share U.S. priorities for how such assistance will be used.[14] While partners may share a specific threat with the United States, they also face other, greater threats from a variety of sources that receive a higher priority.[15] For example, now that ISIS has lost its territorial foothold, divergent threat perceptions and political differences have made it more challenging to consolidate gains.[16] This highlights the degree to which U.S. policymakers are often overly optimistic about the power of security assistance to shape a partner's behavior.

Almost two decades after massive increases in security assistance in the Middle East were made in the name of counterterrorism, it is clear that security assistance will not change a partner's calculus regarding how it prioritizes or perceives threats. This creates situations where, at best, assistance is not used effectively, and, at worst, it is reoriented or misused in ways that are diametrically opposed to U.S. interests. For example, Saudi Arabia and the United Arab Emirates reportedly made unauthorized transfers of U.S. weapons and equipment to al Qaeda–linked groups fighting in the Yemeni civil war in an attempt to buy their loyalty and bolster their capabilities against the Houthis. The Saudi military also reportedly airdropped American-made tube-launched anti-tank missiles in areas where al Qaeda in the Arabian Peninsula (AQAP) was known to be operating.[17]

Efforts to build partner capacity are likely to fail to achieve U.S. objectives even where threat perceptions are aligned, if other structural deficiencies in regional forces are not addressed. Militaries in the Middle East and North Africa are often corrupt, poorly motivated and trained, burdened with mediocre or incompetent leadership, undereducated at all but the more senior levels, and lacking in legitimacy among the population. According to Mara Karlin, who has studied capacity building in fragile states, American officials must be deeply involved in "sensitive military matters"—such as the appointment of senior personnel and the organizational structure of the armed forces—in order to have any hope of professionalizing partner forces and building strong institutions. She also asserts that antagonistic external actors must be deterred from undermining the partner in question.[18] Yet the type of intensive intervention Karlin describes is often unrealistic in terms of what the United States is prepared to undertake and what most partner nations in the Middle East would accept.

The Dark Underbelly of Assistance

Any discussion of security assistance to countries in the Middle East region must acknowledge that many of the threats in the region exist in no small part because most of these countries are led by autocrats who frequently use the power of the state to violently suppress internal dissent and in some cases destabilize their neighbors. The U.S. provision of security assistance can lead recipient governments to believe they can engage in bad behavior—domestically or regionally—because the U.S. government is reliant on them or invested in their stability.[19] When the United States continues to provide assistance or sell arms to a country in spite of such behavior, it may reinforce this perception and make the recipient even more resistant to change by defraying the costs of staying the course.

Rulers in the Middle East typically have little interest in using security assistance to support reforms necessary for improving governance or rule of law. For example, Jordan is considered one of America's most reliable Arab security partners. The single greatest threat to the government, and thus to its partnership with the United States, is internal pressure that could cause the monarchy to collapse. Yet the overwhelming majority of security assistance the country receives—on average, over US$475 million annually over the past decade—goes to supporting the military instead of domestic programs that could address these pressures.[20]

The risks that lethal assistance will be used as a tool of repression are well known. The chances are also growing that the United States may sell or otherwise provide artificial intelligence or other cyber capabilities that enable mass surveillance. This presents a considerable threat to societies across the Middle East, and could undermine U.S. efforts to promote freedoms, human rights, and the free flow of information online. Meanwhile, transfers of security assistance and arms to partner militaries continue to empower the defense, national security, and intelligence arms of Middle Eastern governments, at the expense of already poorly run civilian institutions.

In addition to reinforcing bad governance domestically, the free flow of arms and other assistance has encouraged regional military adventurism by U.S. partners in the Middle East. Most notably, the regimes in Riyadh and, to a lesser extent, Abu Dhabi appeared to believe for a period of time that they had carte blanche to expand their rivalry with Iran. This has contributed to an escalation of sectarian tension that makes stabilizing the Middle East even more difficult, harms American interests, and contributes to humanitarian crises.

The Yemeni civil war is the most glaring example in which U.S. assistance has enabled reckless regional policies by American partners. Saudi pilots flying American-made F-15s and dropping American-made bombs have killed thousands of civilians in Yemen.[21] As part of sales agreements, American mechanics service the aircraft. Because the Saudis are not allowed access to some targeting software and other classified technology, U.S. technicians on the ground have also performed upgrades and troubleshot other maintenance issues.[22] Until November 2018, Saudi jets benefited from aerial refueling from U.S. aircraft.[23] The United States has also provided targeting intelligence in an unsuccessful effort to stop the Saudis from killing Yemeni civilians.

American forces may not be fighting in Yemen, but U.S. assistance has made America a party to the conflict. The Houthis launched missile attacks against the USS *Mason* near the Bab al Mandab Strait in October 2016, leading the U.S. military to destroy three radar sites in Yemen in response. Moreover, Iranian support for the Houthis has grown as the conflict has dragged on. Iranian-supplied anti-ship cruise missiles endanger freedom of maritime navigation in and around the Arabian Peninsula.[24] As a result, the Houthis are now able to threaten the flow of commercial vessels, especially ones carrying oil and gas, a core U.S. interest. In addition to these direct threats to U.S. interests, continuing to sell arms to the Saudis and Emiratis also contributes to the severe humanitarian crisis occurring in Yemen and has raised the issue of U.S. legal culpability in possible war crimes committed by the Saudi-led coalition.[25]

The Trump administration's predilection for prioritizing arms transfers over other instruments for engagement in the Middle East exacerbates the negative externalities long associated with U.S. assistance to the region. The emphasis on arms sales reflects the increasingly crowded global arms market and the administration's ambition to stimulate domestic manufacturing growth.[26] In the case of sales to Saudi Arabia and the United Arab Emirates, both of which are responsible for thousands of civilian casualties in Yemen, this emphasis is also a result of U.S. reliance on them for its maximum pressure campaign against Iran.[27] Congress has made multiple attempts to limit or end U.S. arms transfers to the two Gulf states, including the passage of bipartisan legislation blocking the administration's approval of over US$8 billion in arms sales to Saudi Arabia and the UAE, which was based on the premise of a false national emergency that Trump used to circumvent the need for congressional consent.[28] Trump vetoed this legislation, setting up additional congressional challenges.[29]

Doing Less with Less

Future U.S. policymakers should have realistic ambitions about what they can achieve in the Middle East. It is not presently a place of opportunity for the United States. Rather, the region is currently a place where the United States must prevent, contain, or mitigate crises that threaten it directly or risk distracting it from other pressing priorities. Potential crises include an international terrorist attack or the acquisition by terrorists of game-changing capabilities, another round of massive migrations into Europe, and long-term disruptions in the free flow of oil or to freedom of navigation through choke points such as the Bab al Mandab Strait and Strait of Hormuz. The United States will also face ongoing challenges from Iran, which not only threatens U.S. interests directly but also contributes to the warped policies pursued by America's partners in the region.

These are existing challenges, and, as such, many of the major objectives for U.S. security assistance in the Middle East will remain unchanged. The hurdles to using it effectively, outlined in the previous section, are not going away, regardless of whether or not the United States reduces its overall commitments in the region. One might be tempted to surmise that the U.S. government will need to "do more with less," to use the common policy platitude. Far too often, this is a pipe dream. It suggests the problem is purely one of using resources poorly or of ineffective planning, and ignores the impossibility of some problems that are simply outside of U.S. control.

If the United States may not be able to do more with less in the Middle East, it could arguably do less with less without sacrificing its core interests. This will require confronting tough tradeoffs, such as balancing legacy security assistance commitments to countries that may no longer be as important as they once were with emerging needs and threats. In some cases, this will require convincing old partners not only to accept less assistance than in the past, but also different types of assistance that may be less appealing to them but more useful for the challenges ahead. U.S. decisionmakers, meanwhile, must have greater willingness to accept risk in certain instances. For example, U.S. military planners will have to separate critical from convenient access, and must be willing to consider reducing or pausing assistance or arms sales even if doing so risks leading the recipient to express dissatisfaction by curtailing access.

The United States will confront new challenges as well, chief among them growing competition from Russia and China in the Middle East. This competition could replace counterterrorism as a rationale for using security assistance in the Middle East, in this case as an instrument of relationship maintenance. But U.S. officials should resist the temptation to use assistance to compete with Russia and China when it comes to arms sales. Most countries in the region simply are not strategically important enough to grant them this type of leverage over the United States. Moreover, those that are critical to U.S. national interests are also longtime recipients of security assistance and purchasers of American arms, meaning they are already reliant on U.S. trainers and support systems and are therefore less likely to purchase arms from U.S. competitors. These countries may be able to diversify their arms sourcing, but they will find it difficult to shift completely from the United States to another primary patron. Effectively deterring adversaries—whether Iran or Russia—also has less to do with arming partners, who may behave irresponsibly. Instead, such deterrence demands clearly articulating redlines and retaining prepositioning agreements and emergency basing rights for military access, as discussed in chapter 11 by Melissa Dalton and Mara Karlin.

Implications and Recommendations

The U.S. government maintains an interest in the security and stability of its Middle Eastern partners, which, although imperfect, can still play an important role in advancing American interests in the region. Unfortunately, these partners engage in practices that threaten their own stability and sometimes U.S. interests by extension.

Greater professionalism, transparency, and accountability are needed across Arab states' security sectors, not just in their militaries. No matter how operationally and tactically capable their militaries are or how many advanced weapons these states have, the United States will fail to achieve its capacity-building goals for security assistance if it does not use it to improve institutions and drive political reform. This requires a fundamental departure from the current approach to U.S. security assistance and arms sales in the region where the emphasis on tactical capabilities and big-ticket conventional weapons systems has further militarized problems related primarily to governance and rule of law.

U.S. policies regarding security assistance and arms sales must be driven by an independent assessment of American interests and a clear-eyed vision of where to accept risk, rather than by legacy priorities and agreements, or the demands of regional partners. The United States must find ways to redistribute assistance globally, use the remaining resources more efficaciously in the region, and mitigate the risks that come with providing or selling lethal equipment to the more problematic Middle Eastern countries.

Establish prioritization and planning processes. If the U.S. government truly aims to align security assistance with overarching foreign policy priorities, then emphasizing coordinated, department-wide planning processes at the Departments of State and Defense is a critical step. Such a process would elevate common interagency objectives for assistance, deconflict competing objectives where necessary, identify security assistance resources projected to be available for the period of time necessary to achieve such objectives, and recommend the allocation of assistance based on U.S. foreign policy priorities, country prioritization, availability of resources, and regional and country-specific assumptions.

In such a process, the appropriate elements within the U.S. government's interagency process would identify top foreign policy objectives and priority countries based on these objectives. Factors to consider when prioritizing recipients might include ways in which security assistance could advance U.S. interests directly against China, Iran, and Russia, as well as in competitive or contested environments where one or more of these countries is trying to make inroads; the extent to which security assistance genuinely helps in the maintenance of existing peace treaties between other countries, such as Egypt and Israel; and where security assistance is most needed and would be most useful for degrading or containing terrorist groups that directly threaten the U.S. homeland.[30]

Implement assessment, monitoring, and evaluation protocols. Congress mandated that the Department of Defense, which dispenses a growing amount of security-assistance funding, institute assessment, monitoring, and evaluation (AM&E) protocols. While development of these protocols is still underway at the Department of Defense, the State Department has lagged. Some bureaus have developed sophisticated processes, whereas others have not. The State Department needs to develop a department-wide program. Other departments and agencies involved in the execution of security assistance should, too. Although it may be unrealistic and ultimately unhelpful to develop a single, common interagency process, all of the relevant departments and agencies should at least pursue a common framework for coordination on AM&E.

Identify and enforce redlines. The days of continuing to support governments and militaries in the Middle East regardless of their behavior need to end. This does not mean the United States should preemptively shut down assistance or cease arms sales to every country in the region that does not unfailingly comport itself in line with American values or always act in the U.S. interest. Nor should the U.S. government retroactively cut off assistance or arms sales every time a country steps out of line. Rather, it is time for the United States to identify and communicate to regional partners the conditions under which the United States may restrict or end security assistance or arms sales. Critically, the U.S. government must enforce these redlines when necessary, while simultaneously providing a partner with a clear off-ramp that it can take in order to end an "embargo."

Pursue positive conditionality. Conditioning assistance more effectively could help mitigate some of the ways in which partners hinder U.S. interests and reinforce the more positive aspects of their behavior. Research suggests conditionality works best when a donor does not have critical interests in the recipient country and the recipient's vulnerability—defined as its need for assistance—is high. Conditionality is least successful in cases where the donor perceives core interests to be at stake and the recipient is prepared to leave assistance on the table to secure other interests.[31] In practice, this means the cost of noncompliance for the partner must be higher than that of adherence, and the United States must be prepared to stand firm if conditions are not met. Yet once a recipient is providing goods that America is loath to lose, this makes it easier for that country to refuse entreaties on other issues and still keep U.S. assistance or arms sales flowing. To help overcome this challenge, the U.S. government should pursue multiyear compacts with governments in the region that identify mutually agreed-upon objectives and conditions under which it would increase or expand security assistance in line with progress. Formalizing understandings on security assistance will hopefully both encourage U.S. policymakers to enforce their terms and leave no doubt as to U.S. expectations. Willingness to sign up for such compacts and progress on them should be factored into the planning process that prioritizes recipients of assistance.[32]

Focus on the whole security sector. Security assistance has been focused on partner militaries at the expense of civilian security forces and institutions. This is partly a result of restrictions imposed by Section 660 of the Foreign Assistance Act, which prohibits international police training. The U.S. government has found various workarounds, but it has not developed a comprehensive program focused on improving the capacity, capabilities, and professionalism of civilian security forces and institutions. Congress should amend or repeal Section 660 and authorize the secretary of state to create a dedicated program for this purpose. Such a program should emphasize democratic policing, respect for human rights and due process of law, investigative and forensic capabilities, prison reform, border security, and judicial sector capacity. It should be implemented following a U.S. government assessment that the country's leaders have exhibited the willingness to enhance rule of law, protect human rights, and create accountable and transparent civilian security sector forces and institutions.

Conclusion

The Trump administration's approach to the Middle East—backing Saudi Arabia and the United Arab Emirates to the hilt in their sectarian struggle as part of a misguided push for regime change in Iran, encouraging the Israeli government's worst impulses against the Palestinians in pursuit of political gains at home, and writing autocratic partners a blank check to pursue whatever domestic policies they please—has exacerbated many of the challenges that already existed in the region. Even a smarter approach will founder, however, unless policymakers find ways to optimize the benefits and mitigate the risks associated with security assistance.

Notes

1. This data is from Security Assistance Monitor (http://securityassistance.org). The percentage for FMS is based on deliveries, not authorizations or notifications, through 2017.

2. The Departments of Justice, Homeland Security, Treasury, and others also implement security assistance.

3. Data on foreign assistance is from "Foreign Aid: An Introduction to U.S. Programs and Policy," Congressional Research Service, updated April 16, 2019 (https://fas.org/sgp/crs/row/R40213.pdf). Data on security assistance is from Security Assistance Monitor.

4. The Department of Defense has authorities to assist nonmilitary security forces in certain instances.

5. Data is from Security Assistance Monitor. Security assistance amounts are available through 2020; FMS amounts are through 2017.

6. David Kirkpatrick, "Secret Alliance: Israel Carries Out Air Strikes in Egypt, with Cairo's O.K.," *New York Times*, February 3, 2018.

7. "Israel Bluntly Told the United States Not to Cut Aid to Egypt," *Times of Israel*, October 15, 2013.

8. Data on FMF for Egypt is from Jeremy Sharp, "Egypt: Background and U.S. Relations," Congressional Research Service, updated March 12, 2019 (https://fas.org/sgp/crs/mideast/RL33003.pdf).

9. In addition to withholding Apache helicopters, the administration also canceled planned cash transfers of economic aid and halted delivery of F-16 aircraft, Harpoon missiles, and M1A1 tank kits to Egypt.

10. Jen Psaki, "U.S. Assistance to Egypt," U.S. Department of State press statement, October 9, 2013 (https://2009-2017.state.gov/r/pa /prs/ps/2013 /10/215258.htm).

11. Oren Dorell, "Egypt Slams U.S. Aid Cut; Allies Concerned," *USA Today*, October 11, 2013.

12. Marcia Recio, "Rep. Granger Urges Obama to Send Arms Owed to Egypt," *McClatchy*, February 23, 2015; Dafna Rand and Stephen Tankel, "Security Cooperation and Assistance: Rethinking the Return on Investment," Center for a National American Security, August 5, 2015.

13. There is a related danger of overtaxing elite forces, which are not easily replaced.

14. For instance, the 2011 National Strategy for Counterterrorism asserts that "building strong, enduring partnerships based on shared understandings of the threat and common objectives is essential to every one of our overarching CT objectives." White House, National Strategy for Counterterrorism, 2011. See also, White House, "Fact Sheet: Strategy to Counter the Islamic State of Iraq and the Levant (ISIL)," September 10, 2014.

15. Stephen Tankel, *With Us and Against Us: How America's Partners Help and Hinder the War on Terror* (Columbia University Press, 2018).

16. U.S. support for the Syrian Democratic Forces also further strained the U.S. relationship with Turkey.

17. "House Foreign Affairs Committee Presses Administration for Answers on U.S. Weapons with Al Qaeda Groups in Yemen," Committee on Foreign Affairs of the U.S. House of Representatives, February 26, 2019 (https://foreignaffairs.house.gov/2019/2/house-foreign-affairs-committee-presses-administration-for-answers-on-u-s-weapons-with-al-qaeda-groups-in-yemen).

18. Mara E. Karlin, *Building Militaries in Fragile States: Challenges for the United States* (University of Pennsylvania Press, 2018).

19. Mara Karlin and Tamara Cofman Wittes, "America's Middle East Purgatory: The Case of Doing Less," *Foreign Affairs*, January/February 2019.

20. Assistance spiked to over US$1 billion in 2016 and 2017 in response to the conflict with ISIS.

21. As of November 2018, 6,872 civilians had been killed and 10,768 wounded in Yemen, the majority by Saudi Arabia–led coalition air strikes, according to the Office of the United Nations High Commissioner for Human Rights (OHCHR). Unofficial estimates put the actual number of civilian

casualties much higher. "Bachelet Urges States with the Power and Influence to End Starvation, Killing of Civilians in Yemen," U.N. Office of the High Commissioner for Human Rights, November 10, 2018 (www.ohchr.org/EN/NewsEvents/Pages/DisplayNews.aspx?NewsID=23855&LangID=E).   On unofficial estimates, see Karim Fahim, "The Deadly War in Yemen Rages On. So Why Does the Death Toll Stand Still?" *Washington Post*, August 3, 2018.

22. Declan Walsh and Eric Schmitt, "Arms Sales to Saudis Leave American Fingerprints on Yemen's Carnage," *New York Times*, December 25, 2018.

23. Phil Stewart and Nayera Abdallah Mahmoud, "U.S. Ends Refueling Support in Yemen War as Pressure Builds on Saudi Arabia," Reuters, November 10, 2018.

24. Andrew Exum, "What's Really at Stake for America in Yemen's Conflict," *The Atlantic*, April 14, 2017.

25. "Yemen: United Nations Experts Point to Possible War Crimes by Parties to the Conflict," U.N. Office of the High Commissioner for Human Rights, August 28, 2018 (www.ohchr.org/en/NewsEvents/Pages/DisplayNews .aspx?NewsID=23479&LangID=E).

26. Melissa G. Dalton, "The Risks and Tradeoffs of Security Cooperation," *Texas National Security Review*, November 20, 2018.

27. "Yemen: United Nations Experts Point to Possible War Crimes by Parties to the Conflict."

28. Merrit Kennedy, "Trump Vetoes Bills Intended to Block Arms Sales to Saudi Arabia," NPR, July 25, 2019.

29. See, for example, "Prohibition on the Use of Emergency Authorities for the Sale or Transfer of Defense Articles and Services to Saudi Arabia and the United Arab Emirates," amendment to the House of Representatives Rules Committee Print 116-19 of the National Defense Authorization Act of 2020; "Restriction on Emergency Authority Relating to Arms Sales Under the Arms Export Control Act," amendment to the House of Representatives Rules Committee Print 116-19 of the National Defense Authorization Act of 2020.

30. The U.S. government might consider developing a separate framework for prioritizing recipients of arms transfers.

31. Stephen Biddle, "Building Security Forces and Stabilizing Nations: The Problem of Agency," *Daedulus*, Fall 2017 (www.amacad.org/publication/building-security-forces-stabilizing-nations-problem-agency).

32. For more on how positive conditionality might work, see Stephen Tankel and Melissa G. Dalton, "How to Improve Return on Investment for Security Assistance," *Lawfare* (blog), August 27, 2017 (www.lawfareblog.com/how-improve-return-investment-security-assistance); Tommy Ross and Melissa Dalton, "A Roadmap for Better Choices from Security Partners," *War on the Rocks* (web publication), January 17, 2020.

THIRTEEN

Toward Strategic Investments in Foreign Assistance

The Tunisia Experiment

DAFNA H. RAND

Civilian Assistance and Leveraging Change

For decades, the United States has given more foreign aid to Middle Eastern and North African states than to Africa, Latin America, and Asia combined.[1] Israel, Egypt, Jordan, and Iraq have been among the top ten recipients of U.S. foreign assistance globally for nearly two decades, with assistance to Israel and Egypt together totaling nearly 12.2 percent of the annual foreign aid budget in 2018.[2] The aid packages to Israel, Egypt, and Jordan—each of which in total exceeds US$1 billion—largely consist of the security assistance and training programs detailed in chapter 12 by Stephen Tankel, primarily in the form of foreign military financing (FMF).

Yet alongside the vast sums of security assistance to the region, the United States also offers a smaller civilian aid package comprising disparate economic development, humanitarian, rule of law, governance, and educational programs. The current size and type of civilian assistance packages to Egypt, Iraq, Iran, Jordan, Lebanon, Tunisia, Morocco, Algeria, Yemen, and the Syrian and Palestinian people reflect the policy legacies and commitments of U.S. presidents since the 1970s. For instance, in the wake of the Camp David Accords, the United States began providing Egypt nearly half a billion dollars in civilian grant assistance.[3] Forty years later, the civilian aid package to Egypt endures, albeit at a reduced level, even though the Egyptian government now considers strategic cooperation with Israel as deeply beneficial and would maintain its peace agreement with Israel without the incentives of U.S. assistance.[4]

In other cases, today's civilian assistance packages reflect post-9/11 policy priorities, such as significant investments in Iraqi reconstruction after the 2003 war or the programs associated with the George W. Bush administration's "Freedom Agenda," which prioritized democratization programs in the Arab world. Since 2011, the protracted civil crises in Syria, Yemen, and Libya, and their grave civilian consequences, have significantly shaped the aid landscape in the region. Billions in U.S. foreign aid dollars have gone to the humanitarian response effort in Syria and Yemen, and foreign assistance to Jordan and Lebanon has expanded given the economic toll of their hosting millions of Syrian refugees. Meanwhile, Tunisia—the lone democracy that has survived since the 2011 Arab Spring protest movement—has received new types of assistance to buttress its democratic transition, although not as much as the Tunisian leaders expected or need.[5]

This chapter argues for a clear approach to regional civilian aid—one that respects the U.S. taxpayers' money, demands a return on their investment, and prioritizes improving the rule of law, governance, and human rights in the region. This approach will inevitably look different in each country and will be driven by divergent and changing short- and long-term U.S. objectives and humanitarian imperatives to save lives. The importance of tough prioritization when it comes to U.S. aid in the region will be particularly critical in the post–COVID-19 era. U.S. policymakers will have to resist state pressure when it comes to choosing the types and modalities of assistance in countries such as Morocco, Jordan, Algeria, and Egypt. At times, U.S. foreign assistance packages can become captive to Middle Eastern state and even substate interests in a manner that makes it difficult for the United States to ensure that civilian assistance is always achieving its strategic intent. In order to correct for this bias, the United States, as the benefactor, will need to improve its effort to measure success based on outcomes over time rather than the current practice of evaluating project-level effectiveness. This approach will also have to prioritize countries beyond the headlines, such as Tunisia, where more significant levels of U.S. investment could still help to solidify the region's first stable and secure democratic transition.

This approach takes seriously the Trump administration's skepticism about how U.S. foreign aid has been used but does not reject foreign aid itself. Skepticism should lead to a greater investment in the evaluation of impact in each sector (that is, livelihoods, education, health, and governance). In the aggregate it should involve more frequent analyses of whether U.S. investments advance U.S. interests and values, including countering corruption, building the rule of law into institutions and political culture, devolving highly centralized state authority, expanding rights for minorities and women, and protecting basic civil liberties. Greater scrutiny over the budgetary and programmatic process should ensure that the same funding and programs do not repeat year after year without yielding results. Finally, this approach necessitates the involvement of allies and partners in civilian assistance to share the resource burdens—but not by threatening them or suddenly suspending U.S. assistance, as Trump has done in the case of Syria and the Palestinian Authority. Rather, as discussed in chapter 4 by Megan Doherty, persistent diplomacy is also necessary to leverage U.S. partners' help in sharing the burden of assistance efforts.

Current political scrutiny of the return on the investment of U.S. foreign aid is merited. Yet evaluating returns requires greater strategic clarity about the goals—in particular, which combination of U.S. objectives motivates each assistance effort. Assistance should be tailored to the specific security and desperate human consequences of the civil conflicts and political challenges impeding development progress across Syria, Yemen, Libya, and perhaps again in Iraq—challenges with massive destabilizing effects regionally. U.S. assistance that seeks to improve security, stability, prosperity, and good governance within Middle Eastern states must account for continued demographic realities—particularly the youth bulges that are exacerbating the problems of underemployment and unemployment for college-educated youth.[6] Finally, economic assistance must take into account the greatest societal grievances against the state emerging across the Maghreb, in the Levant, and the Gulf: the illegitimacy, weakness, and corruption of local and state governments and institutions. These deficits will continue to drive youth and disenfranchised communities to support violent extremism and generate other types of medium-term instability.[7]

Future U.S. policymakers should avoid taking a pan-regional approach to civilian assistance, given the internal diversity of the Middle East's states. Instead, assistance strategies are likely to differ dramatically depending on whether U.S. assistance is targeting (1) a divided state with multiple and overlapping governance authorities (Yemen, Libya, Palestinian territories); (2) a centralized state where U.S. assistance must be invested in a way that, at a minimum, does not strengthen authoritarianism (Egypt, Morocco, Jordan, Algeria); or (3) a state in transition, where the combination of humanitarian, economic, and security assistance must be carefully integrated (Iraq and Tunisia).

Finally, U.S. policymakers must approach this arena with humility. U.S. assistance packages are relatively small, and, taken alone, incapable of transforming states or societies in the region. The strategic goal of civilian assistance should be to catalyze reform in the region by generating broader internal changes in Middle Eastern governments and their relationships with societies, by building the capacity of local reformers, and by encouraging leaders to make internal social and economic investments.

The U.S. Civilian Assistance Budget to the Middle East and Its Foundations

Since 2017, each year the Trump administration has proposed cutting the foreign affairs budget by at least 20 percent. Each year, Congress has promptly rejected these proposals and instead maintained traditional foreign aid levels, including security and civilian assistance, at US$56 billion annually—on par with a ten-year average under the administrations of George W. Bush and Barack Obama.[8] Nonetheless, in both the budgets submitted and proposed by the Trump administration and the budgets enacted by Congress, similar patterns emerge: the Middle East continues to receive the greatest percentage of foreign aid globally—approximately US$7.4 billion enacted in FY18, close to President Obama's requests for the Middle East, which were US$7.6 billion for FY16 and US$8.6 billion for FY17.[9] The vast preponderance of this aid, nearly 70 percent, goes to Egypt and Israel in the form of security assistance. Overall, 80 percent of total aid to the Middle East consists of security assistance programs.[10]

The total sum of approximately US$7.6 billion on average for the Middle East excludes the billions in humanitarian aid dedicated to the civilian needs associated with the civil wars in Syria, Libya, and Yemen, and, previously, Iraq. The Middle East has received the largest share of the U.S. global humanitarian aid package since at least 2003, with over US$7.7 billion dedicated to emergency food and other relief to the people of Syria alone between 2011 and 2018.[11]

The Policies that Have Forged the Civilian Assistance Budget for the Middle East

The approximate US$2 billion to US$3 billion in annual aid to the Middle East that is neither military assistance nor humanitarian aid reflects a complex set of historic agendas, vestiges of earlier policies that date back to at least the 1980s. Presidential administrations have inherited the foreign assistance priorities of their predecessors. Congress contributes to these path dependencies, as it is often reluctant to abandon programs requested by earlier administrations. During the Cold War and in its immediate aftermath, consecutive administrations used foreign aid to bolster key allies in the region, whether Anwar Sadat in Egypt, King Hassan of Morocco, or the Shah of Iran.[12] Economic assistance complemented U.S. private sector investments in the region, whether to the energy sector in 1960s Iran or to the growing Egyptian private sector in the 1980s and 1990s.[13]

In the post-1991 era, after the momentous Madrid peace conference, the United States rewarded with economic assistance those regional leaders who supported the Arab-Israeli peace process. Today, Egyptian and American officials disagree about the history of the aid, and whether or not it represents an entitlement earned by Egypt through the very act of making peace with Israel at Camp David. Yet the large package of foreign aid remains a testament to Egypt's regional policies in the late 1970s. Later, in the mid- and late-1990s through the 2000s, Jordan received significant assistance—as well as a free trade agreement—when successive U.S. presidents chose to reward the former king of Jordan, King Hussein, and then his son, King Abdullah II, for signing a peace agreement with Israel in 1994.[14]

The Post-9/11 Order: Counterterrorism and Democracy Promotion

In the wake of the 9/11 attacks, two concurrent policy priorities of the Bush administration drove U.S. foreign assistance strategy. First, the Freedom Agenda generated new funds prioritizing democratization and the strengthening of civil society across the region, from Morocco to the UAE. The Middle East Partnership Initiative (MEPI) allowed individual U.S. ambassadors to make small grants at their discretion directly to nongovernmental recipients.[15] Meanwhile, over the course of the Bush administration, the efforts to support democratization and human rights in Iran led to the creation of the Iran Democracy Fund (later renamed the Near East Regional Democracy (NERD) program), which peaked in size in 2006 at US$75 million as requested by the George W. Bush administration.[16] Second, a range of Middle Eastern states, such as Jordan, Morocco, Lebanon, and Algeria, became important partners in U.S. efforts to combat terrorism. Security-sector assistance to the Middle East ballooned in size as a result, leading to the challenges described by Stephen Tankel in chapter 12. Finally, in the wake of the 2003 Iraq War, the Bush administration spent billions in support of the reconstruction of Iraq.[17] In the 2000s, U.S. assistance to Jordan skyrocketed after 9/11 and the Iraq War, as U.S. officials feared for the stability and economy of this landlocked country confronting spillover threats from the war and growing radicalization threats at home.[18]

Over time, much of the government-to-government aid to Egypt, Iraq, Jordan, Lebanon, and Morocco has served to shore up particular ministries and ministers—evolving into both an instrument of development assistance as well as a signal of U.S. political support. Jordan has become particularly skilled at lobbying the U.S. Congress for funding to sustain its national budget, which was weakened after decades of economic instability.[19]

In other cases, U.S. assistance has reflected concrete U.S. policy goals in the region. Successive U.S. presidents had maintained high levels of economic and security assistance to the Palestinian Authority, and later directly to the Palestinian people, as part of the broader U.S. priority of forging Israeli-Palestinian peace through a two-state solution to the conflict. Many U.S. policymakers saw the aid as an investment in a future Palestinian State—a way to shore up reformers and build institutions within the Palestinian Authority.[20] (This was true despite the fact that, over the past twenty years, an increased percentage of the US$200 million in annual average funding bypassed government ministers and officials in favor of development and humanitarian projects.)[21] By 2014, due to congressional restrictions, the entirety of the direct funding to the Palestinian Authority consisted of a program that trained and built the capacity of the Palestinian security forces in the West Bank. All other funding went directly to nongovernmental organizations implementing development projects, avoiding concerns in Washington that U.S. funds would enrich Palestinian officials, some of whom may have valorized violence.[22]

The Arab Spring and Its Aftermath: Conflict, Democratic Idealism, and Dashed Expectations

Before the Arab Spring, the Obama administration was reticent to build on key Bush administration democratization and human rights initiatives, which had caused controversy in the Arab world due to their direct association with the unpopular 2003 Iraq War. President Obama de-emphasized the MEPI and NERD programs, while increasing funds to address the root causes of grievances fueling terrorism in the region. For example, as part of his 2014 strategy to confront terrorism globally by building partnership capacity, he dedicated US$550 million in new funding to the State Department's Counterterrorism Bureau to address the social, economic, governance, and ideological drivers of individual support for groups such as ISIS.[23]

The Arab Spring protests of 2011, particularly the promise of citizen-led democratic transitions in the region, generated new energy within the Obama White House to elevate U.S. assistance in support of political and economic reform efforts in the Middle East.[24] In the first few years after the Egyptian, Tunisian, Libyan, and Yemeni transitions, President Obama tried to support the weak post-uprising governments in power. He designed new assistance programs to each country, including reprogramming US$65 million in the spring of 2011 to support democratization programs in Egypt, most of which went to independent actors rather than the state.[25] Obama officials worked with Congress to offer new forms of loan guarantees and enterprise funds to the transitional governments in Tunis and Cairo in order to promote economic reform while helping the struggling postrevolution economies in both countries. The reality, however, was that any amount of new U.S. aid would be insufficient to address the vast economic challenges that these new governments faced: the protesters had asked for more inclusive and accountable governance, and now expected better jobs and economic opportunities as well. Many in the Obama White House grew frustrated that despite their intention to help the democratic transitions with new forms of economic support, there were inherent limits to any U.S. aid package. No amount of aid could fundamentally restructure local impediments to growth, including underlying problems with the rule of law that hindered economic growth, rampant corruption, and low levels of intraregional trade. To many U.S. officials who had aspired to transform the economies of the Middle East's new transitioning democracies, the lesson of 2011–13 involved the limits of U.S. assistance to solve short-term economic and political problems as well as the dangers of overpromising U.S. economic support.[26]

Trump's Approach: Assistance as a Lever to Move Diplomacy

President Trump's approach to civilian assistance in the region has reflected his overall skepticism of U.S. foreign aid globally. In addition to proposing cuts of nearly 30 percent to the foreign affairs budgets on at least two occasions, he unexpectedly made a series of significant aid cuts to signal a dramatic discontinuity from traditional U.S. policy approaches in the Middle East.

First, in 2018, Trump abruptly suspended and then ended all economic aid to the Palestinians, US$227 million that supported economic, educational, health, and livelihood goals for the Palestinian people.[27] To many involved in the twenty-five years of the four previous administrations' efforts to negotiate an Israeli-Palestinian agreement, this money was considered a principal lever necessary to further the goal of a two-state solution. It represented an investment in building the foundations of an eventual Palestinian state by addressing Palestinian economic, social, educational, and health gaps. Trump cut this funding—in many cases in the middle of an ongoing program taking place on the ground—allegedly as a lever to put pressure on the PA to negotiate his "deal of the century," despite the fact that nearly all of this aid bypassed the West Bank–based government.[28] Trump fundamentally misunderstood this assistance, which barely supported the PA leadership and therefore would do little to move Palestinian politics. He also misunderstood how much this assistance was not a favor to the Palestinians, but instead a means to further a specific high-priority U.S. policy goal: a two-state solution.

In 2018, Trump also suddenly canceled, via tweet, U.S. assistance to address the post-ISIS stabilization needs in northeastern Syria, which his secretary of state Rex Tillerson had pledged just months earlier. The White House was unconvinced by arguments in support of this aid mustered by the Department of Defense and its allies, particularly that these funds would build a foundation for stability and security in the area formerly occupied by ISIS. Trump instead tried to leverage Gulf states such as Saudi Arabia to foot the bill in northeastern Syria, a strategy that produced decidedly mixed results as of late 2019.[29]

Recommendations for a Strategic Civilian Assistance Approach

Adhering to strong organizing principles would improve the strategic allocation of the limited civilian assistance funds offered to each Middle Eastern state. First, from education programs to women's programs to prison reform, diplomats, rather than technical experts, should weave the civilian assistance efforts into a strategy that complements diplomatic priorities, rather than allowing for a string of discrete and often inchoate programs guided by siloed bureaus and agencies within the State Department and USAID. Second, policymakers must be humble, recognizing the relatively small size of

U.S. foreign assistance dollars compared to, for example, the flow of private capital, foreign direct investment, and other sources of foreign aid, particularly from the Middle East's resource-rich states to poorer neighbors. While the U.S. taxpayer may consider the sums too large, the hundreds of millions in civilian assistance offered to Middle Eastern states is often too little to address deeply rooted socioeconomic and governance challenges, such as institutional gaps among the Middle East's police forces or inadequate jobs for graduating college students. U.S. policymakers should consider civilian assistance as a catalyst—investments, not subsidies, that can engender internal political and economic reforms or improve the prestige and credibility of those internal reformers pushing for change. Finally, in many cases, small but consistent U.S. assistance in support of a priority, such as judicial reform or education reform, can mobilize complementary assistance efforts among U.S. allies, particularly in Europe.

Moreover, policymakers must be more explicit about and prepared to enforce positive conditionality associated with this aid. In some cases, where aid is directed to local communities or civil organizations, local buy-in and absorptive capacity is necessary for success. In other cases, however, local buy-in may divert the United States from achieving its goals. In the case of human rights and democratization assistance, U.S. embassies must independently grant assistance to non-state actors, even if this approach irritates the local governments. Often, U.S. officials need to be tougher on aid recipients. With Jordan, for example, U.S. diplomats could push harder to ensure that the Jordanian ministries receiving U.S. budgetary support in the name of the Syrian refugee burden are using these funds explicitly and prudently to offset and improve health and education investments for Jordanian refugee-hosting communities.[30] Rather than unconditionally transferring cash from the U.S. Treasury to the Jordanian Ministry of Finance, diplomats must ask for information—and offer counsel—on how Jordan is using U.S. budgetary support in a way that supports the refugee absorption process.

The bottom line is that policymakers will need to make a greater effort in order to ensure that civilian assistance does not become a legacy, reward, or entitlement with key political constituencies and government officials in the Middle East, without regard to the United States's own objectives in the country. Policymakers need to be tougher in their expectations of outcome-level success (not just project-level success) within a reasonable medium-term timeframe. To do so, they must demand more rigorous, fact-based analysis and program assessments to ensure investments are yielding desired returns.

Finally, policymakers must assess the impact of civilian assistance in conjunction with the burgeoning U.S. security assistance programs in the Middle East. The security assistance components of aid packages to Middle Eastern states are likely to continue to dwarf the civilian assistance efforts in size. At times, some of these security assistance projects impede economic and political reform because they stunt any efforts to balance civilian-military relations in the region. In many of these states, civilian authorities are already weak when compared to their military colleagues. U.S. aid that disproportionately builds up the Middle East's security apparatuses can exacerbate these imbalances. In some cases, U.S. security assistance has empowered the very same units that commit egregious human rights violations, generating public grievances against the state and derailing more inclusive, rights-based governance. In effect, across the Middle East there is a danger that the two parts of the U.S. assistance bureaucracy are canceling each other out. Policymakers overseeing civilian assistance accounts are often shut out by and insufficiently coordinated with security sector implementers. And yet these very same decision-makers are the ones who can assess whether security assistance that strengthens authoritarian institutions, particularly ruling militaries, should be discontinued. To rectify these internal conflicts will require greater discipline on ending security sector programs with negative, distortive outcomes, and better management within embassy teams to link together those working on assistance programs.

The above principles should guide country-specific assistance strategies that advance U.S. interests in Middle Eastern states, including the promotion of more inclusive, just governance and universal rights. Interests will vary by country but civilian assistance should prioritize the following three objectives in the coming years:

Provide stabilization and humanitarian assistance in conflict regions.
Humanitarian relief should continue to be a principal goal of civilian
assistance, given the level of human need persistent across the Middle
East. The United States has given nearly US$8 billion since 2011 to
address the humanitarian needs of the Syrian people and over US$1
billion to the Yemenis for food, water, medical relief, and other needs
since the start of the 2015 conflict.[31] Humanitarian assistance must
be accompanied by greater attention to access for humanitarian implementers, who often have a hard time delivering relief in areas of
Syria, Yemen, and Libya. In order to ensure that U.S. taxpayer money
reaches communities in need, the United States must put greater pressure on the United Nations organizations that often oversee humanitarian delivery to prevent the co-optation of the humanitarian system
by Russia or other international actors. These actors are less committed to the neutrality and impartiality principles of international
humanitarian law, and have begun to see international civil society
organizations as a threat.[32]

Meanwhile, in those areas where terrorists once ruled, whether
parts of Libya, Iraq, or Syria, humanitarian and development aid may
not be sufficient. Given the extreme security constraints, policymakers need new models to achieve stabilization. The State Department
has already begun considering innovations that will provide stabilization assistance to these liberated areas, but efforts must continue
to ensure that often remotely delivered assistance can complement
direct diplomacy and improved local governance efforts.[33]

Enable economic recovery. U.S. civilian assistance is not sufficient
or significant enough to remake the economies of the region—
many of which are perpetually on the verge of crisis (for example,
Jordan or Egypt). One mistake the Obama administration made in
the post-2011 Arab Spring period was to overestimate the potential
of U.S. civilian assistance to ameliorate the deep-seated economic
challenges facing the fledgling democratically elected governments in
Tunis, Tripoli, Sanaa, and, for a short time, Cairo. In soaring rhetoric, key U.S. officials promised packages of economic aid to reward
new democracies, but, ultimately, U.S. officials had only modest loan
guarantees and enterprise funds to offer.[34] Policymakers both over-

estimated and overpromised what they and Congress could deliver, and, in the meantime, undervalued the imperative that the transitional governments undertake difficult economic reforms internally.

With this in mind, economic assistance should focus on those areas where tough economic reforms are necessary, and areas that would help to develop the workforce and improve those economies' global competitiveness. Private capital can ultimately do far more to revive the economies of Iraq, Tunisia, and Lebanon than U.S. economic assistance, but U.S. assistance programs can improve the competitiveness of the labor market through vocational training programs and English-language programs. Similarly, there is more room to promote entrepreneurship and technology-based economic growth in Jordan, Tunisia, Lebanon, and elsewhere in the region.

Advance universal rights, reform institutions, and build accountability. Supporting democratization and human rights in the Middle East is a core U.S. interest, as Miller and I discussed in chapter 1 of this book. While U.S. efforts have sometimes been unenforced, contested, or deprioritized, promoting democracy and human rights has always been part of U.S. foreign policy in the region. The Trump administration has broken with this historical precedent. Whether shielding Mohammed bin Salman from congressional sanctions related to his role in the gruesome killing of a Saudi journalist, or embracing President Abdel Fattah al Sisi even as he flagrantly deepens authoritarianism in Egypt, Trump has at times seemed to celebrate autocratic excesses in the region.

In the post-Trump period, the region will be more authoritarian. The security forces across the region will be less inclusive and more unaccountable than at any time over the past two decades. As discussed above, the Middle East's robust security apparatuses are in no small part a product of U.S. security training and assistance efforts; while in some cases, this newfound capacity will benefit U.S. security interests, in other cases, it will make it harder to reform security institutions. There will be more political prisoners, fewer rights for civil societies, foreign or domestic, and less freedom of expression or protections for journalists, whether traditional or social media voices.

As future administrations try to undo the harm done by the

Trump administration's embrace of authoritarians, they should not double down on the well-meaning but often flawed efforts of past administrations. Both the Bush and Obama administrations struggled with the right combination of programmatic efforts—as well as the appropriate balance of diplomatic sticks and carrots—to improve democratic outcomes. At times before and after the Arab Spring, U.S. objectives in this realm often focused on deterrence: how to prevent the incarceration of political dissidents or rapacious abuses by the security sector.

Diplomats will always have to try to deter bad behavior among partners, and should be more clear and consistent in how they articulate U.S. expectations when it comes to universal rights, free expression, and other core issues. But an overarching strategy befitting the post-Trump landscape could be more effective if it focused on building rule-of-law cultures and promoting reformers across different institutional domains. U.S. officials should begin integrating components of security-sector reform—such as police reform, prison reform, and prosecutorial reform—into country-specific "rule of law" assistance packages. To do this will require greater policy creativity and mergers of programs that were often siloed but that touch on human rights, police reform, or countering violent extremism.

The Tunisia Experience

U.S. civilian aid to Tunisia since the revolution that ousted the country's longtime dictator, president Zinedine Ben Ali, in 2011 reflects the potential as well as the limits of American assistance. Before the revolution, Tunisia was not a priority for U.S. assistance or policy in the region, and the limited embassy staff in Tunis focused mostly on commercial and trade issues. In the aftermath of 2011, the Obama administration prioritized an increase in its economic assistance to the transitional government through endeavors such as congressionally authorized enterprise funds, loan guarantee efforts, and bilateral economic assistance. The regime of Ben Ali had strictly prohibited any local or international organizations to work on democracy and governance issues at the grassroots level, and had suppressed Tunisia's once vibrant civil society. When Tunisian nongovernmental organizations began to emerge after 2011, the United States started investing in training programs, civil society capacity building, youth employment programs, civic action campaigns, and support for elections.

As of 2020, Tunisia stands out as the only state that emerged from the Arab Spring revolutions to proceed toward a relatively peaceful democratic transition, albeit marked with some periodic instability. That said, U.S. investments were helpful but certainly not the main reasons behind Tunisia's successful transition since 2011. Prior to the revolution, Tunisia had certain characteristics—a robust middle class, a professional military, and strong civil society organizations, among others—that made the country a relatively good candidate for democratization. And, without the courage of the Tunisian people in standing up to a corrupt, repressive regime, their continued participation in the democratic process, and the penchant of Tunisia's political class for compromise, no amount of U.S. aid could have set the country on its current course.

Nonetheless, unlike U.S. aid programs to other Middle Eastern countries, where American support has often propped up dictatorships, U.S. assistance to Tunisia appears to have had a genuinely positive effect on the country's development. With a comparatively modest investment of US$322.5 million from the Economic Support Fund (ESF) between 2012 and 2018 (or US$46.1 million per year), the U.S. government has promoted good governance, civil society capacity, political decentralization, elections, economic growth, and fiscal stability in Tunisia.[35] USAID's Domestic Election Monitoring program, which has helped to train local election monitors, support voter education efforts, and develop the media's capacity to provide critical and balanced coverage of elections, has been particularly important to Tunisia's democratic development. Indeed, through this aid, the United States has supported five separate rounds of free-and-fair elections at the local and national level, setting Tunisia apart from the rest of the region.

U.S. aid to Tunisia has been productive not because of the amount—by comparison Jordan, a slightly smaller country, received nearly sixteen times more in ESF than did Tunisia between 2012 and 2018—but because American programs in Tunisia have largely adhered to the recommendations laid out in this chapter. In contrast to other regional countries such as Egypt or Morocco, Tunisia is a willing and eager recipient of U.S. assistance. Among Tunisian officials, there is little of the suspicion regarding American intentions, even if there are concerns that the investments are too small. U.S. officials in Tunisia, moreover, do not hesitate to provide direct grants to Tunisian civil society organizations even in sensitive areas, such as democracy and political development. Partly because Tunisia has a relatively apolitical military and partly because U.S. aid packages to the country have been more balanced between security and nonsecurity programs, American support for Tunisia has not empowered security agencies at the expense of civilian political structures.

Perhaps most importantly, other tools of U.S. statecraft, such as private and public diplomacy, have complemented and reinforced U.S. aid programs in Tunisia since 2011. Whereas in Egypt, for example, U.S. support for political reform and human rights has been systematically subordinated to the U.S.-Egyptian military relationship, U.S. policy in Tunisia has consistently treated the success of the country's democratic transition as an important priority. Tunisian officials do not regard U.S. assistance as an entitlement and instead understand that its goal is to facilitate real political and economic development. The U.S. Embassy in Tunis has stood up an interagency team to coordinate assistance to the country. At least compared to other U.S. aid programs in the Middle East, U.S. assistance to Tunisia in the period since 2011 has appeared more internally coherent.

None of this is to suggest that U.S. civilian aid to Tunisia is perfect. First, the sum of the assistance granted since 2011 has been insufficient—it is certainly not reflective of how important Tunisia's successful democratic transition is to U.S. strategy. The United States needs to do a better job of leveraging its aid to Tunisia to secure additional commitments from like-minded countries, particularly European countries who, owing to their geographical proximity, have a direct stake in Tunisia's success. It also seems likely that Tunisia could absorb additional American assistance. However, although USAID upgraded its presence in the country to a full mission in 2019, personnel limitations constrain the United States's ability to expand its programming in Tunisia. Moreover, the next administration should explore what steps, in addition to increasing aid, the United

States can take to support Tunisia, particularly economically, such as negotiating preferential trade arrangements and making larger-scale private sector investments through the new U.S. Development Finance Corporation. Finally, the economy in Tunisia still struggles. According to the World Bank, the 2019 youth unemployment rate was approximately 35 percent and per capita GDP has been decreasing every year since 2014, with it now dipping below middle-income status at around US$3,500 per person.[36]

Conclusion

U.S. civilian aid has often failed to produce positive change in the Middle East, wasting American taxpayer money or even unintentionally strengthening authoritarianism and economic autarky. Even when assistance programs have yielded positive results, they tend to be modest rather than transformational. Yet, as U.S. aid to support Tunisia's democratic transition demonstrates, American assistance programs can make a difference. A new U.S. president should learn from both the successes and failures of U.S. assistance to the Middle East, and seek to deploy aid on behalf of the type of strategic, yet realistic, purposes that warrant the investment of the American taxpayer.

Notes

1. U.S. Department of State, "Congressional Budget Justification Department of State, Foreign Operations, and Related Programs: Fiscal Year 2020," March 11, 2019 (www.state.gov/wp-content/uploads/2019/05/FY-2020-CBJ-FINAL.pdf).

2. Ibid.

3. Jeremy M. Sharp, "Egypt: Background and U.S. Relations," Congressional Research Service, August 12, 2008 (www.everycrsreport.com/files/20080812_RL33003_eb2608abafbafd9c8d5d0e04158f579574bfb7b7.pdf).

4. Maged Mandour, "Growing Cooperation between Egypt and Israel Will Have Implications on Cairo's Ability to Play Its Traditional Role as Mediator in the Palestinian Peace Process," Carnegie Endowment for International Peace, March 20, 2018 (https://carnegieendowment.org/sada/75840).

5. U.S. Department of State, "Congressional Budget Justification Department of State, Foreign Operations, and Related Programs: Appendix 2: Fiscal Year 2020," March 11, 2019 (www.state.gov/wp-content/uploads/2019/05/State-and-USAID-Appendix-2.pdf).

6. Nader Kabbani, "Youth Employment in the Middle East and North Africa: Revisiting and Reframing the Challenge," Brookings Doha Center, February 26, 2019 (www.brookings.edu/research/youth-employment-in-the-middle-east-and-north-africa-revisiting-and-reframing-the-challenge/).

7. Ibid.

8. U.S. Department of State, "Congressional Budget Justification Department of State, Foreign Operations, and Related Programs: Fiscal Year 2020."

9. Andrew Miller, Seth Binder, and Louisa Keeler, "President Trump's Third Foreign Affairs Budget," Project on Middle East Democracy, June 2019 (https://pomed.org/wp-content/uploads/2019/06/BudgetReport_FY20.pdf).

10. Ibid.

11. "Fact Sheet: U.S. Assistance to the People of Syria," USAID, January 26, 2018 (www.usaid.gov/news-information/press-releases/jan-26-2018-fact-sheet-us-assistance-people-syria).

12. Suzanne Maloney, "1979: Iran and America," Brookings, January 24, 2019 (www.brookings.edu/opinions/1979-iran-and-america/).

13. Privatization Coordination Support Unit, "The Results and Impacts of Egypt's Privatization Program," USAID, August 2002 (www1.aucegypt.edu/src/wsite1/Pdfs/Results%20and%20Impacts%20of%20Privatization%20in%20Egypt.pdf).

14. Jeremy M. Sharp, "U.S. Foreign Assistance to the Middle East: Historical Background, Recent Trends, and the FY2011 Request," Congressional Research Service, June 15, 2010 (https://fas.org/sgp/crs/mideast/RL32260.pdf).

15. Stephen McInerney, "The Federal Budget and Appropriations for Fiscal Year 2010," Project on Middle East Democracy, July 2009 (https://us.boell.org/sites/default/files/fy10-budget-analysis-paper-final.pdf).

16. J. Scott Carpenter, "After the Crackdown: The Iran Democracy Fund," Washington Institute, September 8, 2009 (www.washingtoninstitute.org/policy-analysis/view/after-the-crackdown-the-iran-democracy-fund).

17. Amy Belasco, "The Cost of Iraq, Afghanistan, and Other Global War on Terror Operations Since 9/11," Congressional Research Service, December 8, 2014 (https://fas.org/sgp/crs/natsec/RL33110.pdf).

18. Miller, Binder, and Keeler, "President Trump's Third Foreign Affairs Budget."

19. Jeremy M. Sharp, "Jordan: Background and U.S. Relations," Congressional Research Service, updated April 9, 2019 (https://fas.org/sgp/crs/mideast/RL33546.pdf).

20. Jim Zanotti, "U.S. Foreign Aid to the Palestinians," Congressional Research Service, July 3, 2014 (www.everycrsreport.com/files/20140703_RS22967_b85493f25e67192545033f6d00f3a83f53062f44.pdf).

21. Ibid.

22. Ibid.

23. Barack Obama, "Remarks by the President at the United States Military Academy Commencement Ceremony," May 28, 2014 (https://obamawhitehouse.archives.gov/the-press-office/2014/05/28/remarks-president-united-states-military-academy-commencement-ceremony); John Hudson,

"Growth of Islamic State Forces State Department Overhaul," *Foreign Policy*, February 1, 2016.

24. Barack Obama, "Remarks by the President on the Middle East and North Africa," May 19, 2011 (https://obamawhitehouse.archives.gov/the-press-office/2011/05/19/remarks-president-middle-east-and-north-africa).

25. See also Kristen Chick, "In Egypt, American NGO Workers Head to Court in Civil Society Trial," *Christian Science Monitor*, June 5, 2012.

26. Hillary Clinton, *Hard Choices* (New York: Simon & Schuster, 2014); William J. Burns, *The Back Channel: A Memoir of American Diplomacy and the Case for Its Renewal* (New York: Random House, 2019).

27. Zanotti, "U.S. Foreign Aid to the Palestinians."

28. Amir Tibon, "U.S. Officially Cuts Funding to Palestinian Authority over Payments to Terrorists and Their Families," *Haaretz*, March 24, 2018.

29. Tom DiChristopher, "Saudi Arabia Clarifies Trump Tweet: No New Saudi Pledges to Rebuild Syria," CNBC, December 26, 2018.

30. Sharp, "Jordan: Background and U.S. Relations."

31. USAID, "Syria—Complex Emergency: Fact Sheet #8, Fiscal Year (FY) 2019," August 9, 2019 (www.usaid.gov/sites/default/files/documents/1866/08.09.19_-_USG_Syria_Complex_Emergency_Fact_Sheet_8.pdf); USAID, "United States Announces Additional Humanitarian Assistance to the People of Yemen," February 26, 2019 (www.usaid.gov/news-information/press-re leases/feb-26-2019-us-announces-additional-humanitarian-assistance-people-yemen).

32. The case of the diversion of UN food aid by the Syrian regime offers a cautionary tale. Human Rights Watch, "Rigging the System: Government Policies Co-opt Aid and Reconstruction Funding in Syria," June 28, 2019 (www.hrw.org/report/2019/06/28/rigging-system/government-policies-co-opt-aid-and-reconstruction-funding-syria).

33. Stabilization Assistance Review, "A Framework for Maximizing the Effectiveness of U.S. Government Efforts to Stabilize Conflict-Affected Areas," June 18, 2018 (https://media.defense.gov/2018/Jun/13/2001931133/-1/-1/1/STABILIZATION-ASSISTANCE-REVIEW.PDF).

34. Barack Obama, "Remarks by the President on the Middle East and North Africa"; C-SPAN, "Hillary Clinton on Middle East Uprisings and Transition Process," keynote speech at the National Democratic Institute's 2011 Democracy Awards Dinner, November 11, 2011 (www.c-span.org/video/?302532-1/secretary-clinton-middle-east-uprisings-transition-process).

35. Alexis Arieff, "Tunisia: In Brief," Congressional Research Service, July 5, 2018 (https://crsreports.congress.gov/product/pdf/RS/RS21666/62); and World Bank Statistics, "Tunisia Foreign Assistance" (https://foreignassistance.gov/explore/country/Tunisia).

36. Arieff, "Tunisia: In Brief," and World Bank Statistics, "Tunisia Foreign Assistance."

CONCLUSION

Looking to the Future

DAFNA H. RAND
ANDREW P. MILLER

In offering policy recommendations to the next administration, the authors in this volume underscore that the pursuit of U.S. interests will require elevating diplomacy, de-escalating regional conflicts, and rethinking security partnerships. The authors might disagree internally on the degree of U.S. leverage still available to change or shape outcomes in the region, the nature and success of U.S. engagement in the past, and the likelihood of U.S. influence in the future. Yet they all believe that the United States still has a role to play in the Middle East and North Africa, if a more limited one in some cases. In other words, there are alternatives to either leaning in or retreating from the region—and these alternatives are worth pursuing. The authors' arguments converge with each other when it comes to how core U.S. interests depend on hard-earned global leadership and proactive management of core problems. This pathway for U.S. influence is all the more urgent in the wake of the coronavirus pandemic, and its political and economic consequences across the region.

The authors agree on the need for greater scrutiny regarding the military levers of U.S. statecraft—whether security assistance and cooperation packages, U.S. military force posture, or the use of force more broadly. Many of the chapters in this volume have proposed elevating civilian authority and assistance in U.S. foreign policy in order to pursue key U.S. objectives. The chapters make the case that these civilian levers of statecraft can, over time, push the ongoing political change in the region in a direction more supportive of U.S. interests and values. Reprioritizing civilian-led diplomatic efforts can help the United States regain its moral authority, which the Trump administration has squandered so cavalierly with its very clear messages that human rights conditions and civilian protection are no longer key U.S. objectives in the region.

For the people of the region, the strength of U.S. power will be measured by the U.S. government's willingness to confront the repression deepening within the Middle East's authoritarian states and the insecurity facing civilians in those states where governments and non-state combatants, along with their foreign supporters, are ignoring international humanitarian law, such as in Yemen, Syria, and Libya.

Tough Trade-Offs and Internal Contradictions

Despite the common approaches linking this volume's authors, some of their policy recommendations conflict with each other. For example, Le Mon's road map on how to end the war in Yemen may be hard to reconcile with Benaim's hopeful assessment that a new president could salvage the U.S.-Saudi relationship—albeit on very different terms. Dalton and Karlin's argument for reducing the U.S. military footprint in the Middle East may make it more difficult to rein in adventurous partners, whether in the United Arab Emirates (UAE) or Qatar, or to put pressure on the Assad regime, Iran, and ISIS in Syria. Nowrouzzadeh and Rhee have argued for putting the Iranian people, and their relationship with America, at the heart of U.S. policy toward Iran. Yet this approach will ruffle feathers in Jerusalem and Riyadh, who may see in it naïveté about the depth of control by Iran's revolutionary leadership.

Moreover, this volume has, with the exception of Russia, bracketed the question of how international politics are playing out in the region—particularly the competitive dynamics that the United States will face as it pursues the suggested policies. As Bick makes clear, there are limits to Russian adventurism, projection of power, and interest in the Middle East. Nonetheless, Russian intervention, even at a low level, could shape or change U.S. calculations, particularly in Syria, Iran, and the Gulf. While there are certain key U.S. partner states, such as Israel or Jordan, where Russia's new power projection will not undermine U.S. influence and standing, in other states, the U.S. competitive advantage is less clear. Russia's growing energy interest in Iraq could reduce U.S. influence there, as the Iranian-U.S. standoff in Iraq intensifies. While the Gulf states will be tied for decades to the United States via deep defense relationships, in part because of the preponderance of U.S. defense articles that sustain their militaries, there is a higher potential for Egypt to move more closely toward Russia when it comes to defense sales and security cooperation.

Finally, global U.S. foreign policy priorities will affect how the United States approaches policies specific to the Middle East. For example, the United States will need to rebuild the strength of NATO as an institution and U.S. relationships with key NATO allies. In doing so, it will have to navigate whether to push Turkey westward, back into the NATO orbit. The crises in the region since 2011 have had the cumulative effect of moving Turkey away from the Western alliance, motivating Turkey to expand its regional power projection. Future U.S.-NATO policies will have to contend with these shifts within Ankara, and even grapple with the appropriateness of Turkey's continued membership. Whether Turkey and the United States are able to collaborate in Syria will be a key factor in the post-October 2019 period following Turkey's intervention in northeastern Syria. After the Trump administration abruptly called for a withdrawal of U.S. troops from northeast Syria, within twenty-four hours Turkey and its proxies launched Operation Peace Spring, gaining approximately fifteen hundred square kilometers of new territory, including more than sixty towns that had been under control of the U.S.-backed Kurdish administration. Meanwhile, Turkey and its local Arab allies unleashed massive civilian harm on the Kurdish population living in the area, prompting global calls to investigate ethnic cleansing and war crimes. With the encouragement of the Trump administration and U.S. abdication of its commitments to its Kurdish Syrian partners, by 2020 Turkey emerged with new regional leadership momentum. It has become one of the key powers in the Levant with sufficient leverage to determine, or at least heavily influence, events on the ground in Syria, both in the northeast and in Idlib province, which remained the last area west of the Euphrates beyond regime control. Given this momentum, Turkey under President Erdogan is more likely to dictate, rather than follow, Western-leaning approaches in the Levant over the coming years.

Known Unknowns through the 2020s

As the chapters in this volume have explicated, the next few years could bring great uncertainty in the Middle East. COVID-19 may upset the political status quo from Tehran to Beirut, creating instability with unknown geopolitical outcomes. The tanking of oil markets, for example, could dampen Gulf states' willingness to invest in regional adventures from Yemen to Libya. In the first few weeks of 2020, President Trump's targeted killing of the head of Iran's IRGC-QF, Major General Qassem Soleimani, escalated tensions with Iran, bringing the United States to the precipice of a major hot war. Meanwhile, as of this writing, the exit of U.S. forces from Iraq seemed increasingly possible, given growing Iraqi political mobilization around a demand for U.S. withdrawal after the Soleimani killing and continued force protection issues, as groups on the ground in Iraq committed to attacking them. Attacks on U.S. military and diplomatic personnel in Iraq by Iranian-backed groups will continue in the coming months, with each attack carrying the potential for a U.S. retaliation that could, again, invite an intentional or unintentional military confrontation in the Persian Gulf or elsewhere in the region. Iraq's government finds itself caught in the middle—hosting over five thousand U.S. troops and cooperating strongly with the United States on counterterrorism even as Tehran-backed militias have tried to co-opt or control Iraqi state institutions.[1] As the 2020 U.S. presidential election nears, Trump may have even greater political motivations to either dramatically withdraw all troops in Iraq to follow through on his campaign promises or to provoke a confrontation with Iran in order to distract from the administration's political liabilities at home.

President Trump's January 2020 rollout of an Israeli-Palestinian "peace plan" prompted Israeli right-wingers to posture and plan for the annexation of West Bank territory—a move that could set off a new round of intense Israeli-Palestinian violence. In so doing, the administration reversed decades of U.S. policy predicated on a politically negotiated two-state solution, calling into question the ability of the United States to remain the central mediator between Israelis and Palestinians. Meanwhile, Hamas and other actors in Gaza continue to engage in intermittent, albeit low-level, rocket fire; although Israel has thus far responded with restraint, the likelihood of a new major Gaza war remains high. Generally without claiming credit, Israel continues to attack Iranian assets, including IRGC and Hezbollah weapons depots and outposts in Lebanon, Syria, and Iraq.[2] While the United States is not actively involved in these operations, Iran and its proxies perceive Israeli escalation as a tacit extension of U.S. policy in the region and could conceivably retaliate against the United States. The situation in the northeast of Syria remains highly precarious, and continued instability there could allow for the more rapid reconstitution of ISIS.

Although the UAE chose to redeploy its troops away from active conflict zones with the Houthis in the summer of 2019, the war in Yemen persists and ceasefire efforts are tenuous.[3] With internal rivalries between the government of Yemen and UAE-backed Southern Transitional Council forces in the south intensifying, it appears that the Yemen conflict will not only continue but fracture, drawing regional powers into the country in new ways. Freedom of navigation and the free flow of commerce in the Red Sea and Bab al Mandab have always been key U.S. interests and, given the new levels of bellicosity and anti-Iran sentiment pervading the senior levels of the Trump administration, the chances of military confrontation related to the protection of these equities has dramatically increased.

In Syria, Assad's ongoing military offensive in Idlib province reflects how his regime and its Russian and Iranian patrons are eager to declare formally that all areas of Syria are now under Damascus's control, formally ending the war. And yet the current hold by the regime on reconquered opposition areas, particularly in the south, south central, and northwest, may be shaky. As long as the underlying grievances that motivated the 2011 uprisings in Syria remain, political instability will persist, with intermittent fighting among various militias and forces. There will also continue to be significant humanitarian consequences in terms of refugee flows and loss of life, the import of which extend beyond the region.

It seems unlikely that the degradation of human rights in most Middle Eastern states will ameliorate any time soon. President al Sisi's repressive de-democratization in Egypt has benefited from the Trump administration's willingness to overlook Egypt generally—and the country's domestic politics in particular. With Saudi Arabia, Trump has been unwilling to pressure Mohammed bin Salman when it comes to domestic matters, even on relatively modest requests such as the release of women's rights activists. Indeed, his continued defiance of Republican and Democratic leaders in Congress and his own intelligence community to protect Mohammed bin Salman after his involvement in the heinous murder of Jamal Khashoggi has signaled America's retreat from basic international norms. In Jordan, Morocco, and elsewhere where regimes practice lower levels of repression, trends are moving toward increased political control by intelligence and security forces, tipping the balance even further away from bottom-up political movements and grassroots activism and toward the power of the state. The commercial availability of cyber technologies enabling surveillance will further solidify this trend, as has been seen particularly in the case of the UAE.

Finally, as of early 2020, though the U.S.-led coalition defeated ISIS's territorial caliphate in Iraq and Syria, the threat posed by the terrorist group endures. As tens of thousands of hardened fighters poured out of the last remaining ISIS strongholds in the Euphrates Valley region of northeast Syria, it became apparent that the international community had underestimated the strength of the organization. In the aftermath of the U.S. drawdown of forces in October 2019, whether the al Assad regime, Turkey, and their allies are willing or capable of securing tens of thousands of ISIS detainees in Syria, and the extent to which changing conflict dynamics in Syria will exacerbate the reemergence of ISIS, remain key variables that will affect ISIS's trajectory. In Iraq, the Iraqi government has to balance an effective, inclusive management of the Sunni heartlands in Anbar, Ninewa, and the other areas of Iraq that had fallen to ISIS, with the growing protests among restive Shia populations in Baghdad and southern Iraq. As the past fifteen years have shown, the people and tribal leaders living in the under-resourced Sunni heartlands of Iraq and Syria will choose extremism when the alternatives are far worse for their interests; yet it is also becoming clear that Iraq's Shia have higher expectations of their national leadership.

New Strategies for a New Era

Given the policy recommendations that the authors have advocated throughout this volume, we believe that new strategies and tools will be necessary. The rest of this chapter lays out areas of foreign policy implementation where this book's policy recommendations will demand new approaches.

Reconsider Democracy, Human Rights, and Civilian Protection

To many of the authors in this volume, the United States has fallen short when it comes both to protecting civilians living through the conflicts in Libya, Syria, or Yemen, and stopping authoritarian states from further degrading human rights in Egypt, Saudi Arabia, Iran, and elsewhere. The United States needs new ways to counter these negative trends in the region, or at least impose consequences for state repression and gross violations of human rights.

To effectively construct a U.S. civilian protection infrastructure will first require reckoning with how U.S. policies unintentionally contribute to abuses in the region. The next administration will need to build up the arms sales oversight policies, security-sector training efforts, and Leahy Law implementation work led by the State Department's Bureau of Democracy, Human Rights, and Labor. These efforts should be merged with the oversight over security assistance and cooperation handled by the Bureau of Political-Military Affairs, which oversees the overall security assistance and cooperation tools toward the region. The State Department needs to coordinate, rationalize, and fund these overlapping offices, creating one large and empowered entity that can help U.S. embassies across the Middle East bring together the State Department, the Department of Defense, the U.S. military (particularly U.S. Central Command), and other key experts to ensure that U.S. partner security services are trained and held responsible for preventing civilian casualties, limiting harm to civilian entities such as hospitals and schools, and protecting humanitarian access. Because the security services in the Middle East are the largest recipients, globally, of U.S. security assistance, the State Department, with the support of the Department of Defense, should improve the coherence around these tools to ensure that accountability, professionalism, and human rights become core components of U.S. security partnerships in the region.

Meanwhile, traditional tools of human rights promotion, which focus on public and private messaging and small programmatic investments, need to be overhauled as well. If the next administration wants to get serious about governance and human rights, it will need to do more than just reverse the Trump administration's approach, which has been unique in its overt hostility to these issues. It will also have to synchronize better the delivery of pro-reform messages by various U.S. government agencies. Even prior to the Trump administration, inconsistent messaging between the State Department and the Department of Defense on human rights in Egypt or Saudi Arabia, for instance, has regularly led foreign leaders to conclude it was not a real priority for the U.S. president. A more effective approach will require a concerted effort across departments and agencies to prevent such disconnects from undercutting the impact of future U.S. public statements on governance and political reform. The United States should also review all democracy, governance, justice, rule of law, and governance-related programming to see what has worked over time in different types of Middle Eastern contexts—and to ensure strategic coordination among all of these small grant programs.

A new administration should also take stock of the fact that Congress has become increasingly vocal about human rights issues in the region. The 2016 passage of the Global Magnitsky Act has given a new sanction tool to the executive branch, allowing it to target individuals in Middle Eastern states who have committed serious violations of human rights.[4] Congress has also been on the forefront of calibrating U.S. arms sales to certain regional states when these sales could implicate the United States in violations of international law, such as in the case of U.S. arms sold to Saudi Arabia and used for the war in Yemen. Congressional oversight in this domain will only increase. The next administration would be wise to harness bipartisan congressional interest to its benefit—relying on congressionally mandated accountability tools such as the Leahy Laws, the Arms Export Control Act, the Global Magnitsky Act, the Child Soldier Protection Act, and others.

Finally, when those rare opportunities for democratic progress in the region materialize, the next president should be prepared to invest time and resources. Tunisia, the only Arab Spring country to remain on a democratic trajectory, is the most obvious example. U.S. civilian and security support to Tunisia has helped the country to cope with the many challenges to its sometimes halting transition, and this support should at least continue if not increase. The United States likewise has an interest in supporting the democratic aspirations of the Algerian, Iraqi, and Lebanese peoples, all of whom have recently turned out in the streets to call for more freedom and better governance. A new administration should always be mindful that the United States is not, and should not try to become, the central player in local democratic development, but it must be attuned to opportunities to advance the cause of democracy and human rights in the Middle East.

Right-Size the Role of Economic Statecraft in the Region

While commercial diplomacy has always been an important part of U.S. foreign policy in the Middle East, President Trump has elevated the priority of economic interests to a new, almost perverse extent. Profits, often his family's own, have come to override other considerations—not just human rights but also hard security interests. In the president's mercantilist worldview, arms sales and business contracts—which supposedly generate a significant number of new American jobs—are the metric by which U.S. foreign policy in the Middle East should be judged.

In this volume, we gave comparatively short shrift to economic interests—and commercial diplomacy in particular. This was a conscious decision to correct for the overwhelming importance that President Trump has attached to these issues, and does not reflect a belief on our part that the U.S. government should get out of the business of commercial diplomacy. Indeed, we believe that in a new administration, commercial interests and the politics that surround them should and will continue to be a part of U.S foreign policy in the Middle East. The challenge for U.S. policymakers will be to attend to U.S. economic interests without blowing them out of proportion. This will be especially important for both U.S. energy concerns and arms sales policies.

As we discussed in the preface, the Middle East's primary economic significance to the United States will continue to revolve around energy for the foreseeable future. No single country in the region, however, has the capacity to hold America hostage by driving up energy prices—at least not without doing even more damage to itself. As such, the United States should not hesitate to exert pressure on Gulf oil producers when they take actions that are at odds with U.S. interests for fear of retaliation on energy markets, which seems to be one of the reasons for the Trump administration's gentle response to the 2018 Khashoggi murder.

That said, a scenario in which a large portion of Middle Eastern oil is taken offline for any extended period of time would be disastrous for the global economy in the short term. Presumed Iranian strikes on Saudi oil infrastructure in September 2019, which took 5 percent of the global oil supply off the market for less than a week, temporarily rattled the international economy, underscoring the potential damage disruptions to Gulf oil can cause. U.S. policy should aim to reduce the likelihood of such supply interruptions by establishing effective deterrence. To this end, the next administration should consider reaffirming an updated version of the Carter Doctrine, which stated that "an attempt by any outside force to gain control of the Persian Gulf region will be regarded as an assault on the vital interests of the United States of America, and such an assault will be repelled by any means necessary, including military force."[5]

At the same time, consistent with this volume's emphasis on nonmilitary tools, a new president should discriminate carefully between attacks that represent a fundamental threat to Gulf oil supplies and those that are mere short-term nuisances, including Iran's seizure of individual tankers. When responding to less serious challenges to Gulf oil production, the next administration should favor non-military responses to attacks on Gulf oil installations, such as sanctions. A new president should also take pains to avoid policies that could incentivize countries to strike regional oil supplies, such as the Trump administration's "maximum pressure" campaign on Iran. A public statement explaining how the United States will respond to external attacks on the Gulf states that threaten global energy supply would reassure U.S. partners of our continued interest in their security, while a more sober approach to potential spoilers like Iran would mitigate the risk of challenges to the U.S deterrence regime. This combined policy of deterrence and threat management offers the United States the best chance to stabilize energy markets as progress continues on alternative energies that promise true independence from Gulf oil production, while avoiding repeated standoffs in the Middle East that would exacerbate the American public's fatigue with the region.

Likewise, the next administration should recognize the potential value of arms sales in building partner capacity while placing more emphasis on their negative security externalities and refraining from overstating their economic benefits to American workers. As a start, a new administration should suspend the Trump administration's changes to arms sales policy, which eroded oversight of commercial and government-to-government deals. Ensuring that human rights considerations are systematically incorporated into all sales will help to clarify the process, returning needed oversight into both commercial sales and government-to-government sales.

Rebuild Transatlantic Cooperation on the Middle East

In both the short and the long terms, it is in America's interest to develop partners who can shoulder more of the burden in the Middle East. While President Trump talks often about burden-sharing in terms of economic assistance and troop commitments, the benefits of a partnership model have not been lost on the last several administrations before him. The past few presidents have primarily prioritized finding partners in the region itself. Local partners would be ideal for a variety of cultural, linguistic, and motivational reasons, but the reality is that most U.S. partners in the Middle East lack either the capacity or willingness—or both—to serve as reliable substitutes for the United States. And, as several chapters in this volume make clear, the interests of regional actors, including our traditional partners, are increasingly diverging from our own, making cooperation ever more fraught.

As the U.S. adjusts its footprint in the Middle East, the imperative to identify burden-sharing options will only grow. The United States cannot give up on trying to forge more effective partnerships in the Middle East, but we should also be realistic, given the present limitations generated by the rivalries within the region, and place more emphasis on the role of allies outside of the region. Though the Europeans have their own weaknesses, including military capacity shortfalls, internal differences, and the distraction of Brexit, no other potential U.S. partners are as closely aligned with our interests and have such a direct stake in the Middle East.

The next administration should make it a priority to seek new ways to institutionalize U.S.-European cooperation on the Middle East. A logical place to start would be to hold a regular strategic dialogue—focused exclusively on the Middle East—between the United States, the European Union, and interested member states. These dialogues would provide an invaluable venue for devising common approaches, synchronizing policies, and deconflicting actions. Given that the Europeans will likely be eager to put the Trump era behind them and repair the transatlantic alliance, a new president should be in a strong position to ask the Europeans to fill in gaps that will be created as the United States recalibrates its investments in the region. This will be particularly crucial in North Africa, the part of the Middle East that is less central to U.S. interests but critically important to those of the Europeans.

Empower the State Department's Top Middle East Diplomat
If the next administration is to restore the civilian face of U.S. power in the Middle East, there is no substitute for getting civilians on the

ground. Senior U.S. military officials, for all their strengths, are not
diplomats and often do not have the skills and expertise to conduct
sensitive diplomacy. Given their portfolios, when senior military officials are asked to play diplomatic roles—conducting what we often
have called "military diplomacy"—they tend to concentrate on what
they know best, highlighting certain types of issues at the expense of
others. The bottom line is that diplomacy cannot be outsourced to
other national security agencies any more than military strategy can
be entrusted to Foggy Bottom. And even the most security-centric
issues have inherently political dimensions that necessitate important
roles for the State Department.

Over the past decade, given the sheer number of U.S. military personnel stationed in the region and the constant stream of high-level
Department of Defense visitors, in many places, on many occasions,
civilian diplomatic voices and perspectives were drowned out. The
State Department will never compete with the Department of Defense in terms of sheer manpower, but it can do a much better job of
increasing the commanding presence of its diplomats by taking two
steps.

First, the State Department should have more diplomats permanently based in the region to deal with countries in which the United
States does not have a diplomatic presence, such as Syria, Yemen, and
Libya. Face-to-face meetings are an essential part of diplomacy, but
under current conditions either U.S. diplomats must fly from Washington or foreign leaders must fly to Washington in order to make
them happen. If these diplomats were located next door to a conflict zone, the frequency of such meetings would obviously increase.
Additionally, many of the most important regional conversations on
these conflicts take place within the Middle East, not just during
official discussions but also between them. (Amman, Jordan, for example, has become a hub of diplomatic energy on Yemen.) The limited number of U.S. diplomats dedicated to these issues in regional
capitals puts the United States at an unnecessary disadvantage.

Second, Washington-based Bureau of Near Eastern Affairs (NEA)
officials need to spend more time in the region doing what diplomats
do best, managing U.S. relationships and foreign leaders on a day-
to-day basis. In particular, the NEA assistant secretary should be a

ubiquitous presence in regional capitals, building on the secretary of state's travels and ensuring that important issues receive the high-level follow-up they deserve. Deputy assistant secretaries can stay in Washington to manage the interagency process and staff higher-level meetings, leaving the assistant secretary free to spend more time on the ground. The assistant secretary is arguably the only official senior enough to be listened to by regional countries while having a narrow enough portfolio to concentrate all of their time on the region's issues. Focusing on the staffing and allocation of tasks among the top diplomats working on the Middle East at the State Department is in and of itself a critical strategic decision.

Conclusion

The return of great power competition may suggest that it is time for the Middle East to take a back seat after driving U.S. foreign policy for decades. Due to the persistence of conflict and instability in the region, however, this shift is unlikely to be as fast or sharp as some global strategists desire. This book has nevertheless argued that the Middle East need not be all-consuming for U.S. policymakers. Instead, policy and strategy approaches should be more disciplined, reflecting U.S. interests and values.

To be fair, discipline has never been the hallmark of post–World War II American foreign policy. Foreign policy is a messy business, and the next administration's policies will inevitably diverge from the ideal types set out in this book. Yet we remain optimistic that the United States can pursue a new Middle East policy that protects core U.S. interests at a more modest and sustainable cost. Discipline is easy to abandon when resources are plentiful, but the growing imperative to address emerging challenges elsewhere in the world and at home—which could intensify with COVID-19—should induce greater self-control.

In the final analysis, the greatest threat to the policy we advocate in this book may not be another round of overcommitment in the Middle East, but instead a reckless and precipitous disengagement. The American public's interest in the region will only continue to decline, and political leaders of both major U.S. parties have argued for further retreat. Even if the Trump administration bumbles into another war in the Middle East, the net effect of such a calamitous mistake may be to hasten—rather than to delay—U.S. total with-drawal. In the wake of another calamitous military engagement with Iran, for example, the American people are likely to demand that a new president withdraw completely from the region.

The next administration will thus have to reimagine a new foreign policy to the region, while communicating to the American people why this part of the world still matters. This book set out a vision for a new U.S. approach toward the Middle East, and tried to explain why the region remains important to American interests. As even a reduced level of investment in the Middle East may be unpopular, the burden of proof will be on the next generation of officials and diplo-mats to convince the American people that the region is worth it. We hope that this book will contribute to the ongoing public dialogue about the U.S. role in the Middle East, providing a framework for how to reengage the region with the support of the American people.

Notes

1. Qassim Abdul-Zahra, "Iraq Moves to Limit Influence of Iran-Backed Militias," Associated Press, July 1, 2019.

2. "Hezbollah and Israel: A Timeline of Cross-Border Attack," Al Jazeera, September 9, 2019 (www.aljazeera.com/news/2019/09/hezbollah-israel-time line-cross-border-attacks-190909084547973.html).

3. Aya Batrawy, "UAE Draws Down Troops in Yemen in 'Strategic Rede-ployment,'" Associated Press, July 8, 2019.

4. Global Magnitsky Human Rights Accountability Act, S. 284, 114th Cong. (2016).

5. Jimmy Carter, "State of the Union Address," January 23, 1980 (www .jimmycarterlibrary.gov/assets/documents/speeches/su80jec.phtml).

Contributors

Wa'el Alzayat is CEO of Emgage, a national nonprofit dedicated to voter education and mobilization. He is also a senior fellow at the Middle East Institute. He previously served for ten years at the U.S. Department of State as a Middle East expert, including as senior policy adviser to the U.S. Ambassador to the United Nations Samantha Power, and outreach coordinator for U.S. Ambassador to Syria Robert Ford. He holds a BA in Middle East history and political science from the University of California at Berkeley and an MS in foreign service from Georgetown University.

Daniel Benaim holds fellowships at the Century Foundation and Center for American Progress. He served as a Middle East policy adviser and foreign policy speechwriter at the White House, State Department, and U.S. Senate Foreign Relations Committee.

Alexander Bick is a fellow at the Woodrow Wilson International Center for Scholars and research scholar at the Johns Hopkins School for Advanced International Studies. He served in the Obama administration on the policy planning staff at the U.S. Department of State and as Syria director at the National Security Council. He earned a PhD in history from Princeton University.

Melissa Dalton is a senior fellow and deputy director of the Center for Strategic and International Studies (CSIS) International Security Program and director of the Cooperative Defense Project. Her research focuses on reinforcing the principled foundations of U.S. defense policy and military operations. She also frequently conducts research and writes on U.S. defense policy in the Middle East. Prior to joining CSIS, she served for ten years in a number of policy and intelligence positions at the U.S. Department of Defense. She holds a BA in foreign affairs from the University of Virginia and an MA in international relations from the Johns Hopkins University School of Advanced International Studies. She is a member of the Council on Foreign Relations.

Megan Doherty served as the White House National Security Council director for North Africa from 2015 to 2016. Her tenure included the establishment of the Libyan Government of National Accord and the campaign to defeat ISIS in Sirte. She previously served in the U.S. Department of State as a senior adviser on Libya and the senior coordinator for U.S. assistance to Libya. Before joining the U.S. government, she served in Libya with the National Democratic Institute. Following the 2011 revolution, she helped establish Libya's first citizen election observation network, trained women candidates who won seats in Libya's first elected parliament, and conducted extensive public opinion research on post-Qaddafi Libya.

Jon Finer is an adjunct senior fellow at the Council on Foreign Relations and a nonresident adviser at NYU's Reiss Center for Law and Security. He spent more than seven years in the Obama administration, including as a speechwriter and Middle East adviser in the White House, and at the State Department, where he served as chief of staff and director of policy planning. He began his career as a journalist, covering the invasion of Iraq and its aftermath for the

Washington Post. He co-founded, and now chairs, the International Refugee Assistance Project, a legal services and advocacy organization. He has a law degree from Yale University, an M.Phil in international relations from Oxford University, where he was a Rhodes Scholar, and an undergraduate degree from Harvard University.

Amy Hawthorne is the deputy director for research at the Project on Middle East Democracy (POMED). She served at the U.S. Department of State during the Obama administration as Egypt coordinator and as senior adviser in the Bureau of Near Eastern Affairs. She also previously worked at several think tanks and NGOs, where she focused on Arab politics and U.S. policy in the Middle East. She studied at Yale University and the University of Michigan and was a Fulbright Scholar in Egypt.

Mara Karlin is director of strategic studies at the Johns Hopkins School of Advanced International Studies (SAIS). She is also an associate professor at SAIS and a nonresident senior fellow at the Brookings Institution. She has served in national security roles for five U.S. secretaries of defense, advising on policies spanning strategic planning, defense budgeting, future wars and the evolving security environment, and regional affairs involving the Middle East, Europe, and Asia. Most recently, she served as the deputy assistant secretary of defense for strategy and force development. She has been awarded Department of Defense medals for Meritorious and Outstanding Public Service, among others. She is the author of *Building Militaries in Fragile States: Challenges for the United States.*

Christopher J. Le Mon is Washington director for Crisis Action, an international human rights advocacy organization working to protect civilians from armed conflict. During the Obama administration, he served on the National Security Council (NSC) staff as special assistant to the president and senior adviser for multilateral affairs and human rights, and earlier as director for multilateral affairs; at the White House, as special assistant to the president for presidential personnel (national security); and at the State Department, as senior adviser to the assistant secretary for the Bureau of International Organization Affairs. Prior to government service, he was an international lawyer in private practice.

Sahar Nowrouzzadeh began her tenure as a career civil servant within the U.S. government in 2005. She has focused on Iran in a range of capacities across multiple administrations. She served as a director for Iran and Iran nuclear implementation on the White House National Security Council staff from 2014 to 2016, and was charged with covering Iran on the U.S. Secretary of State's policy planning staff between 2016 and 2017. She is currently on a sabbatical from the U.S Department of State, serving as an associate with Harvard's Belfer Center and pursuing her PhD in political science at Boston University. She earned her bachelor's in international affairs from George Washington University and her master's in Persian studies from the University of Maryland, College Park.

Jane Rhee, a former foreign service officer, served with the State Department and National Security Council (NSC) for more than a decade. As the NSC director for Iran (2012–2014) and for strategic planning (2015–2017), she led and coordinated strategies for the negotiations to achieve a comprehensive accord to curb Iran's nuclear program and long-term strategic threats to U.S. national security, as well as workforce and diversity policies for the national security community. She also served tours in Kabul, Afghanistan, and Dubai, United Arab Emirates, as well as in Washington, D.C., with the Office of Iranian Affairs, policy planning staff, and the U.S. Senate. She has a master's in public affairs from the Woodrow Wilson School of International Affairs at Princeton University, and a bachelor's in government from Harvard College.

Daniel B. Shapiro is a distinguished visiting fellow at the Institute for National Security Studies in Tel Aviv. During the Obama administration, he served as U.S. Ambassador to Israel from 2011 to 2017, and as senior director for the Middle East and North Africa at the National Security Council from 2009 to 2011. In more than twenty years of U.S. government service in the executive branch and the U.S. Congress, he has worked extensively to advance and support a wide range of U.S.-Israel security cooperation initiatives and to promote Israeli-Palestinian peace negotiations from 1993 to 2017. He is a principal at WestExec Advisors in Washington, D.C.

Stephen Tankel is an associate professor at American University and an adjunct senior fellow at the Center for a New American Security. He previously served as a senior fellow on the House Foreign Affairs Committee and as a senior adviser at the Department of Defense. His research focuses on terrorism and counterterrorism, the use of force, and security assistance and cooperation. He has conducted field research on these issues in Afghanistan, Algeria, Bangladesh, India, Kenya, Lebanon, Pakistan, Tunisia, and the Balkans. He is the author of numerous works, including *With Us and Against Us: How America's Partners Help and Hinder the War on Terror.*

Index

Surnames starting with "al" are alphabetized by subsequent part of name.